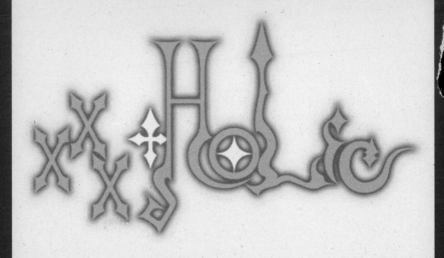

CLAMP

TRANSLATED AND ADAPTED BY
William Flanagan

LETTERED BY
Dana Hayward

BALLANTINE BOOKS • NEW YORK

2005 Del Rey Books Trade Paperback Edition

Published in the United States by Del Rey Books, an imprint of The Random House Publishing Group, a division of Random House, Inc., New York.

Del Rey is a registered trademark and the Del Rey colophon is a trademark of Random House, Inc.

First published in serialization and subsequently published in book form by Kodansha Ltd., Tokyo in 2004, copyright © 2004 CLAMP.

ISBN 0-345-47789-8

Printed in the United States of America

Del Rey Books website address: www.delreymanga.com

9 8 7

Translator and Adaptor—William Flanagan
Lettering—Dana Hayward
Cover Design—David Stevenson

xxxHOLiC crosses over with *Tsubasa*. Although it isn't necessary to read *Tsubasa* to understand the events in *xxxHOLiC*, you'll get to see the same events from different perspectives if you read both series!

Contents

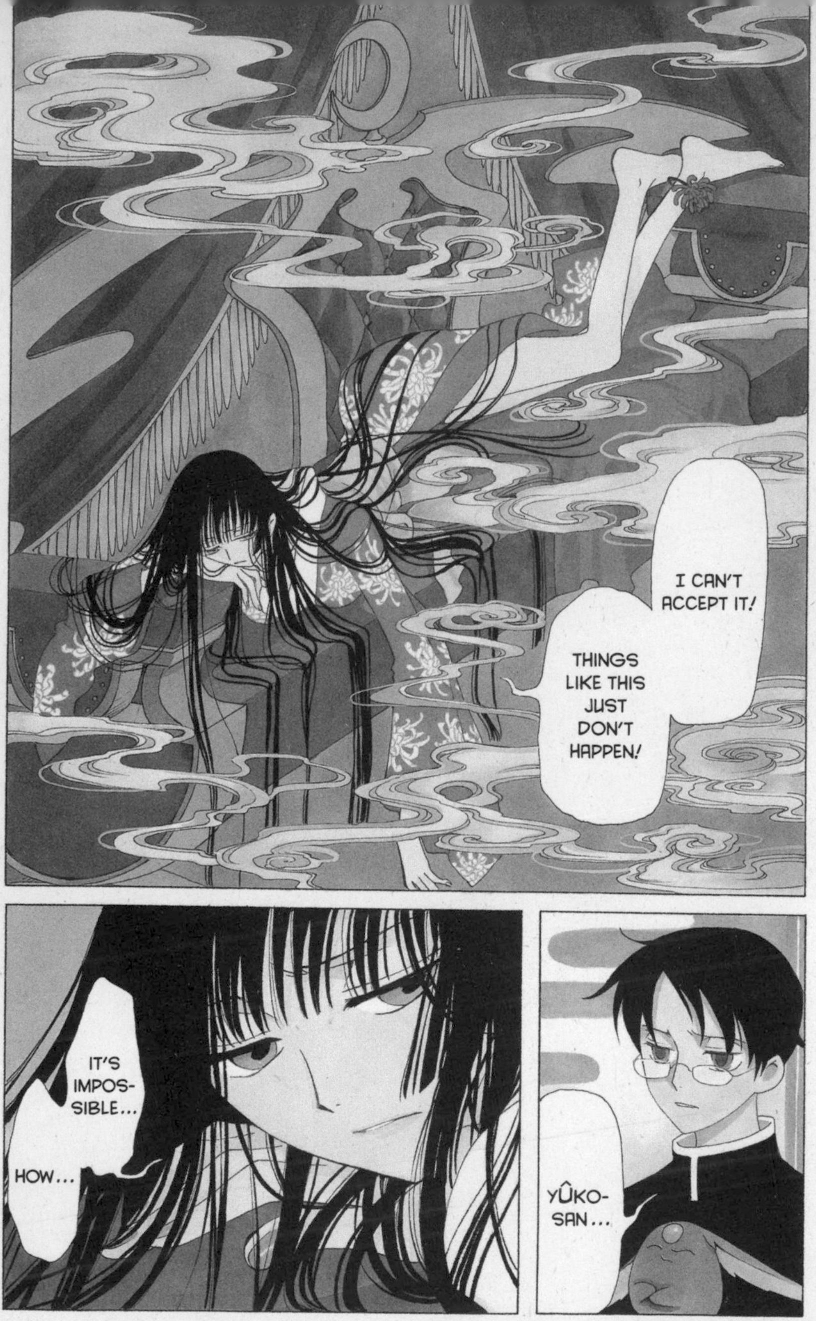
I CAN'T ACCEPT IT!
THINGS LIKE THIS JUST DON'T HAPPEN!
YÛKO-SAN...
IT'S IMPOSSIBLE...
HOW...

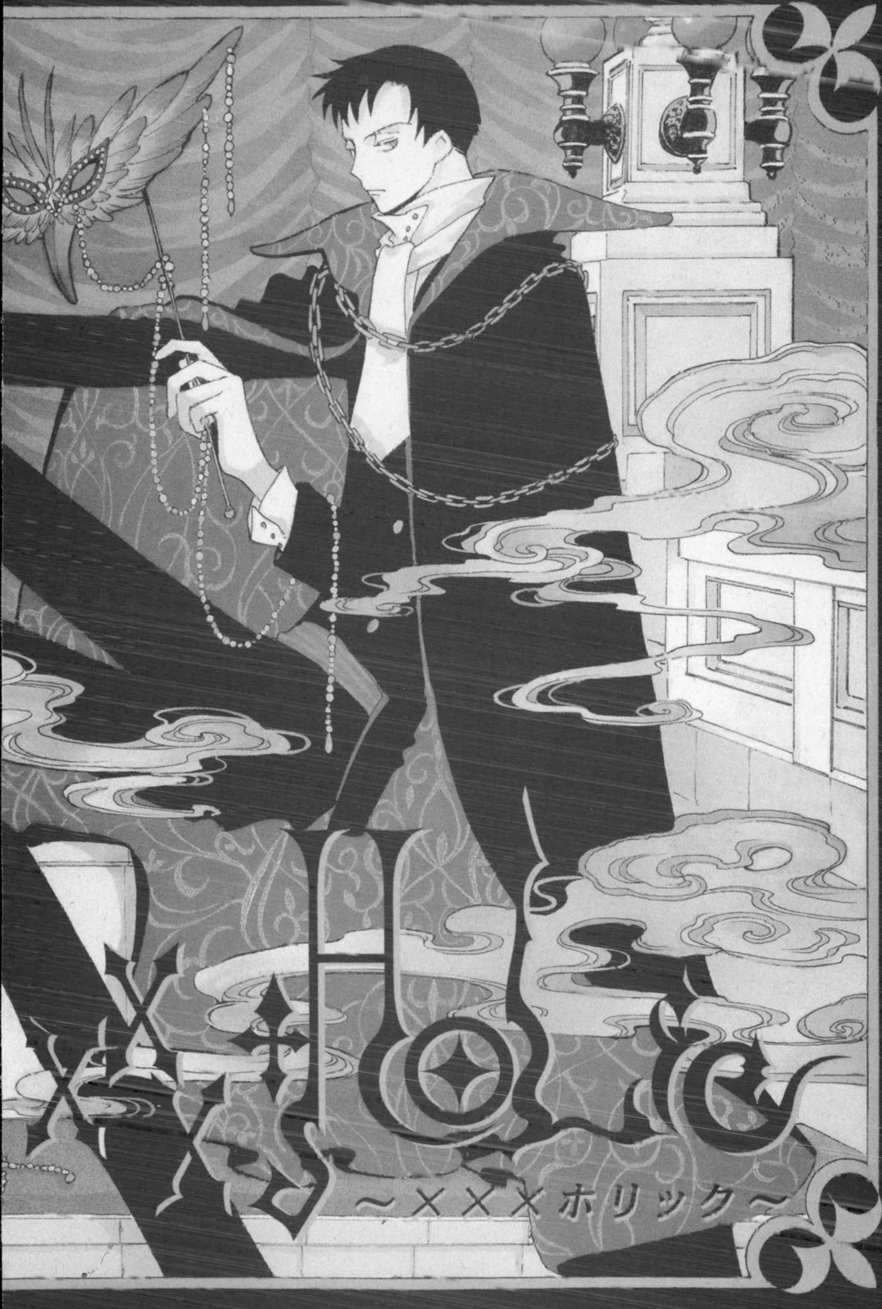
～×××ホリック～

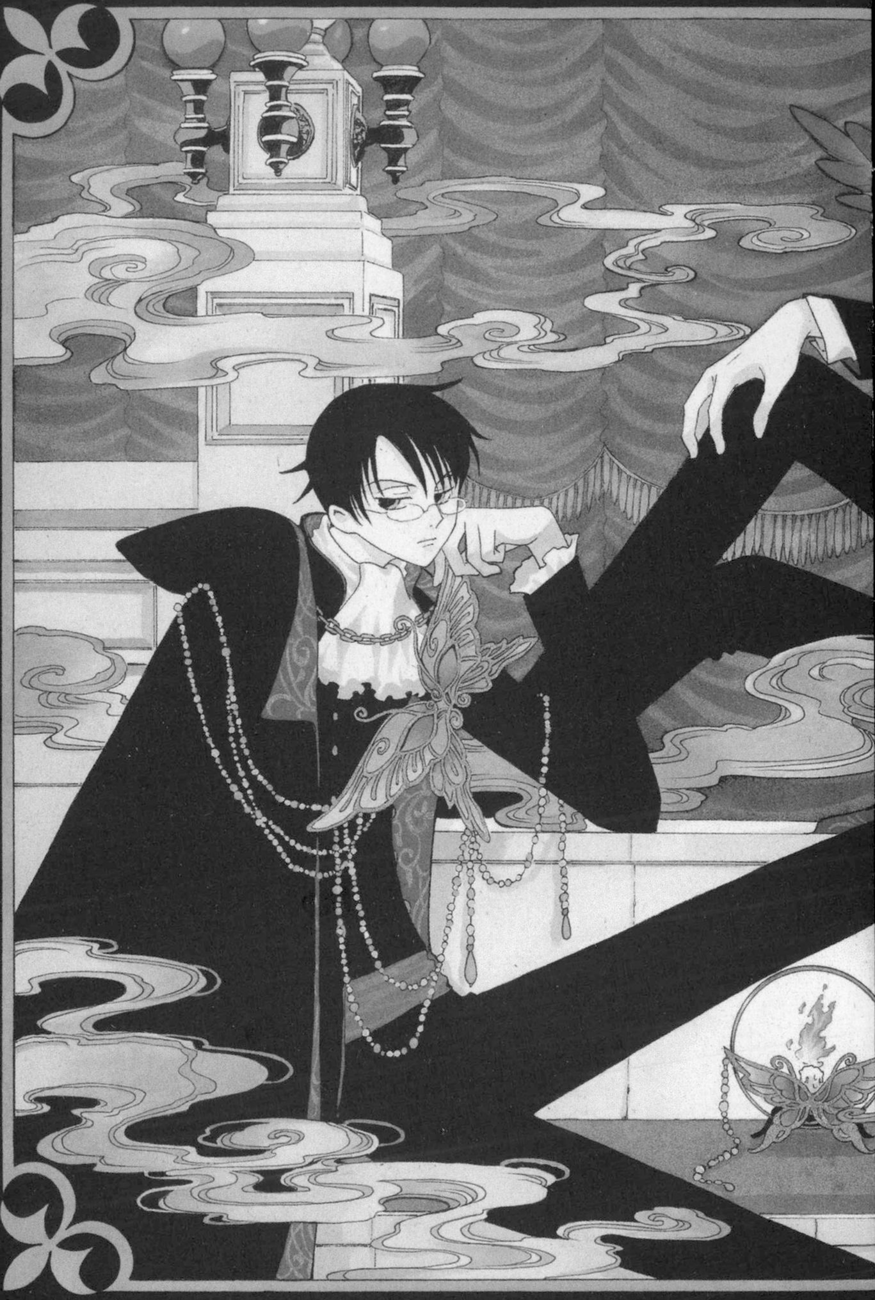

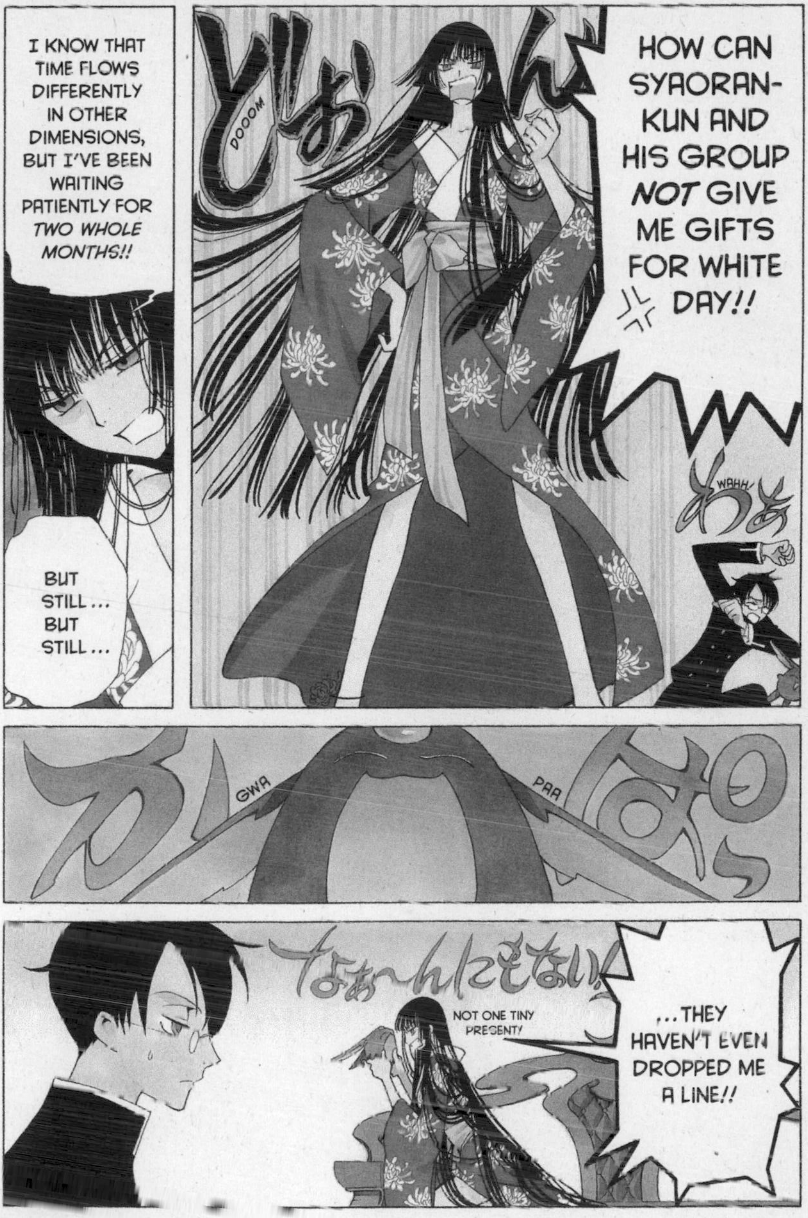
どぉん
DOOOM
HOW CAN SYAORAN-KUN AND HIS GROUP *NOT* GIVE ME GIFTS FOR WHITE DAY!!
わぁ
WAHH!
I KNOW THAT TIME FLOWS DIFFERENTLY IN OTHER DIMENSIONS, BUT I'VE BEEN WAITING PATIENTLY FOR *TWO WHOLE MONTHS!!*
BUT STILL... BUT STILL...
PAA
GWA
...THEY HAVEN'T EVEN DROPPED ME A LINE!!
なぁ〜んにもない!
NOT ONE TINY PRESENT!

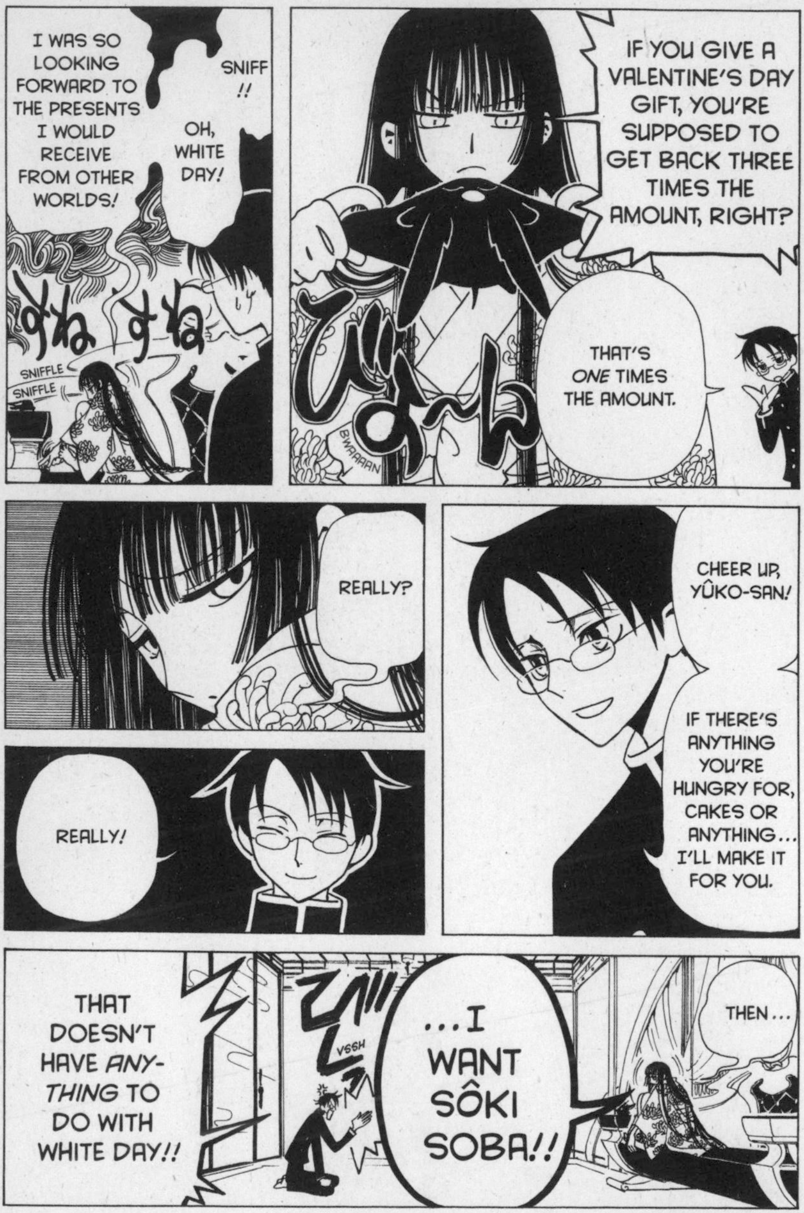
IF YOU GIVE A VALENTINE'S DAY GIFT, YOU'RE SUPPOSED TO GET BACK THREE TIMES THE AMOUNT, RIGHT?
BWAAAAAN
THAT'S *ONE* TIMES THE AMOUNT.
I WAS SO LOOKING FORWARD TO THE PRESENTS I WOULD RECEIVE FROM OTHER WORLDS!
SNIFF !!
OH, WHITE DAY!
すね すね
SNIFFLE
SNIFFLE
CHEER UP, YÛKO-SAN!
IF THERE'S ANYTHING YOU'RE HUNGRY FOR, CAKES OR ANYTHING... I'LL MAKE IT FOR YOU.
REALLY?
REALLY!
THEN...
...I WANT SÔKI SOBA!!
VSSH
THAT DOESN'T HAVE *ANY-THING* TO DO WITH WHITE DAY!!

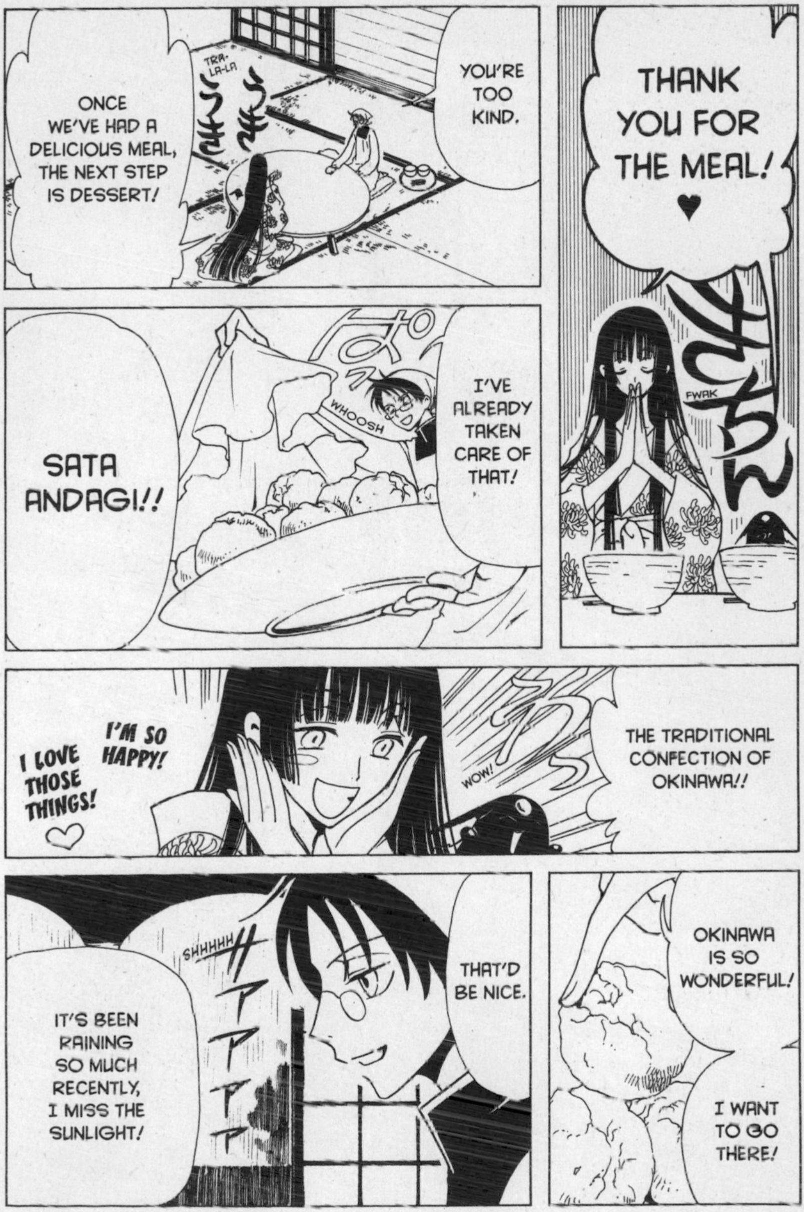
THANK YOU FOR THE MEAL! ♥
FWAK
YOU'RE TOO KIND.
TRA-LA-LA
ONCE WE'VE HAD A DELICIOUS MEAL, THE NEXT STEP IS DESSERT!
I'VE ALREADY TAKEN CARE OF THAT!
WHOOSH
SATA ANDAGI!!
THE TRADITIONAL CONFECTION OF OKINAWA!!
WOW!
I'M SO HAPPY!
I LOVE THOSE THINGS! ♡
OKINAWA IS SO WONDERFUL!
I WANT TO GO THERE!
THAT'D BE NICE.
SHHHHH
IT'S BEEN RAINING SO MUCH RECENTLY, I MISS THE SUNLIGHT!

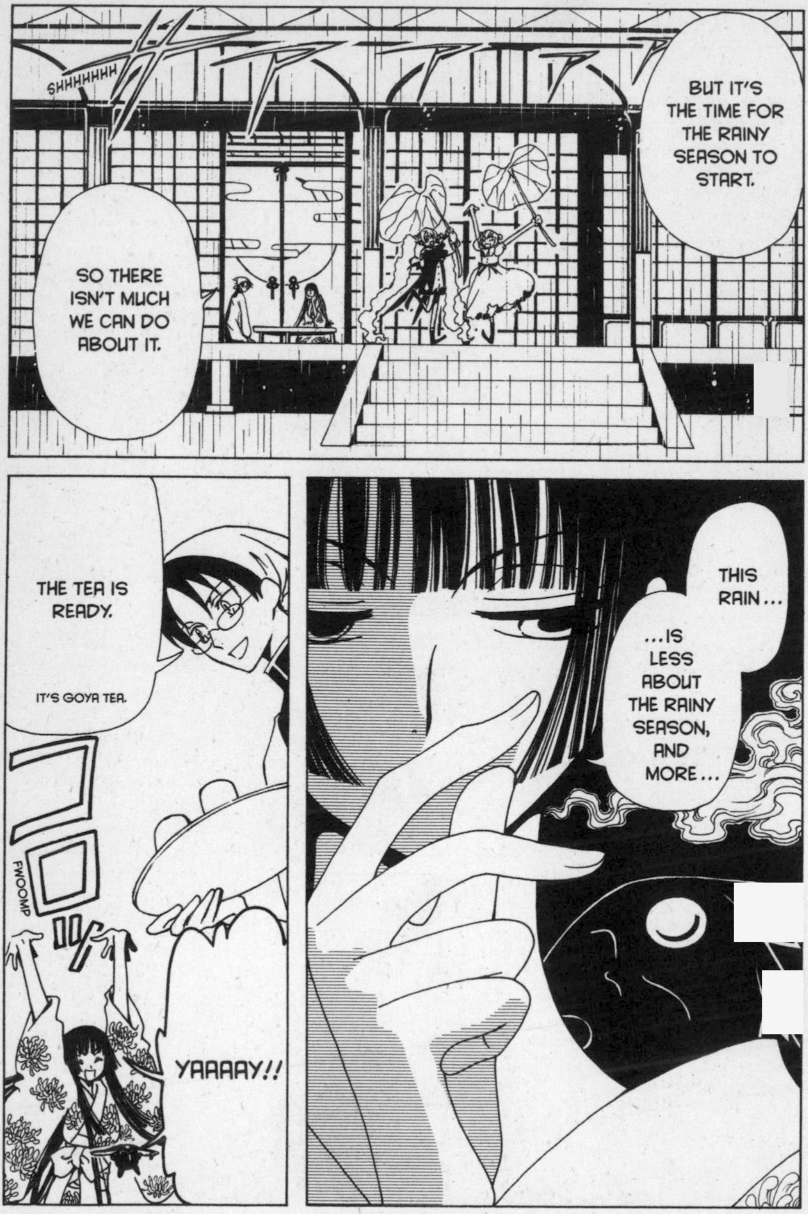
BUT IT'S THE TIME FOR THE RAINY SEASON TO START.
SHHHHHHH
SO THERE ISN'T MUCH WE CAN DO ABOUT IT.
THIS RAIN...
...IS LESS ABOUT THE RAINY SEASON, AND MORE...
THE TEA IS READY.
IT'S GOYA TEA.
FWOOMP
YAAAAY!!

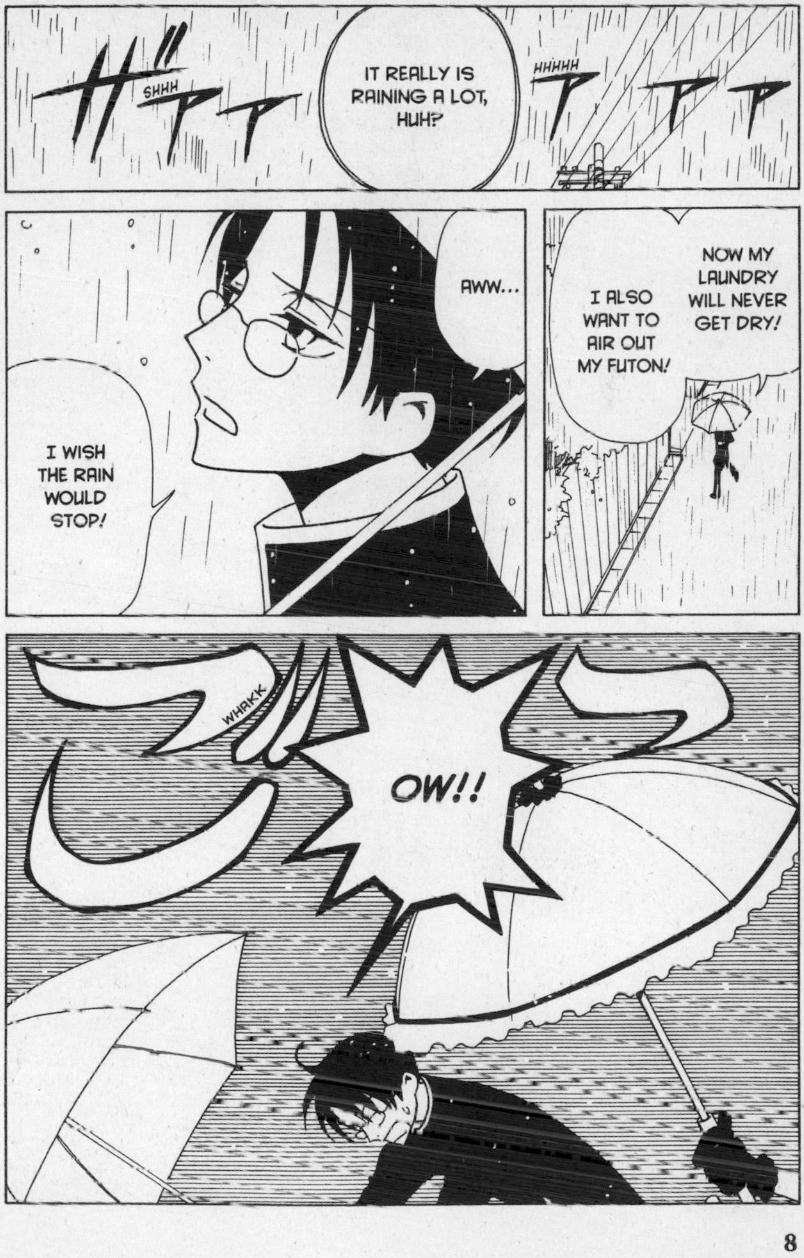
HHHHH
IT REALLY IS RAINING A LOT, HUH?
SHHH
NOW MY LAUNDRY WILL NEVER GET DRY!
I ALSO WANT TO AIR OUT MY FUTON!
AWW...
I WISH THE RAIN WOULD STOP!
WHAKK
OW!!

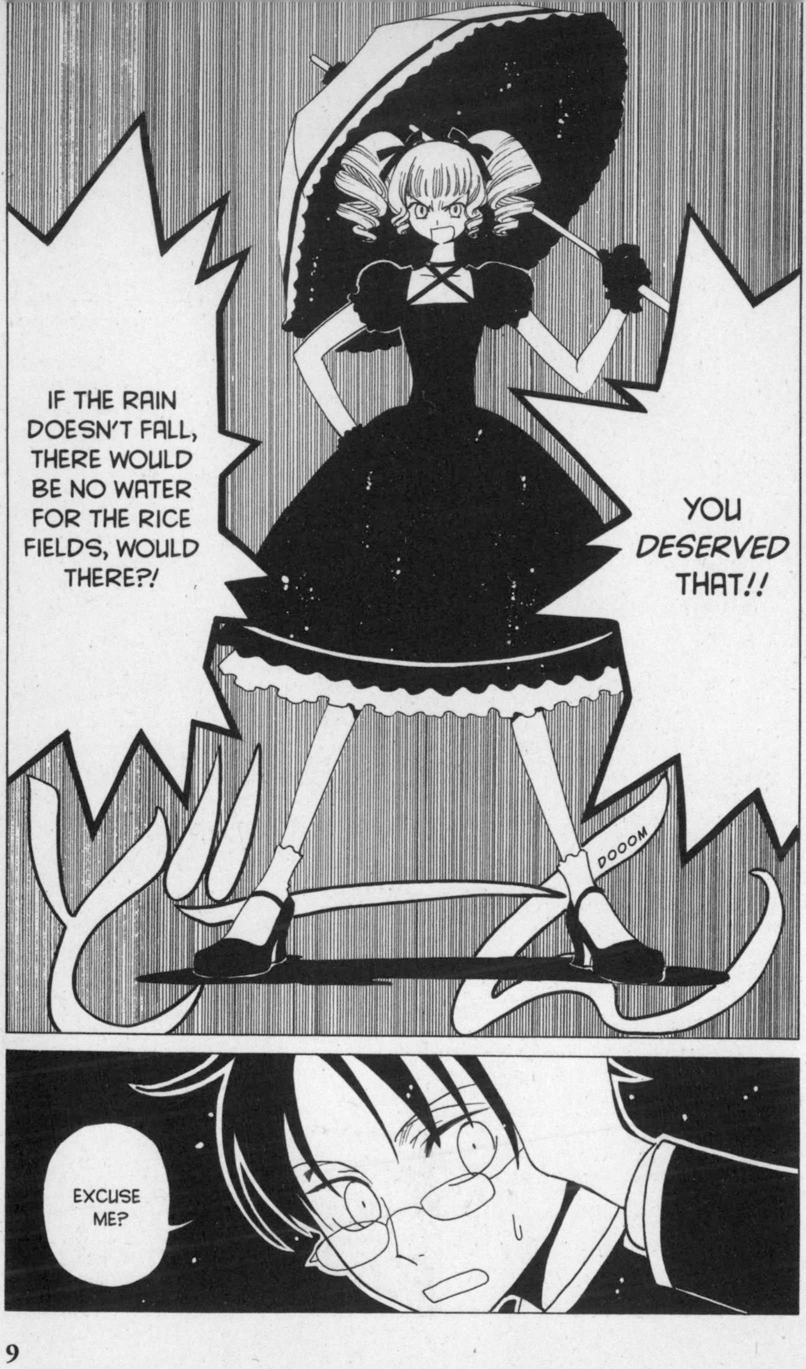
YOU DESERVED THAT!!
IF THE RAIN DOESN'T FALL, THERE WOULD BE NO WATER FOR THE RICE FIELDS, WOULD THERE?!
DOOOM
EXCUSE ME?

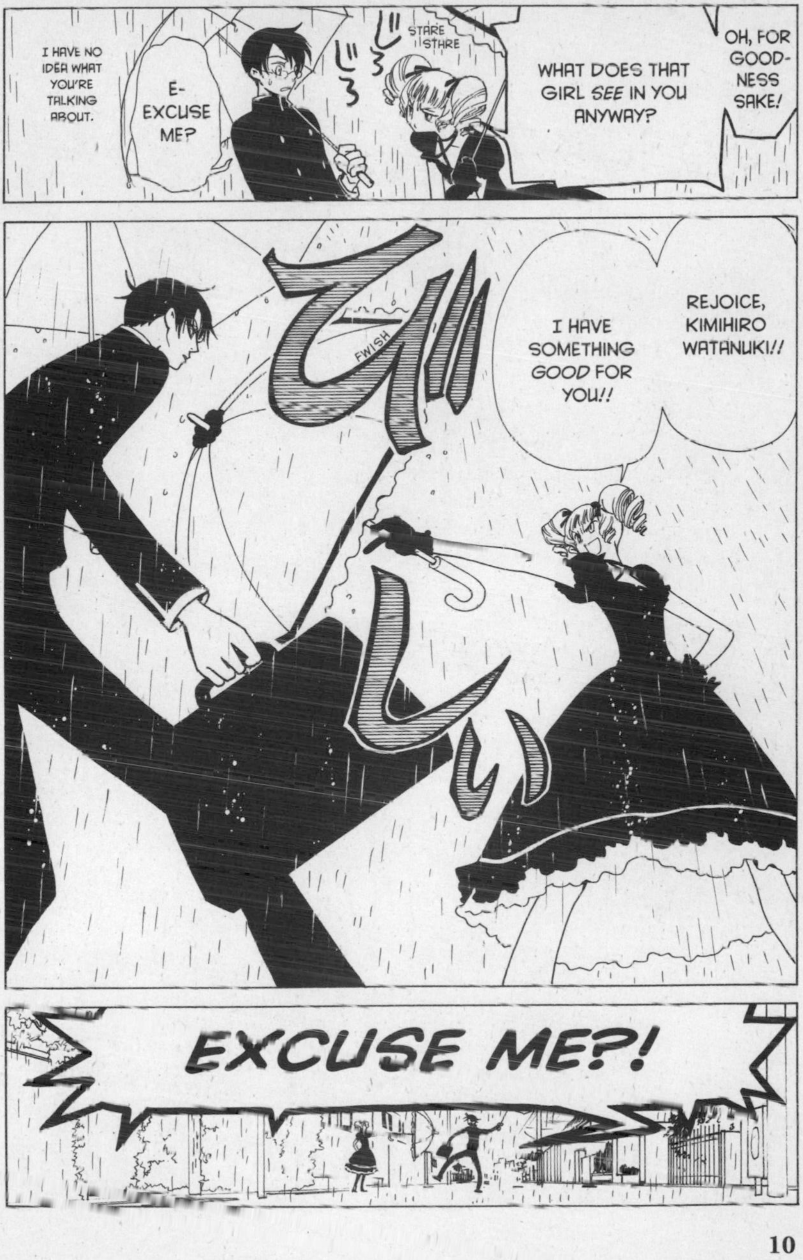
OH, FOR GOODNESS SAKE!
WHAT DOES THAT GIRL SEE IN YOU ANYWAY?
STARE STARE
E-EXCUSE ME?
I HAVE NO IDEA WHAT YOU'RE TALKING ABOUT.
REJOICE, KIMIHIRO WATANUKI!!
I HAVE SOMETHING GOOD FOR YOU!!
FWISH
EXCUSE ME?!

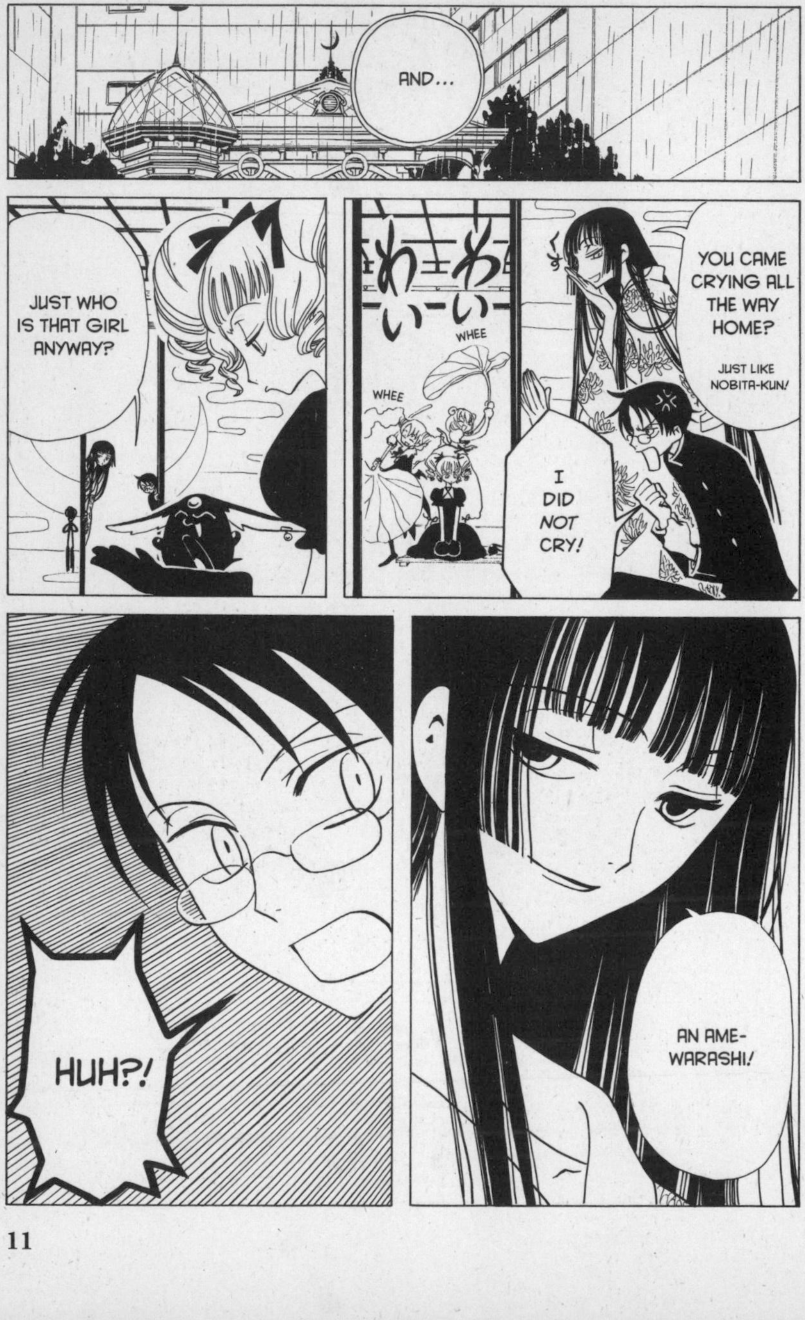
AND...
YOU CAME CRYING ALL THE WAY HOME?
JUST LIKE NOBITA-KUN!
I DID NOT CRY!
WHEE
WHEE
JUST WHO IS THAT GIRL ANYWAY?
AN AME-WARASHI!
HUH?!

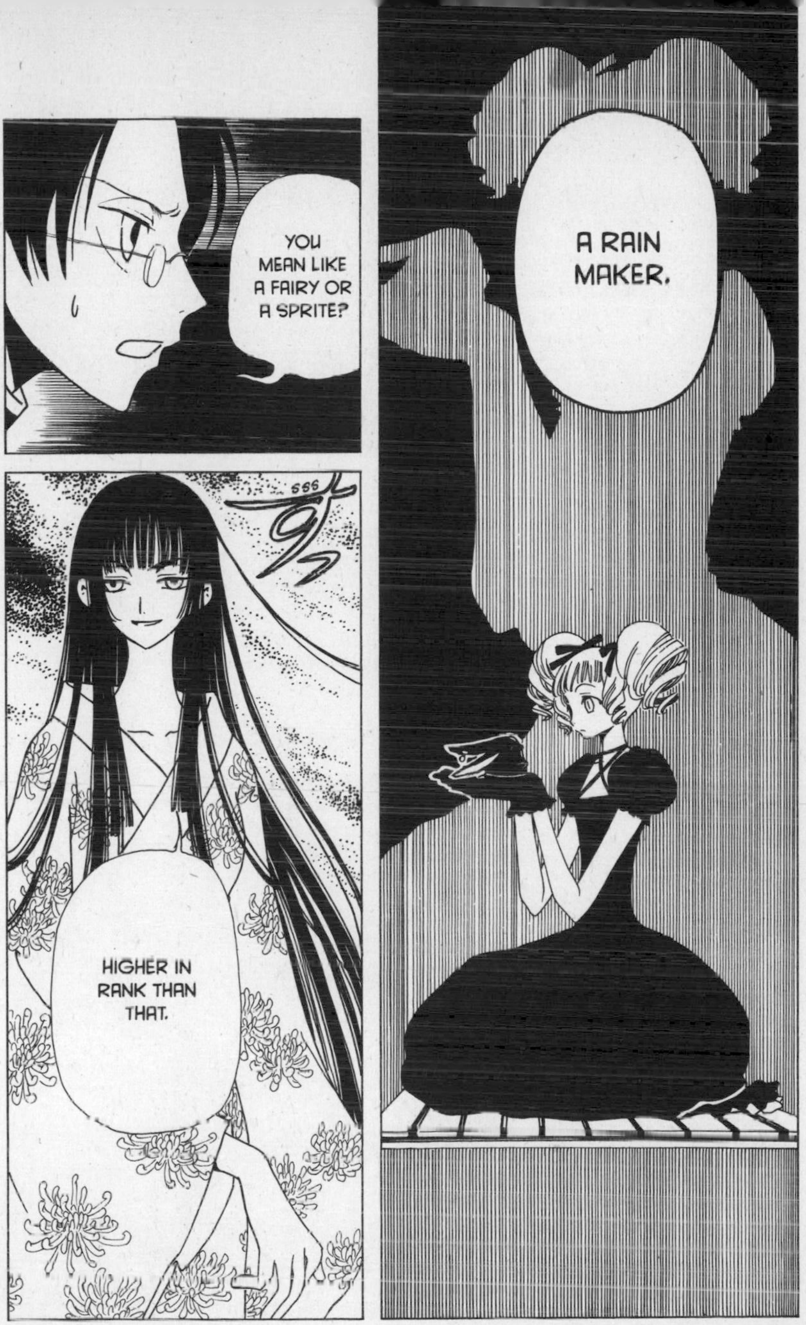
A RAIN MAKER.
YOU MEAN LIKE A FAIRY OR A SPRITE?
SSS
HIGHER IN RANK THAN THAT.

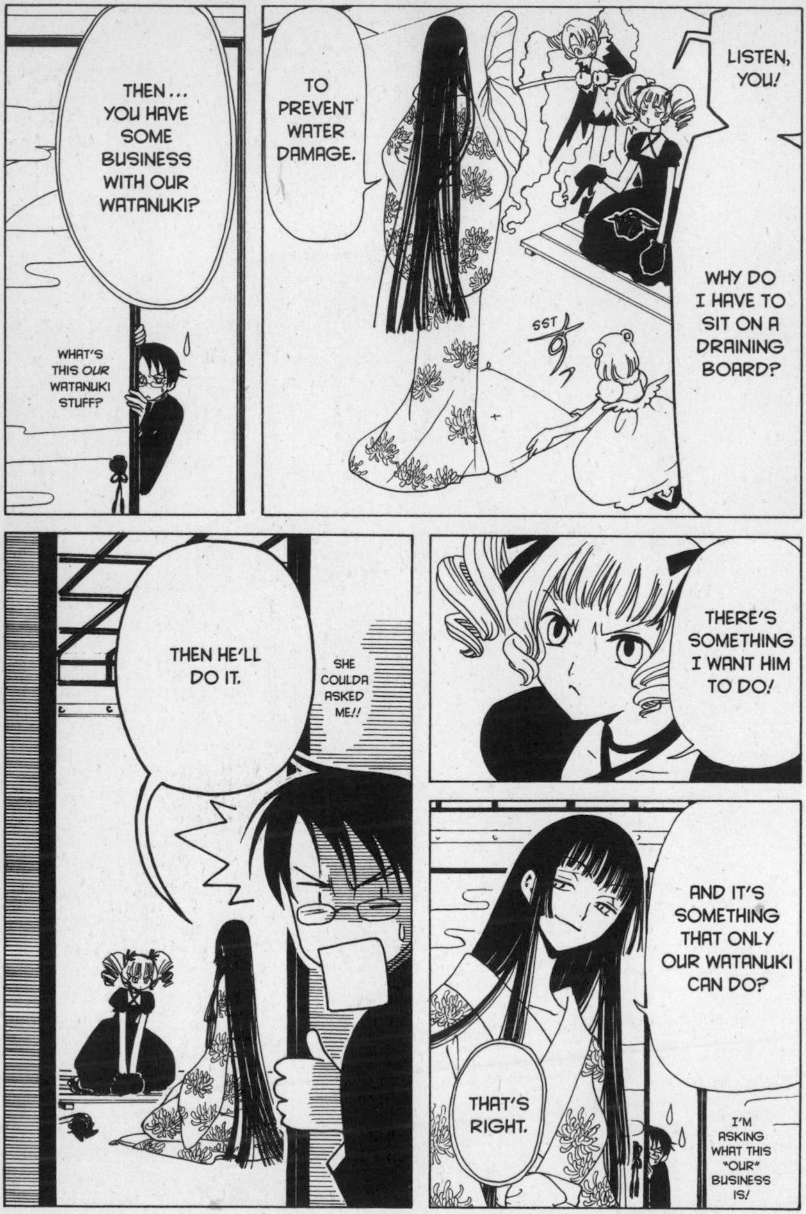
LISTEN, YOU!
WHY DO I HAVE TO SIT ON A DRAINING BOARD?
TO PREVENT WATER DAMAGE.
SST
THEN... YOU HAVE SOME BUSINESS WITH OUR WATANUKI?
WHAT'S THIS OUR WATANUKI STUFF?
THERE'S SOMETHING I WANT HIM TO DO!
AND IT'S SOMETHING THAT ONLY OUR WATANUKI CAN DO?
THAT'S RIGHT.
I'M ASKING WHAT THIS "OUR" BUSINESS IS!
THEN HE'LL DO IT.
SHE COULDA ASKED ME!!

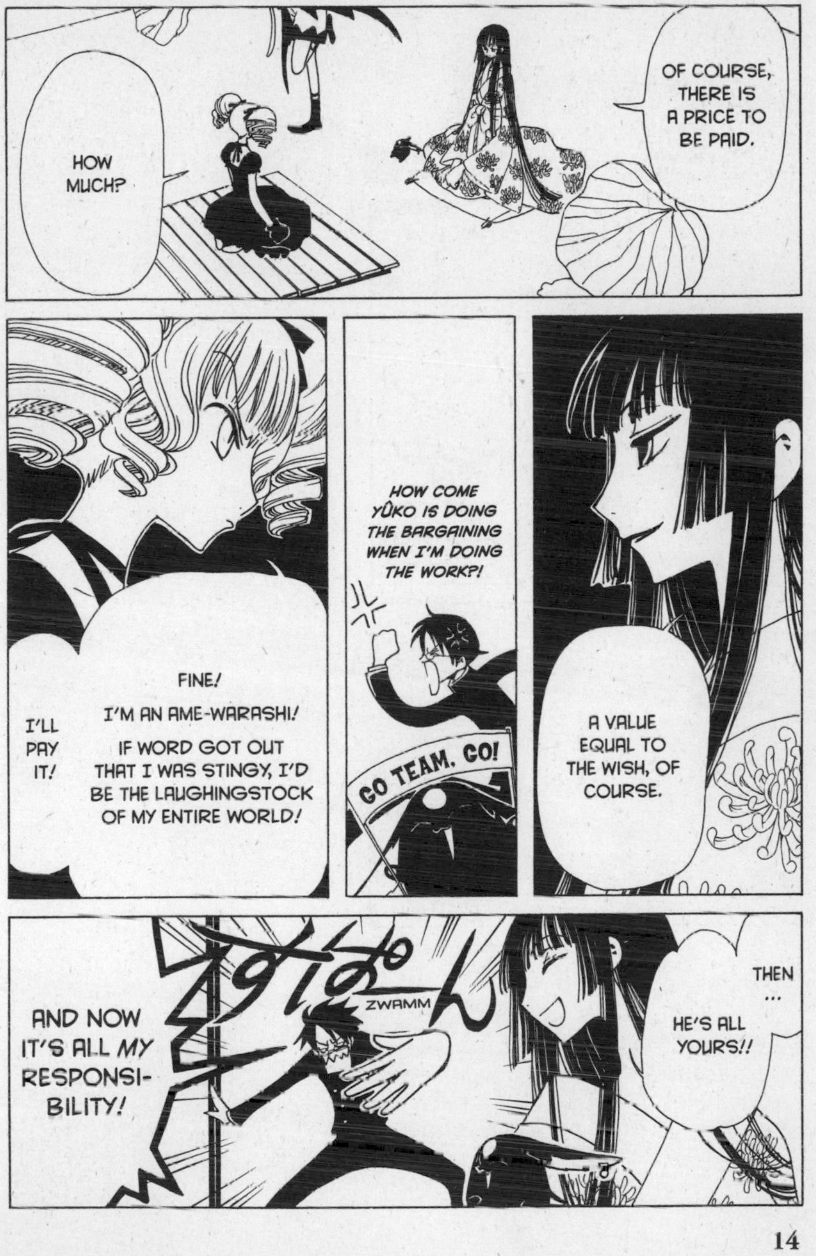
OF COURSE, THERE IS A PRICE TO BE PAID.
HOW MUCH?
A VALUE EQUAL TO THE WISH, OF COURSE.
HOW COME YÛKO IS DOING THE BARGAINING WHEN I'M DOING THE WORK?!
GO TEAM, GO!
FINE!
I'M AN AME-WARASHI!
IF WORD GOT OUT THAT I WAS STINGY, I'D BE THE LAUGHINGSTOCK OF MY ENTIRE WORLD!
I'LL PAY IT!
THEN...
HE'S ALL YOURS!!
ZWAMM
AND NOW IT'S ALL MY RESPONSIBILITY!

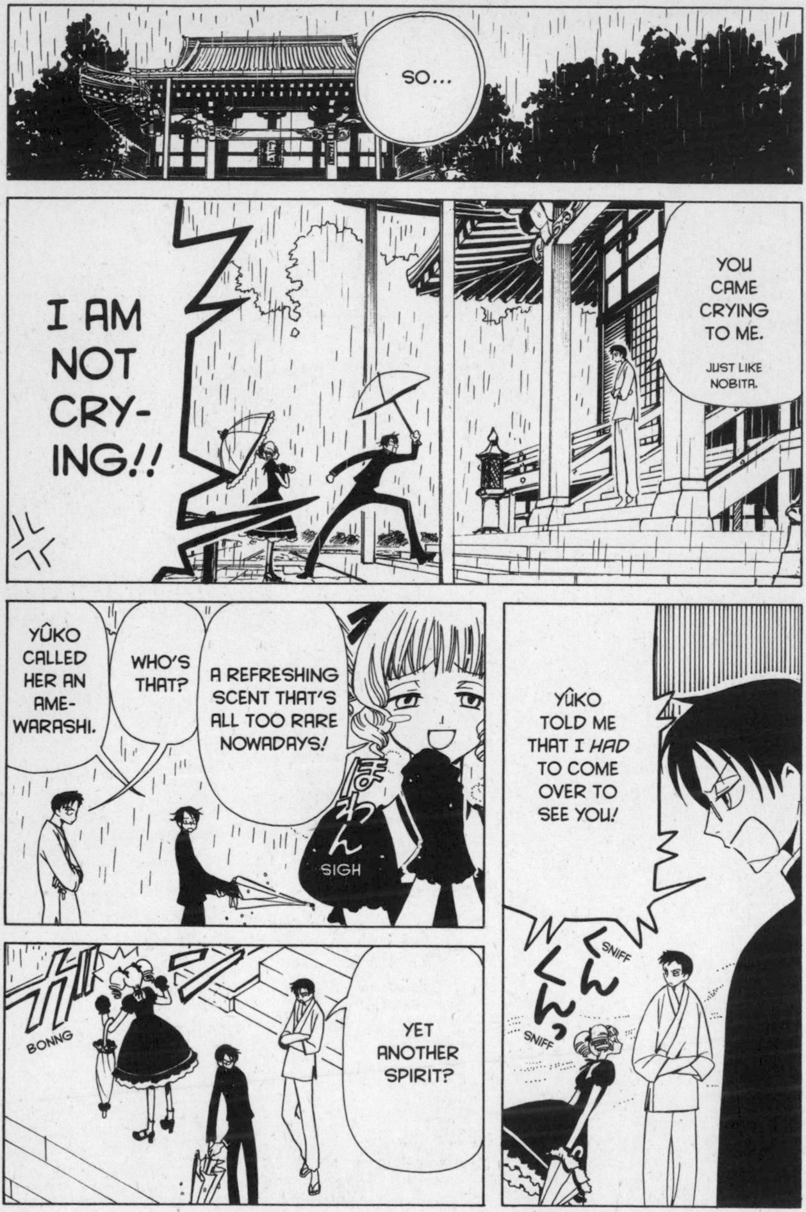
SO...
YOU CAME CRYING TO ME.
JUST LIKE NOBITA.
I AM NOT CRYING!!
YÛKO TOLD ME THAT I *HAD* TO COME OVER TO SEE YOU!
くん SNIFF
くん SNIFF
A REFRESHING SCENT THAT'S ALL TOO RARE NOWADAYS!
ほわん
SIGH
WHO'S THAT?
YÛKO CALLED HER AN AME-WARASHI.
YET ANOTHER SPIRIT?
BONNG

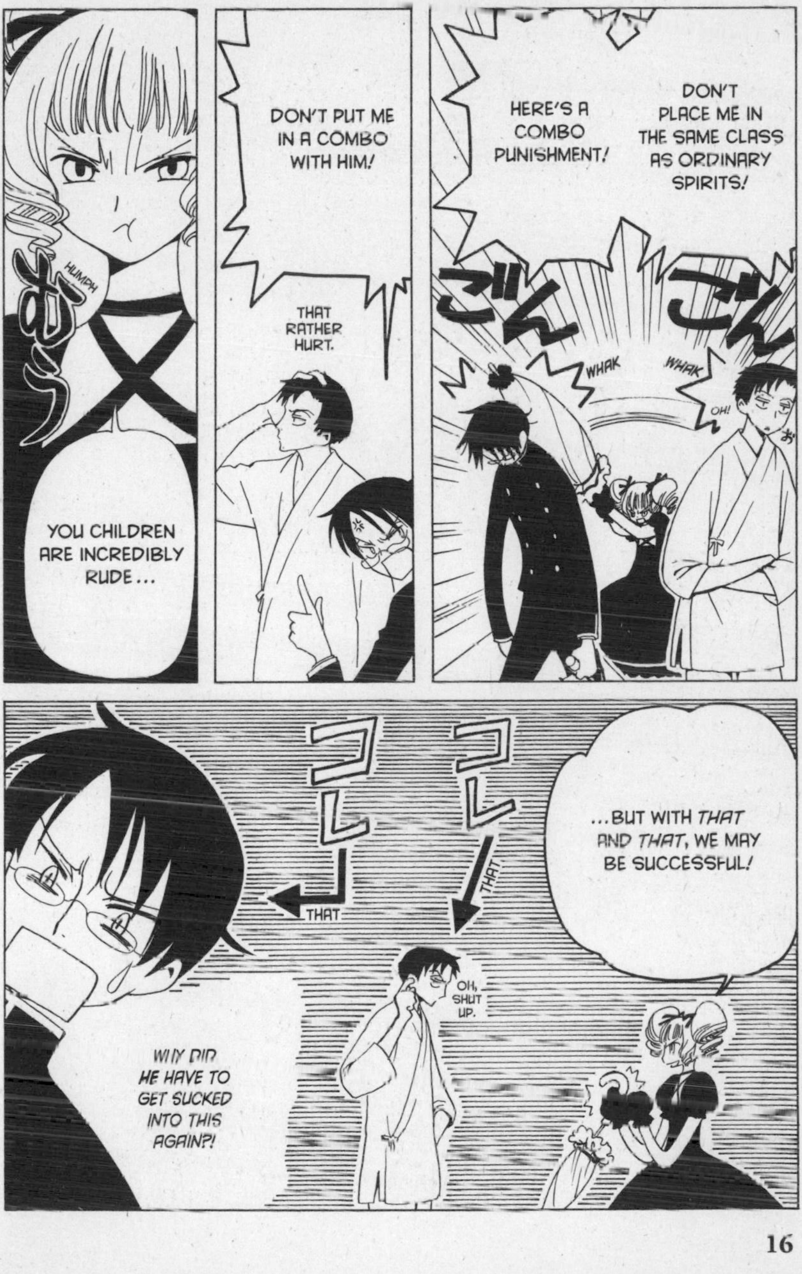
DON'T PLACE ME IN THE SAME CLASS AS ORDINARY SPIRITS!
HERE'S A COMBO PUNISHMENT!
ごん
ごん
WHAK
WHAK
OH!
DON'T PUT ME IN A COMBO WITH HIM!
THAT RATHER HURT.
HUMPH
YOU CHILDREN ARE INCREDIBLY RUDE...
...BUT WITH *THAT* AND *THAT*, WE MAY BE SUCCESSFUL!
コレ
THAT
コレ
THAT
OH, SHUT UP.
WHY DID HE HAVE TO GET SUCKED INTO THIS AGAIN?!

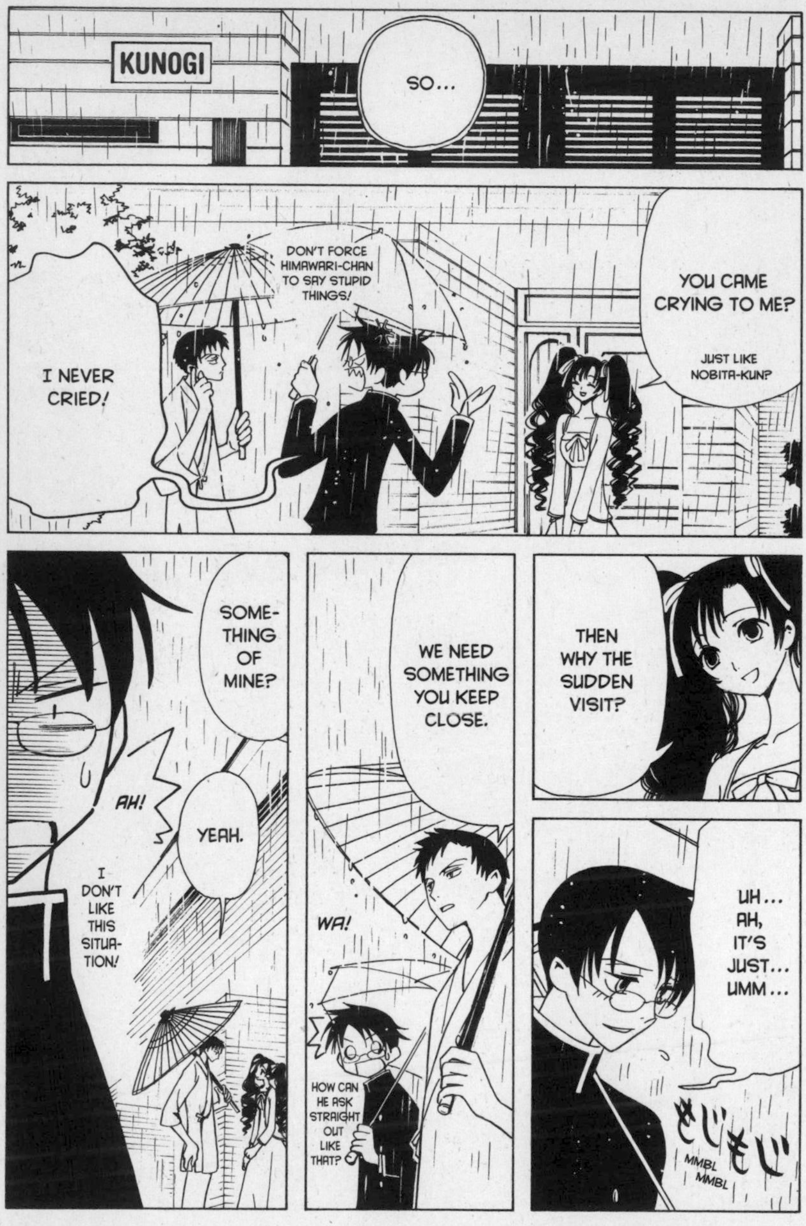
KUNOGI
SO...
YOU CAME CRYING TO ME?
JUST LIKE NOBITA-KUN?
DON'T FORCE HIMAWARI-CHAN TO SAY STUPID THINGS!
I NEVER CRIED!
THEN WHY THE SUDDEN VISIT?
UH... AH, IT'S JUST... UMM...
もじもじ
MMBL MMBL
WE NEED SOMETHING YOU KEEP CLOSE.
WA!
HOW CAN HE ASK STRAIGHT OUT LIKE THAT?
SOME-THING OF MINE?
AH!
YEAH.
I DON'T LIKE THIS SITUATION!

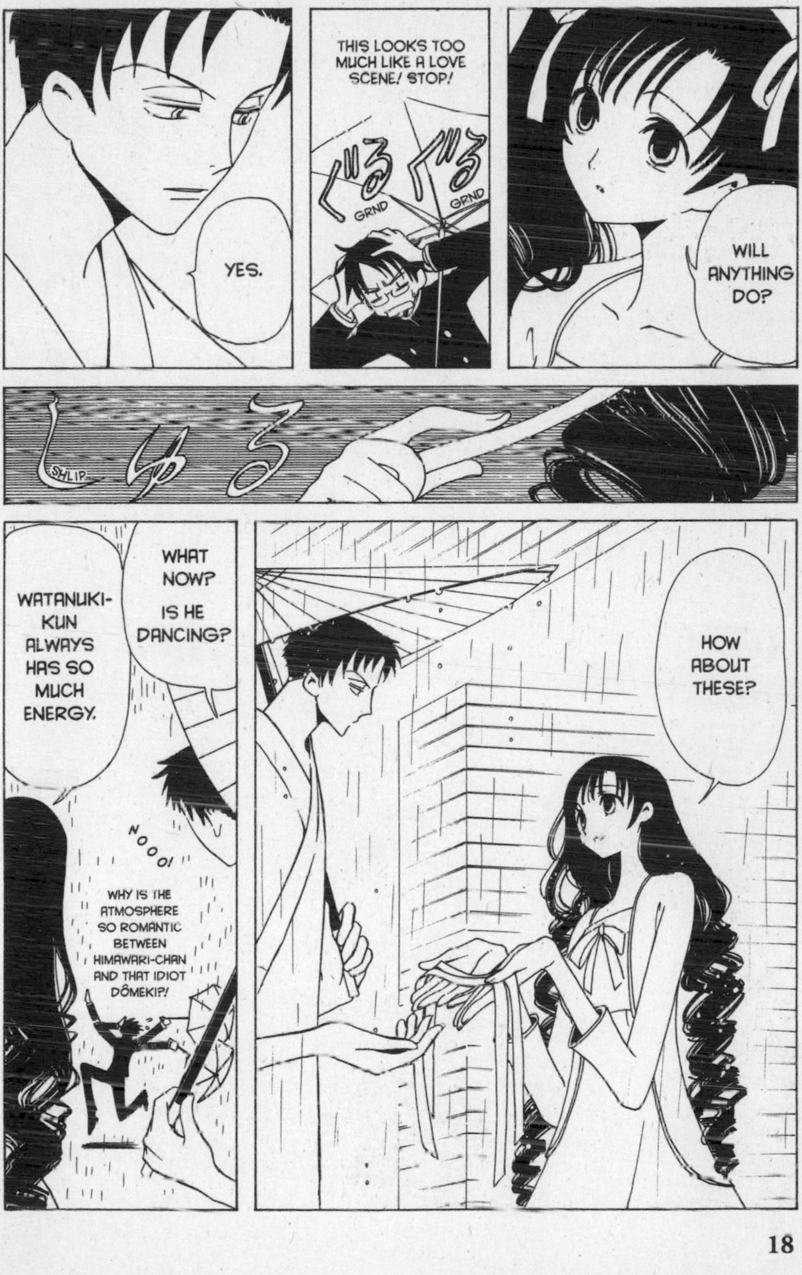
WILL ANYTHING DO?
THIS LOOKS TOO MUCH LIKE A LOVE SCENE! STOP!
ぐるぐる
GRND GRND
YES.
しゅる
SHLIP
HOW ABOUT THESE?
WHAT NOW? IS HE DANCING?
WATANUKI-KUN ALWAYS HAS SO MUCH ENERGY.
NOOO!
WHY IS THE ATMOSPHERE SO ROMANTIC BETWEEN HIMAWARI-CHAN AND THAT IDIOT DÔMEKI?!

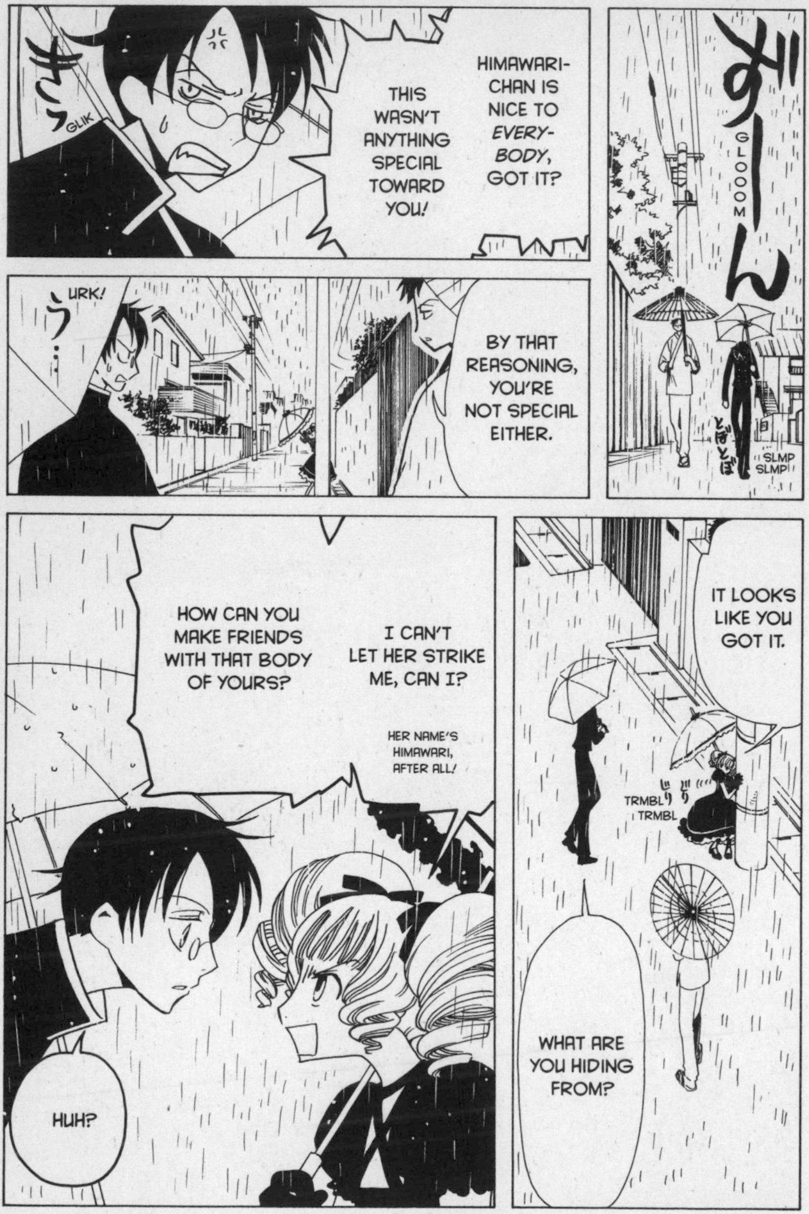
GLOOOM
SLMP SLMP
HIMAWARI-CHAN IS NICE TO *EVERY-BODY*, GOT IT?
THIS WASN'T ANYTHING SPECIAL TOWARD YOU!
GLIK
BY THAT REASONING, YOU'RE NOT SPECIAL EITHER.
URK!
IT LOOKS LIKE YOU GOT IT.
TRMBL TRMBL
WHAT ARE YOU HIDING FROM?
I CAN'T LET HER STRIKE ME, CAN I?
HER NAME'S HIMAWARI, AFTER ALL!
HOW CAN YOU MAKE FRIENDS WITH THAT BODY OF YOURS?
HUH?

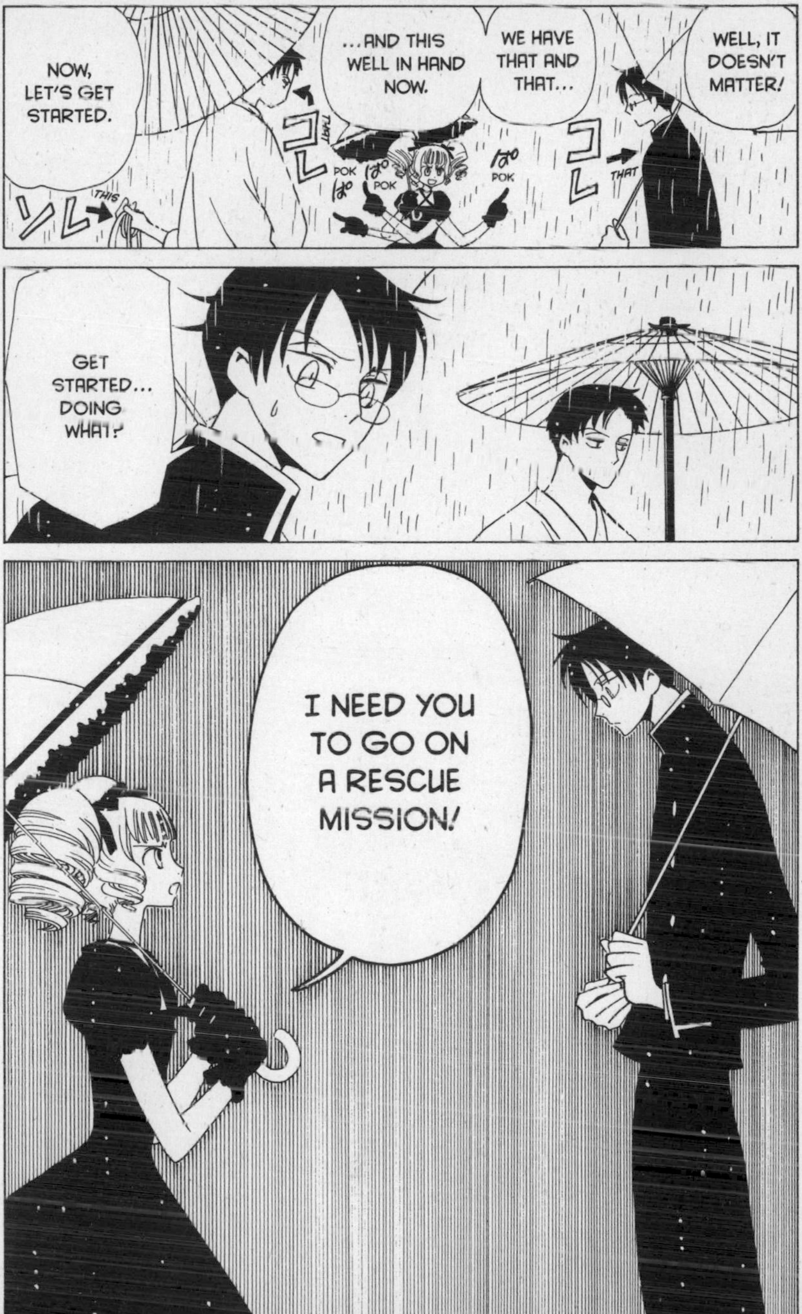
WELL, IT DOESN'T MATTER!
コレ
THAT
WE HAVE THAT AND THAT...
ぽ POK
ぽ POK
ぽ POK
...AND THIS WELL IN HAND NOW.
コレ
THAT
NOW, LET'S GET STARTED.
ソレ
THIS
GET STARTED... DOING WHAT?
I NEED YOU TO GO ON A RESCUE MISSION!

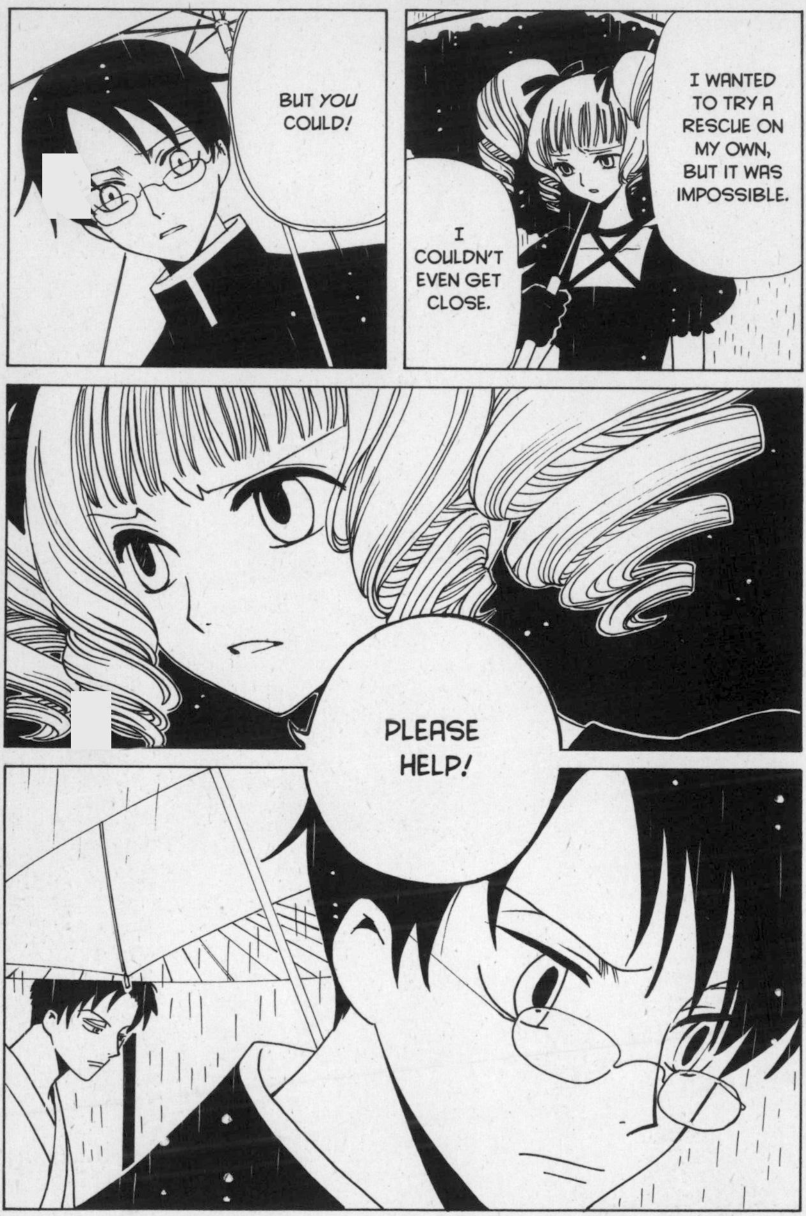
I WANTED TO TRY A RESCUE ON MY OWN, BUT IT WAS IMPOSSIBLE.
I COULDN'T EVEN GET CLOSE.
BUT YOU COULD!
PLEASE HELP!

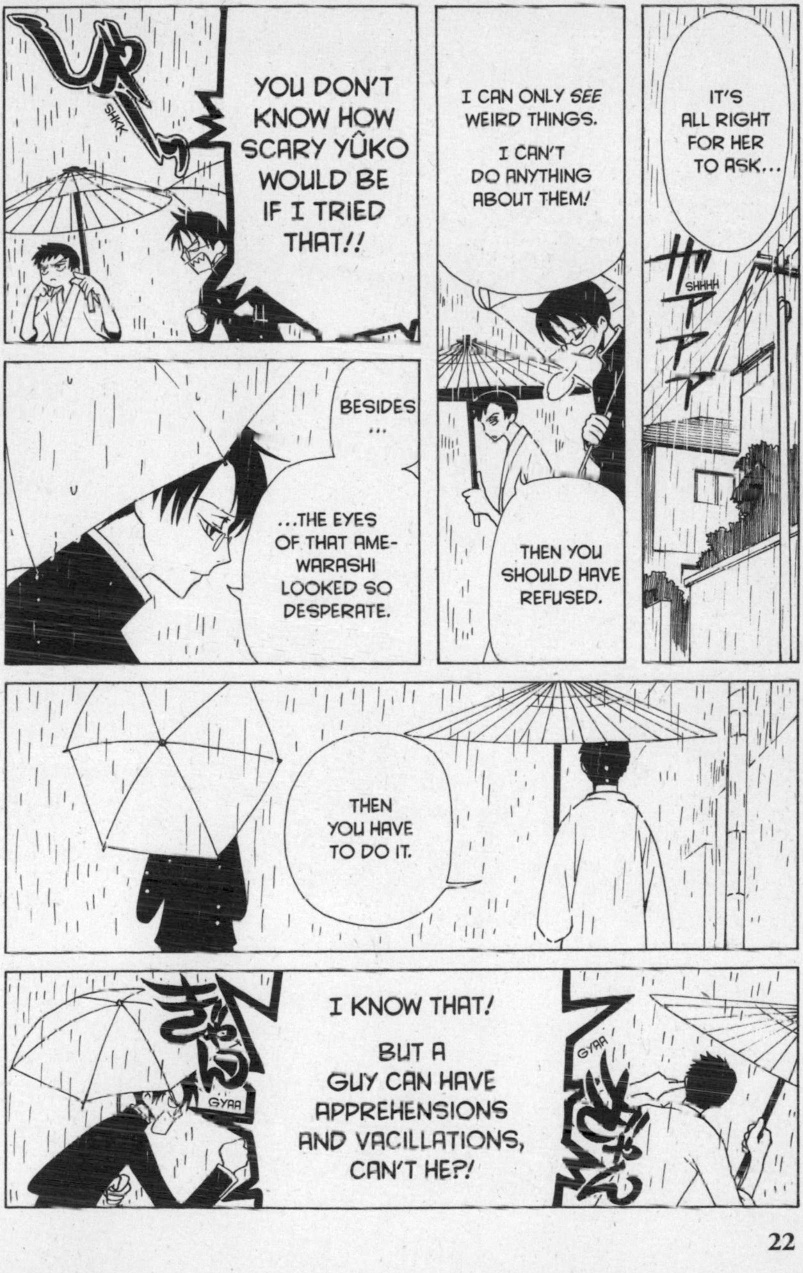
IT'S ALL RIGHT FOR HER TO ASK...
SHHHH
I CAN ONLY *SEE* WEIRD THINGS.
I CAN'T DO ANYTHING ABOUT THEM!
THEN YOU SHOULD HAVE REFUSED.
SHKK
YOU DON'T KNOW HOW SCARY YÛKO WOULD BE IF I TRIED THAT!!
BESIDES...
...THE EYES OF THAT AME-WARASHI LOOKED SO DESPERATE.
THEN YOU HAVE TO DO IT.
GYAA
I KNOW THAT!
BUT A GUY CAN HAVE APPREHENSIONS AND VACILLATIONS, CAN'T HE?!
GYAA

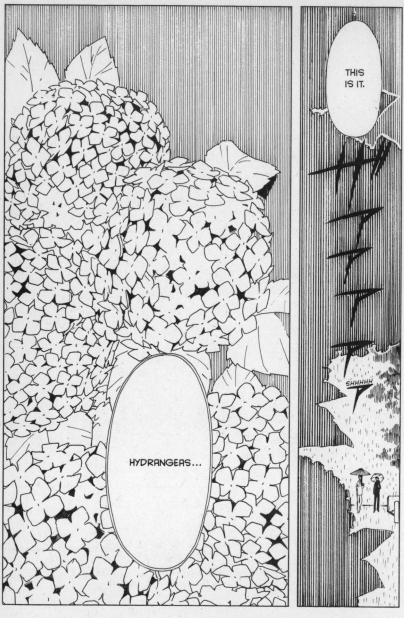

THIS IS IT.

SHHHHH

HYDRANGEAS...

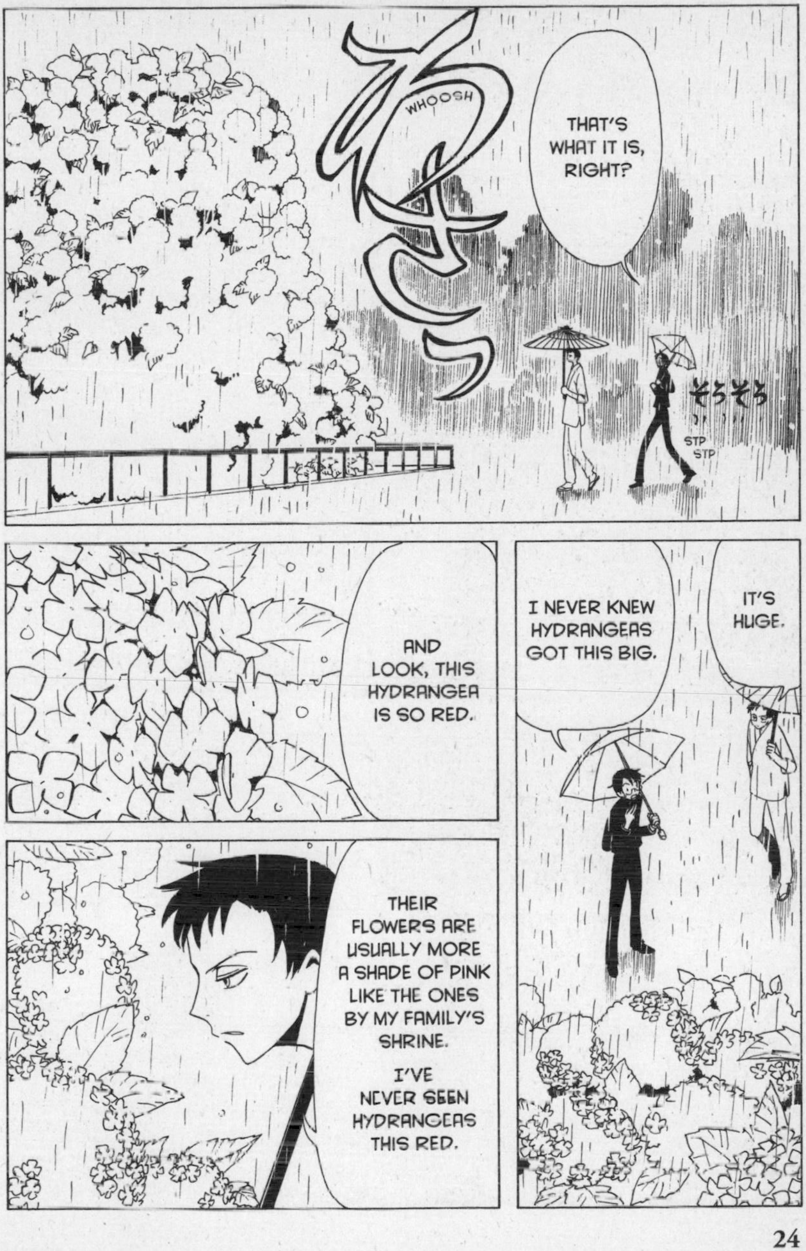
THAT'S WHAT IT IS, RIGHT?
WHOOSH
そろそろ
STP STP
IT'S HUGE.
I NEVER KNEW HYDRANGEAS GOT THIS BIG.
AND LOOK, THIS HYDRANGEA IS SO RED.
THEIR FLOWERS ARE USUALLY MORE A SHADE OF PINK LIKE THE ONES BY MY FAMILY'S SHRINE.
I'VE NEVER SEEN HYDRANGEAS THIS RED.

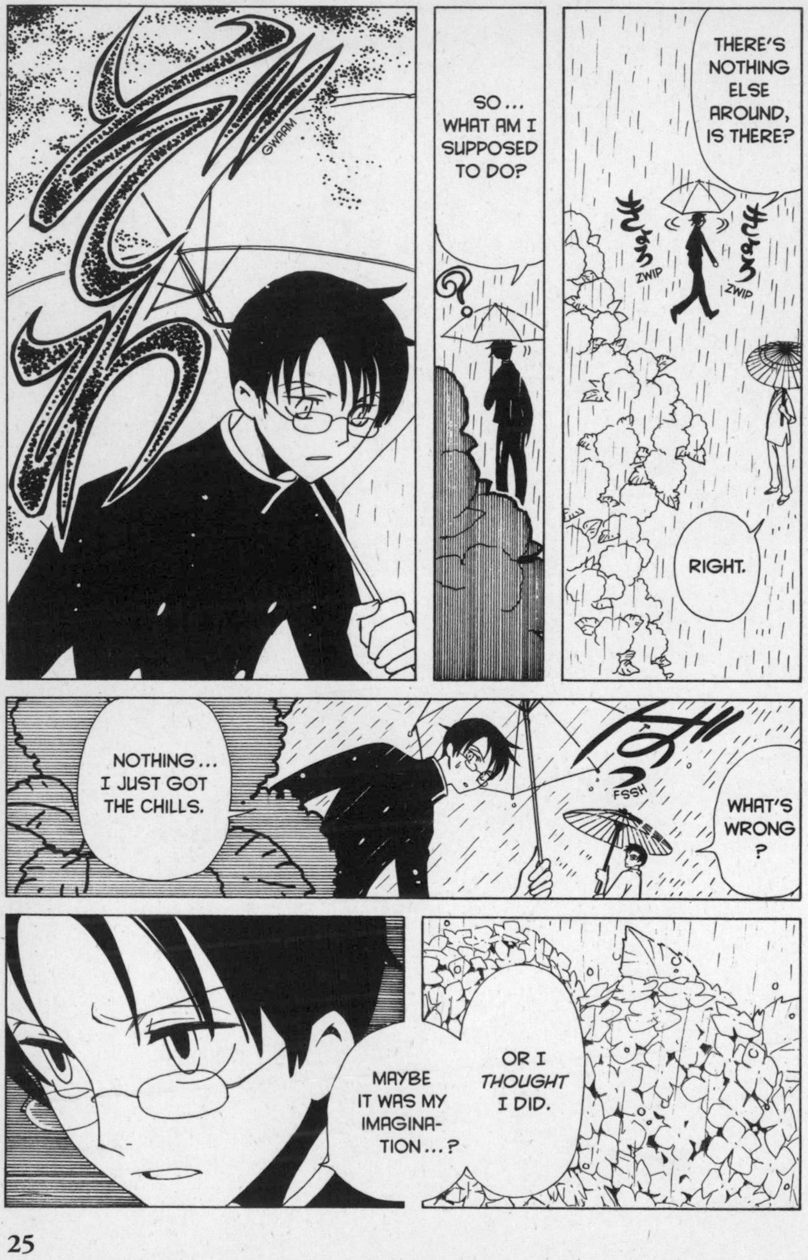
THERE'S NOTHING ELSE AROUND, IS THERE?
きょろ
ZWIP
きょろ
ZWIP
RIGHT.
SO... WHAT AM I SUPPOSED TO DO?
?
GWAAM
WHAT'S WRONG?
FSSH
NOTHING... I JUST GOT THE CHILLS.
OR I *THOUGHT* I DID.
MAYBE IT WAS MY IMAGINA-TION...?

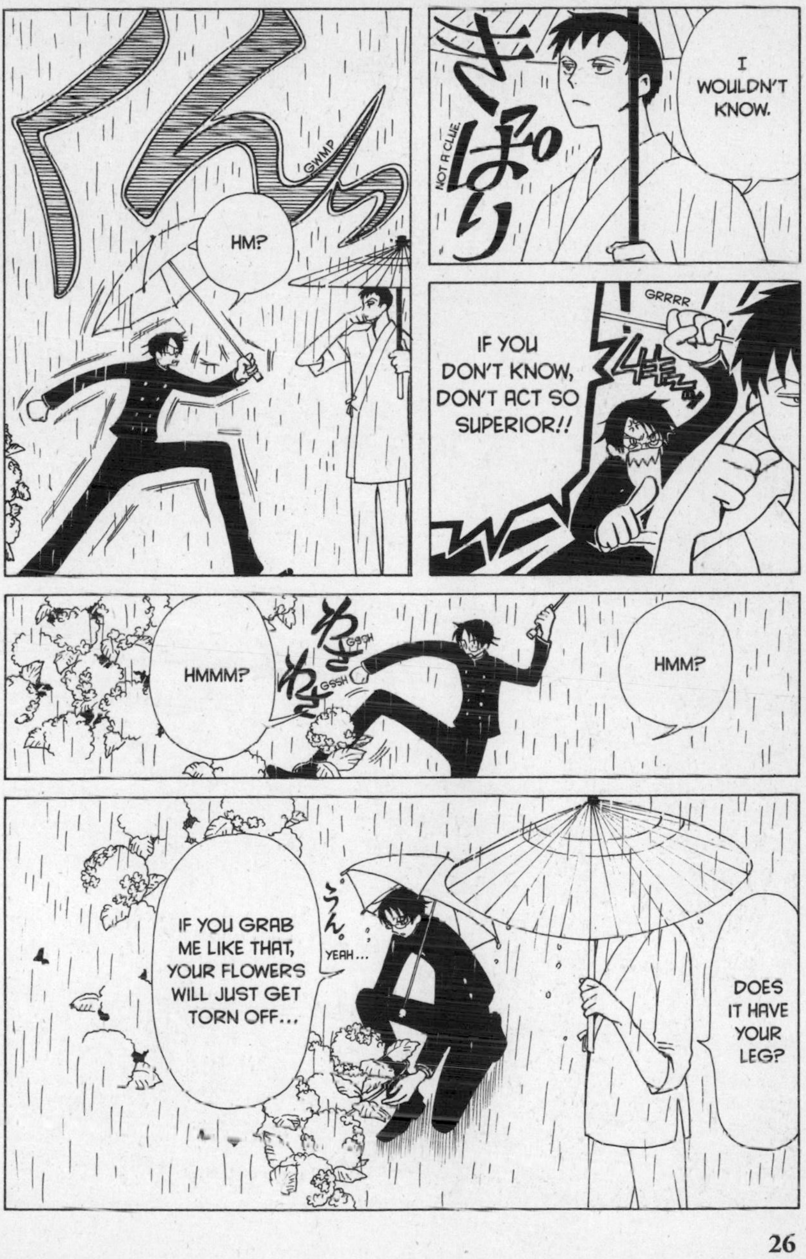

I WOULDN'T KNOW.
きっぱり
NOT A CLUE.
GRRRR
IF YOU DON'T KNOW, DON'T ACT SO SUPERIOR!!
GWMP
HM?
HMM?
わさわさ
GSSH
GSSH
HMMM?
DOES IT HAVE YOUR LEG?
うん。
YEAH...
IF YOU GRAB ME LIKE THAT, YOUR FLOWERS WILL JUST GET TORN OFF...

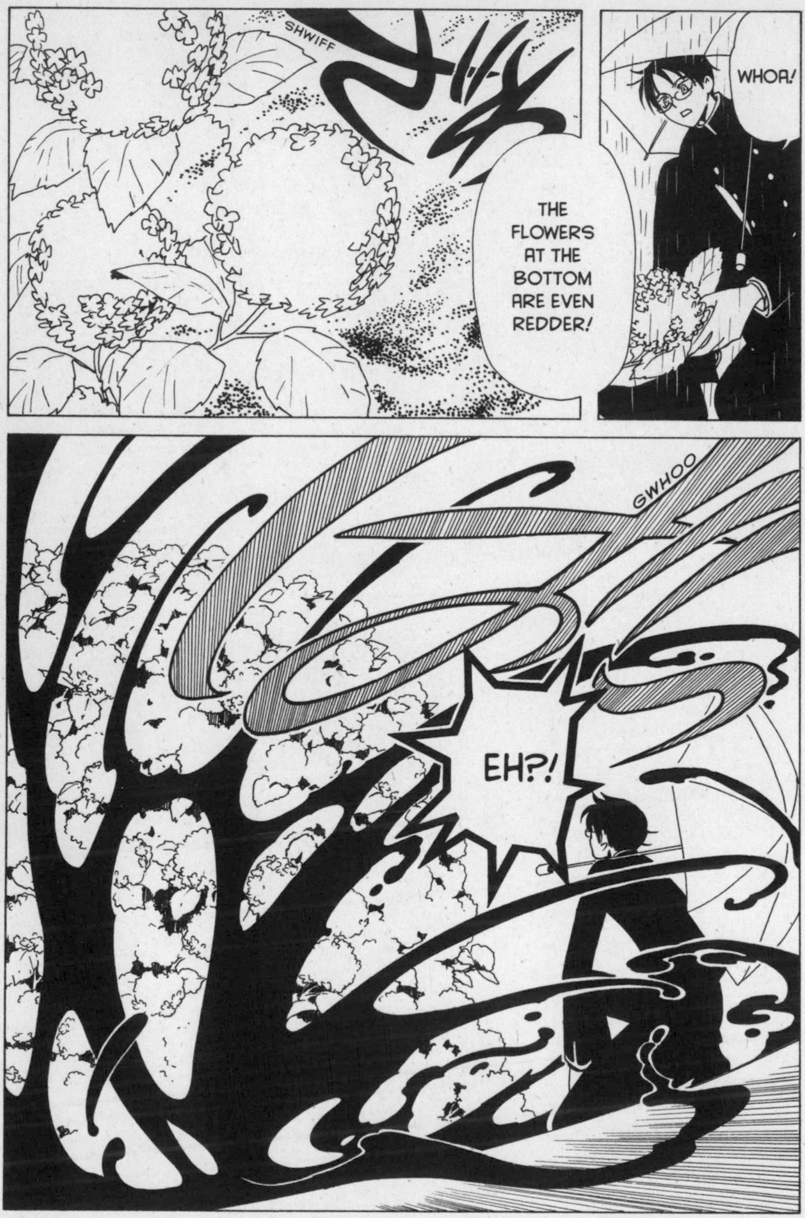
WHOA!
THE FLOWERS AT THE BOTTOM ARE EVEN REDDER!
SHWIFF
GWHOO
EH?!

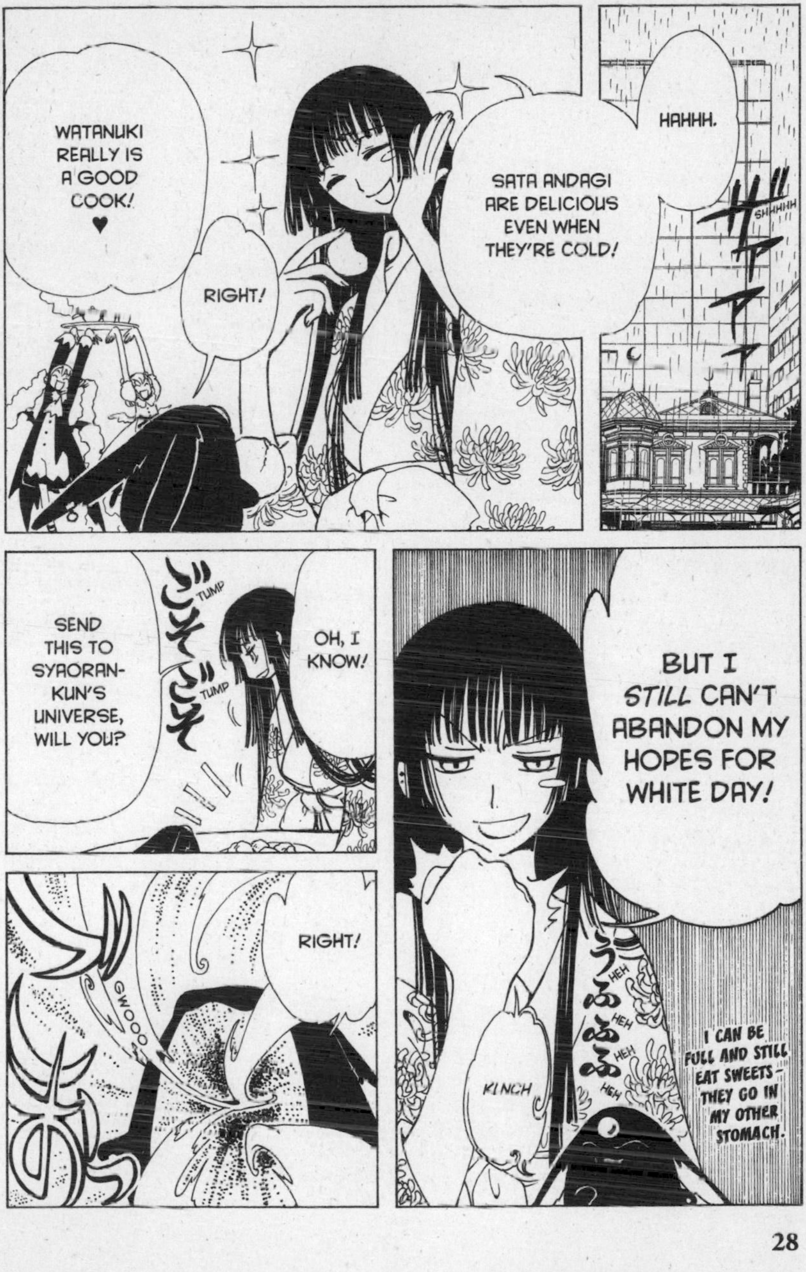
HAHHH.
SHHHHH
SATA ANDAGI ARE DELICIOUS EVEN WHEN THEY'RE COLD!
WATANUKI REALLY IS A GOOD COOK! ♥
RIGHT!
BUT I STILL CAN'T ABANDON MY HOPES FOR WHITE DAY!
HEH HEH HEH HEH
I CAN BE FULL AND STILL EAT SWEETS- THEY GO IN MY OTHER STOMACH.
KINCH
OH, I KNOW!
TUMP TUMP
SEND THIS TO SYAORAN-KUN'S UNIVERSE, WILL YOU?
RIGHT!
GWOOOO

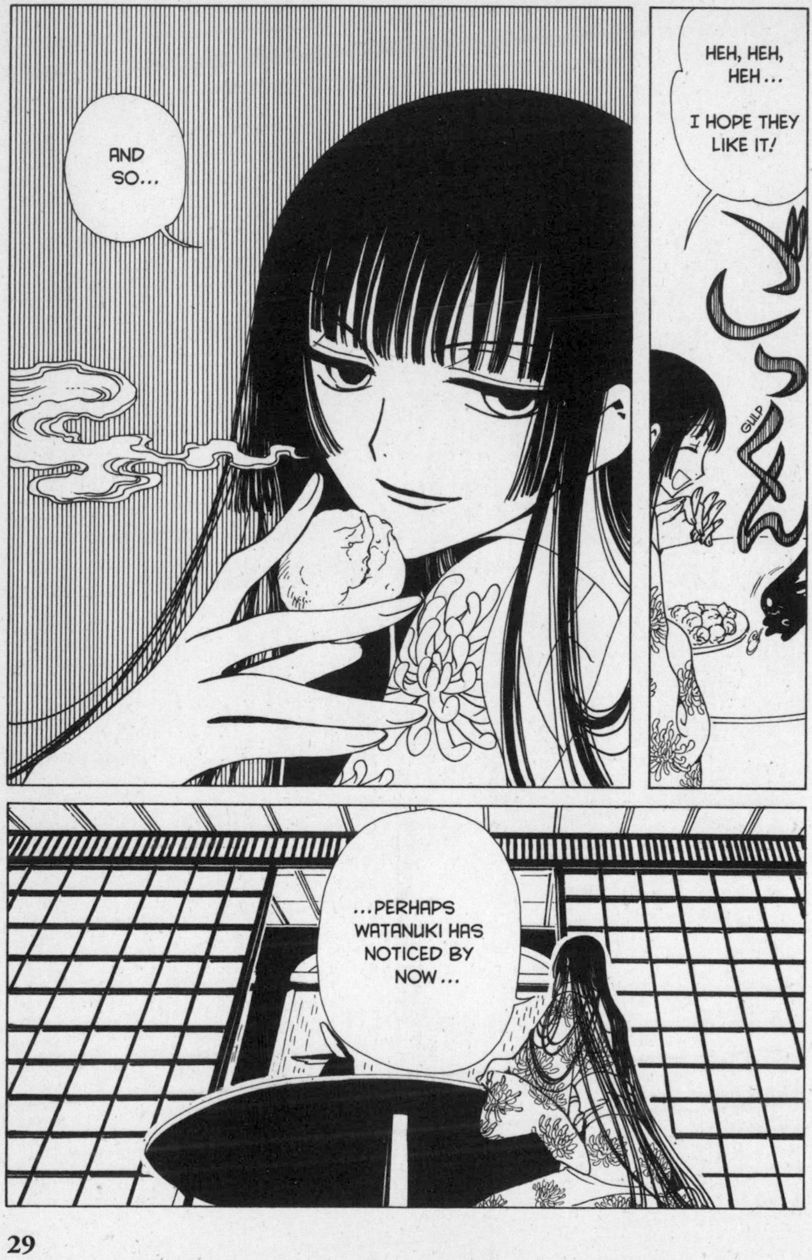
HEH, HEH, HEH... I HOPE THEY LIKE IT!
ごっくん
GULP
AND SO...
...PERHAPS WATANUKI HAS NOTICED BY NOW...

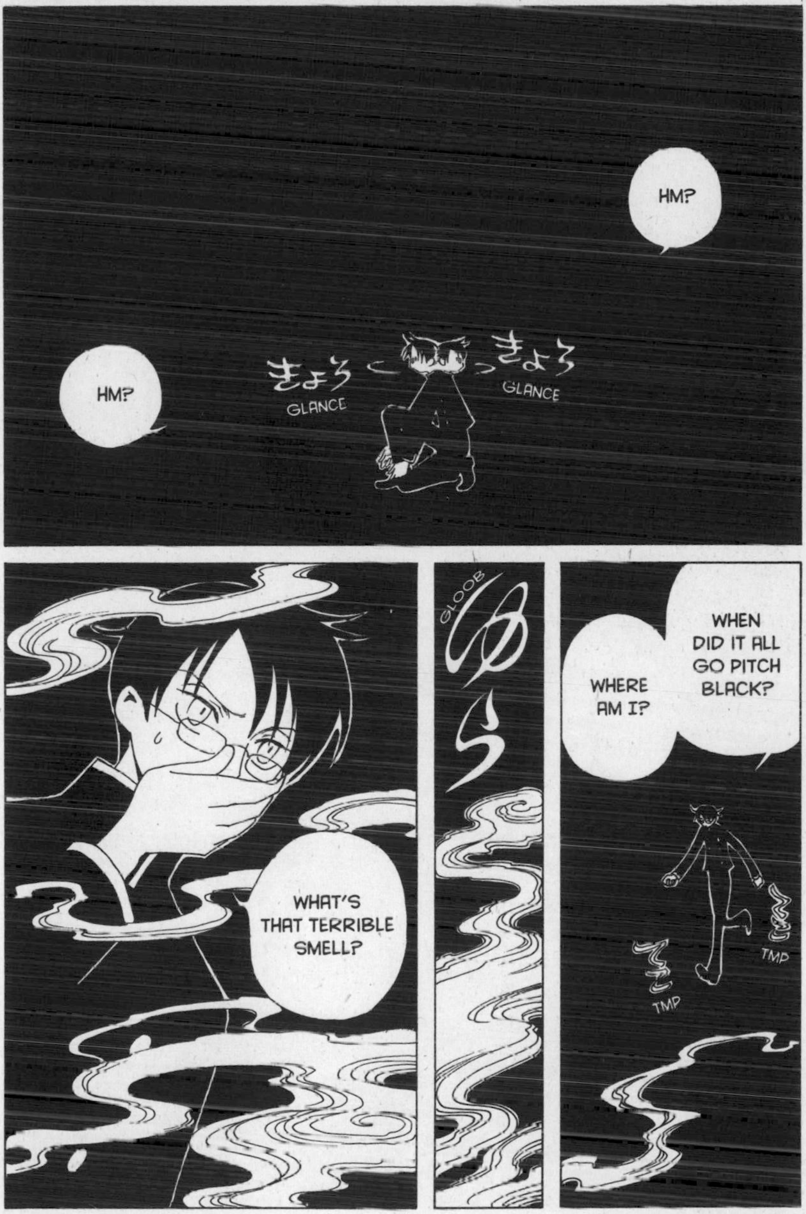
HM?
HM?
きょろ
GLANCE
きょろ
GLANCE
WHEN DID IT ALL GO PITCH BLACK?
WHERE AM I?
TMP
TMP
GLOOB
WHAT'S THAT TERRIBLE SMELL?

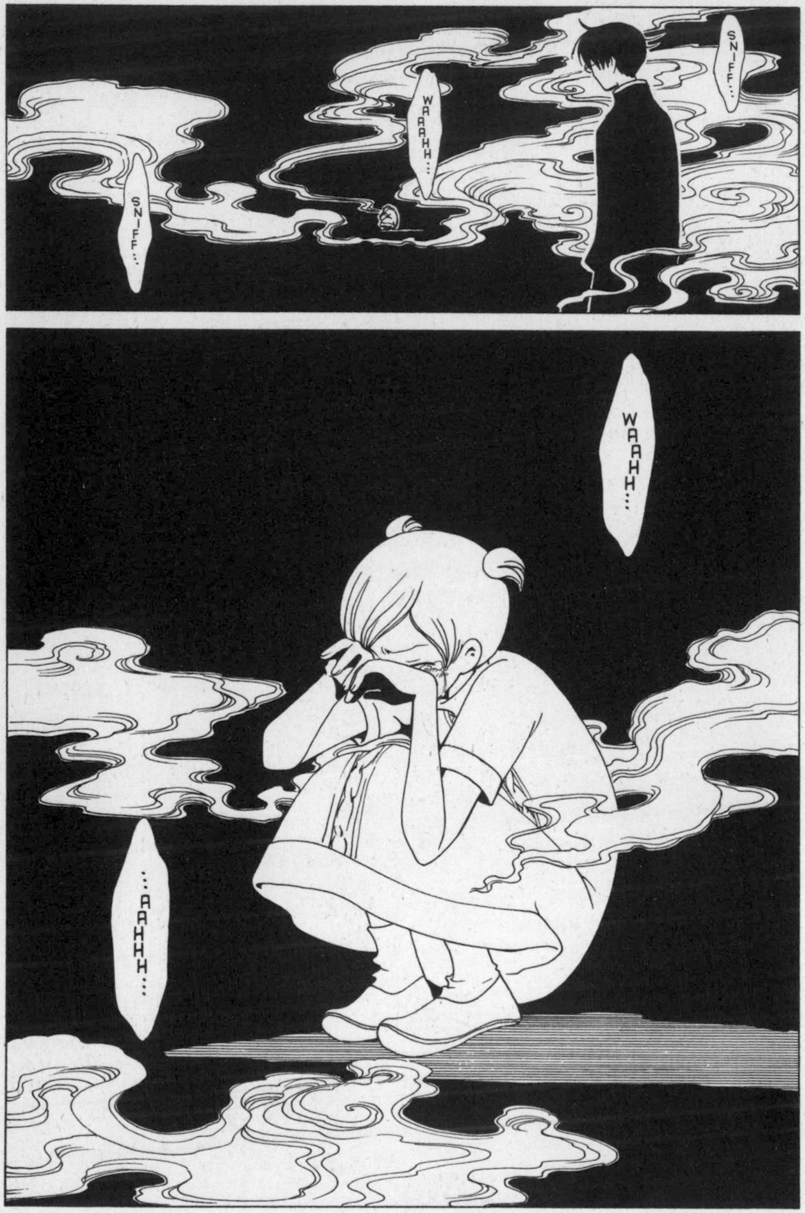
SNIFF...
WAAHH...
SNIFF...
WAAHH...
...AAHHH...

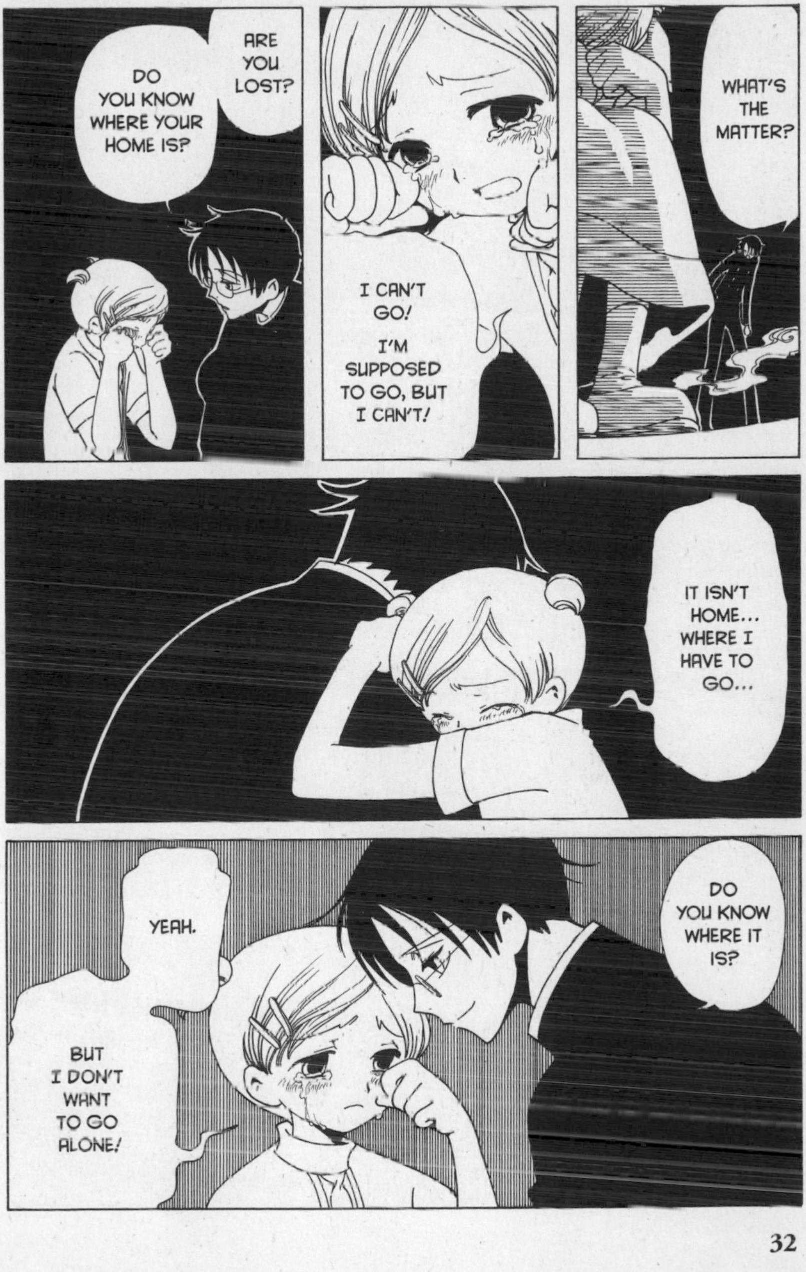
WHAT'S THE MATTER?
I CAN'T GO!
I'M SUPPOSED TO GO, BUT I CAN'T!
ARE YOU LOST?
DO YOU KNOW WHERE YOUR HOME IS?
IT ISN'T HOME... WHERE I HAVE TO GO...
DO YOU KNOW WHERE IT IS?
YEAH.
BUT I DON'T WANT TO GO ALONE!

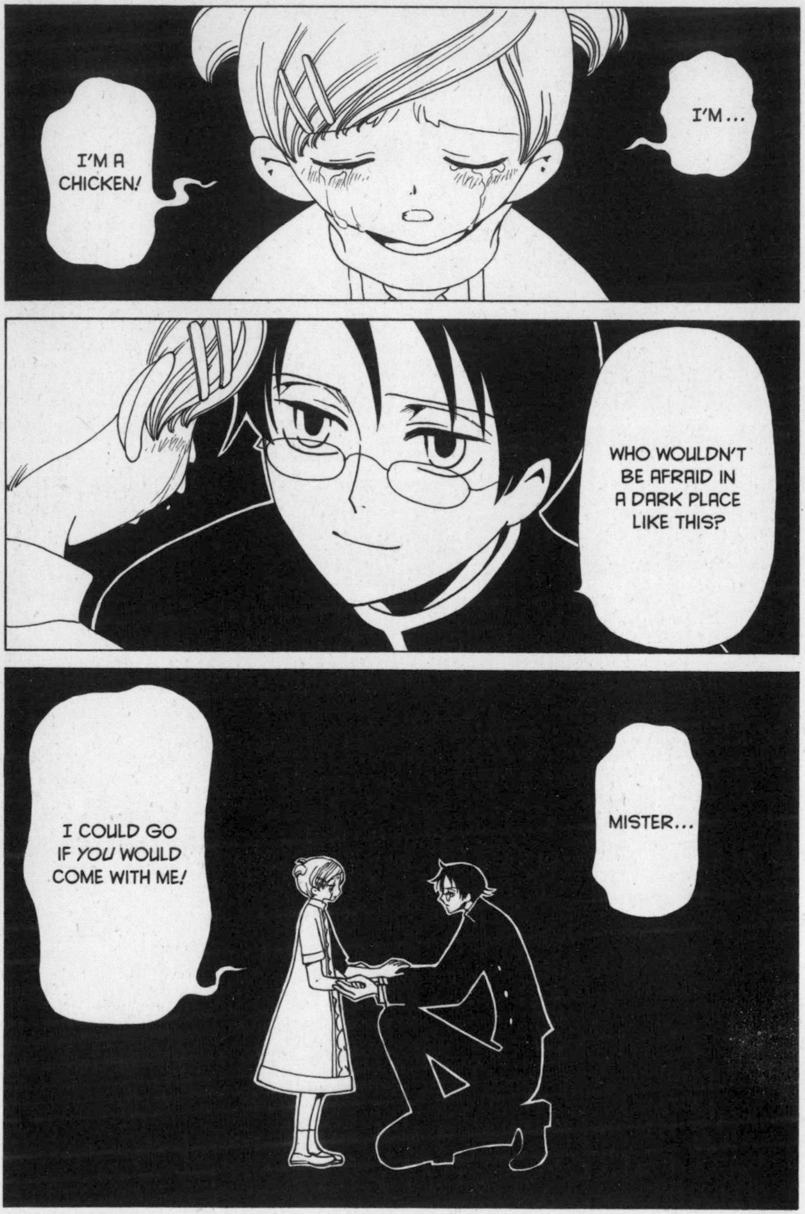
I'M...
I'M A CHICKEN!
WHO WOULDN'T BE AFRAID IN A DARK PLACE LIKE THIS?
MISTER...
I COULD GO IF *YOU* WOULD COME WITH ME!

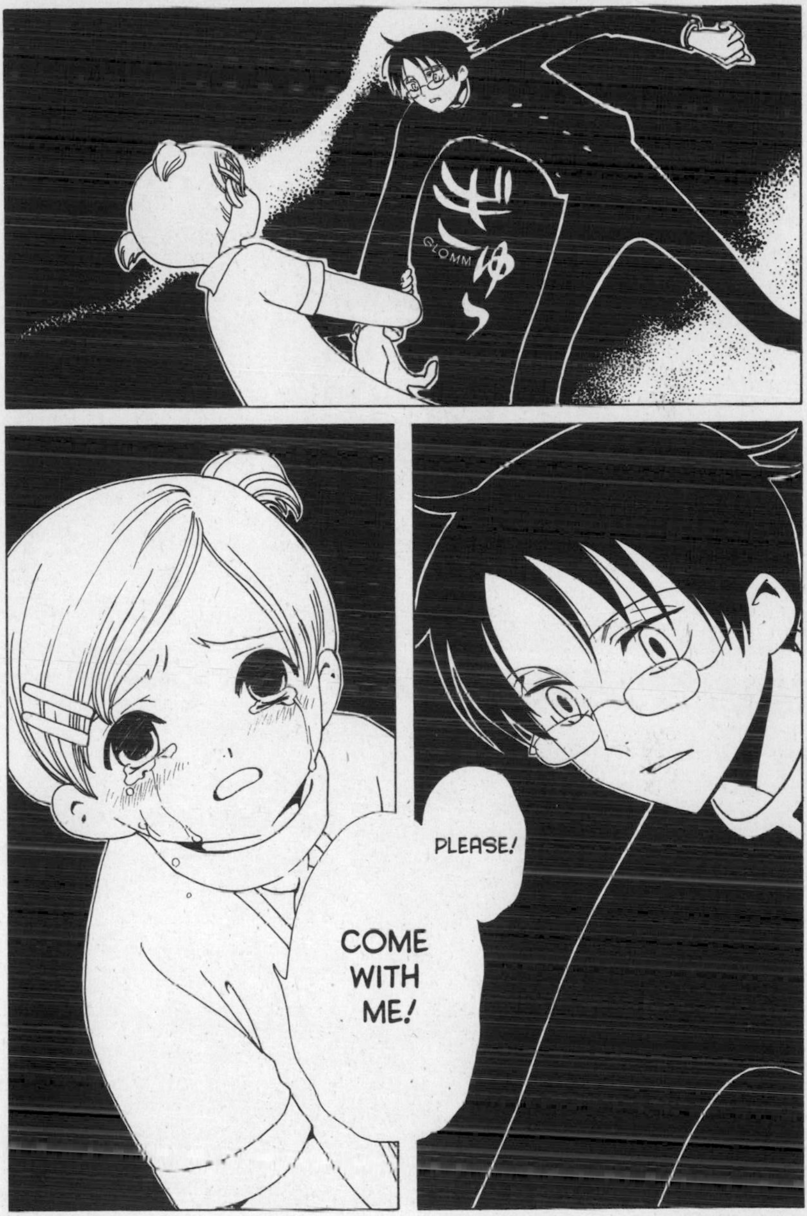
ぎゅっ
GLOMM
PLEASE!
COME WITH ME!

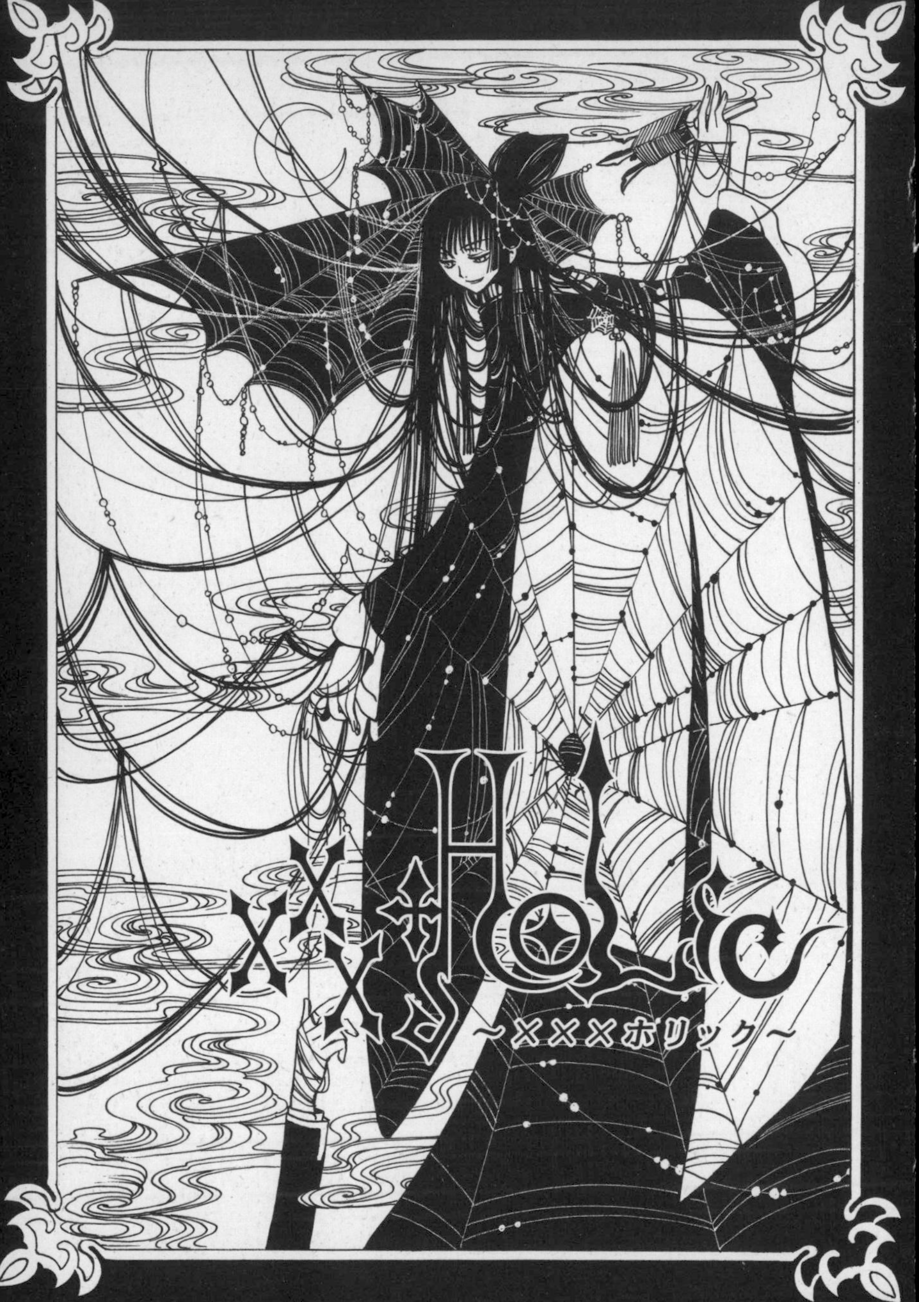
xxxHOLiC
〜×××ホリック〜

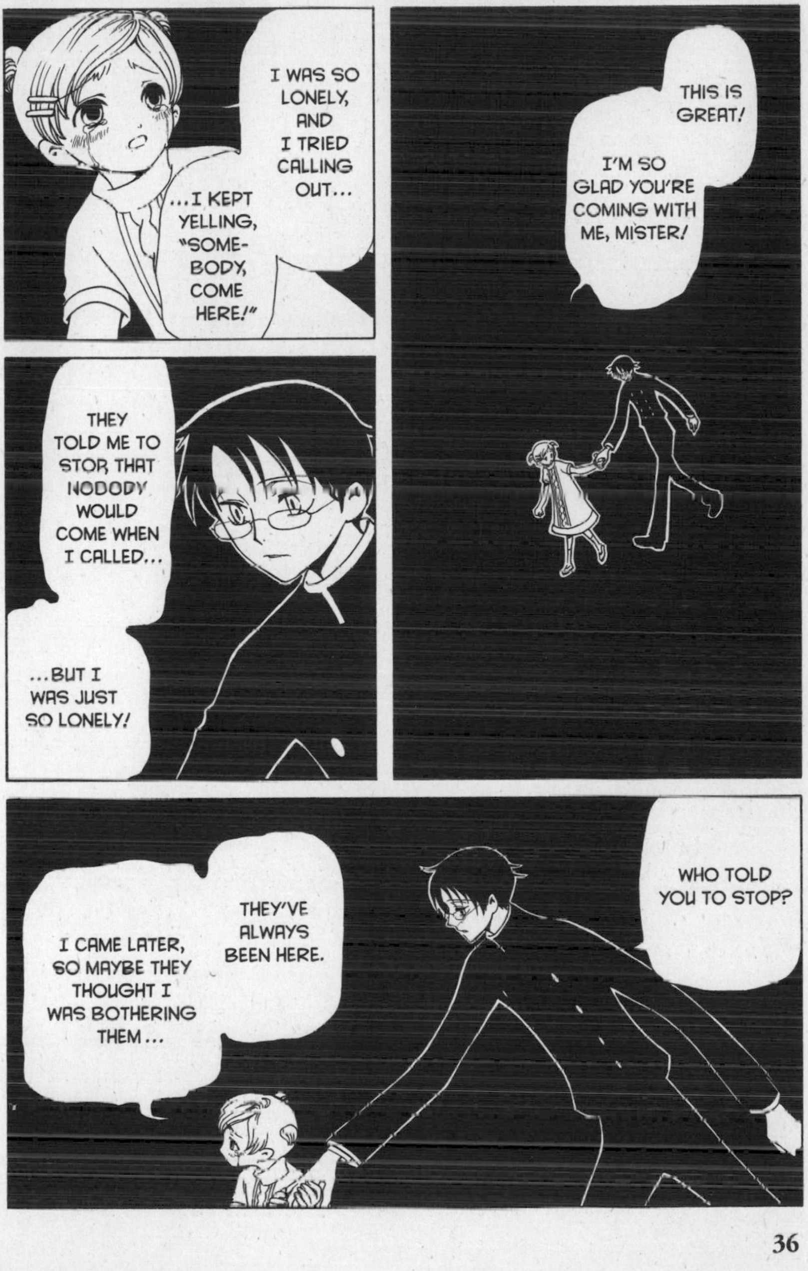
THIS IS GREAT!
I'M SO GLAD YOU'RE COMING WITH ME, MISTER!
I WAS SO LONELY, AND I TRIED CALLING OUT...
...I KEPT YELLING, "SOMEBODY, COME HERE!"
THEY TOLD ME TO STOP, THAT NOBODY WOULD COME WHEN I CALLED...
...BUT I WAS JUST SO LONELY!
WHO TOLD YOU TO STOP?
THEY'VE ALWAYS BEEN HERE.
I CAME LATER, SO MAYBE THEY THOUGHT I WAS BOTHERING THEM...

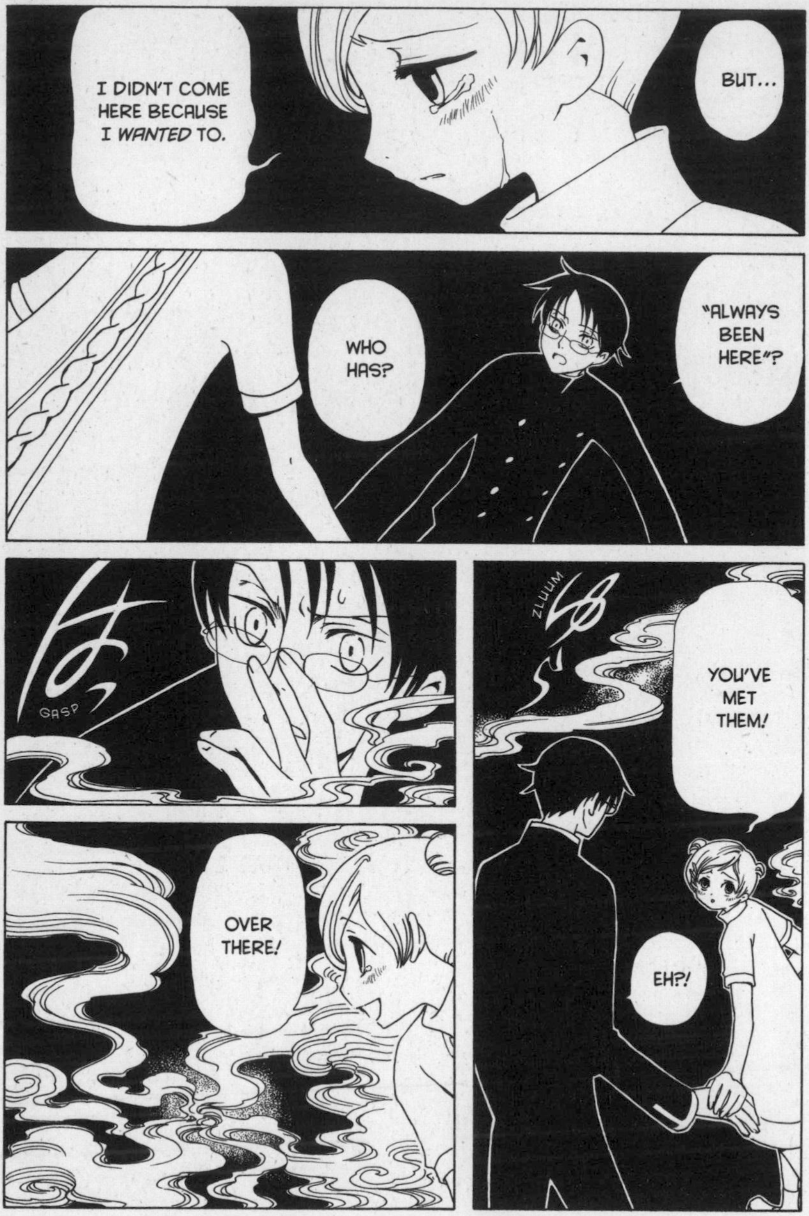
BUT...
I DIDN'T COME HERE BECAUSE I WANTED TO.
"ALWAYS BEEN HERE"?
WHO HAS?
ZLUUM
YOU'VE MET THEM!
EH?!
GASP
OVER THERE!

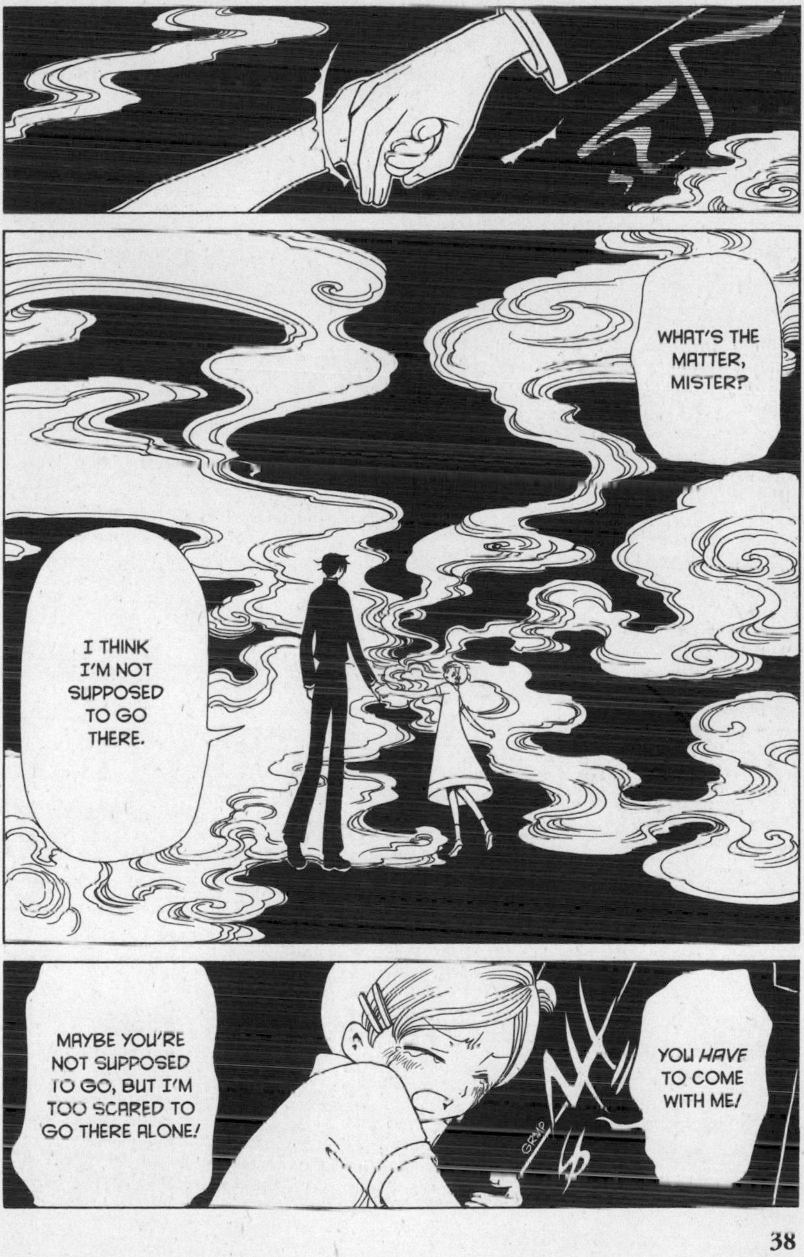
WHAT'S THE MATTER, MISTER?
I THINK I'M NOT SUPPOSED TO GO THERE.
YOU *HAVE* TO COME WITH ME!
GRMP
MAYBE YOU'RE NOT SUPPOSED TO GO, BUT I'M TOO SCARED TO GO THERE ALONE!

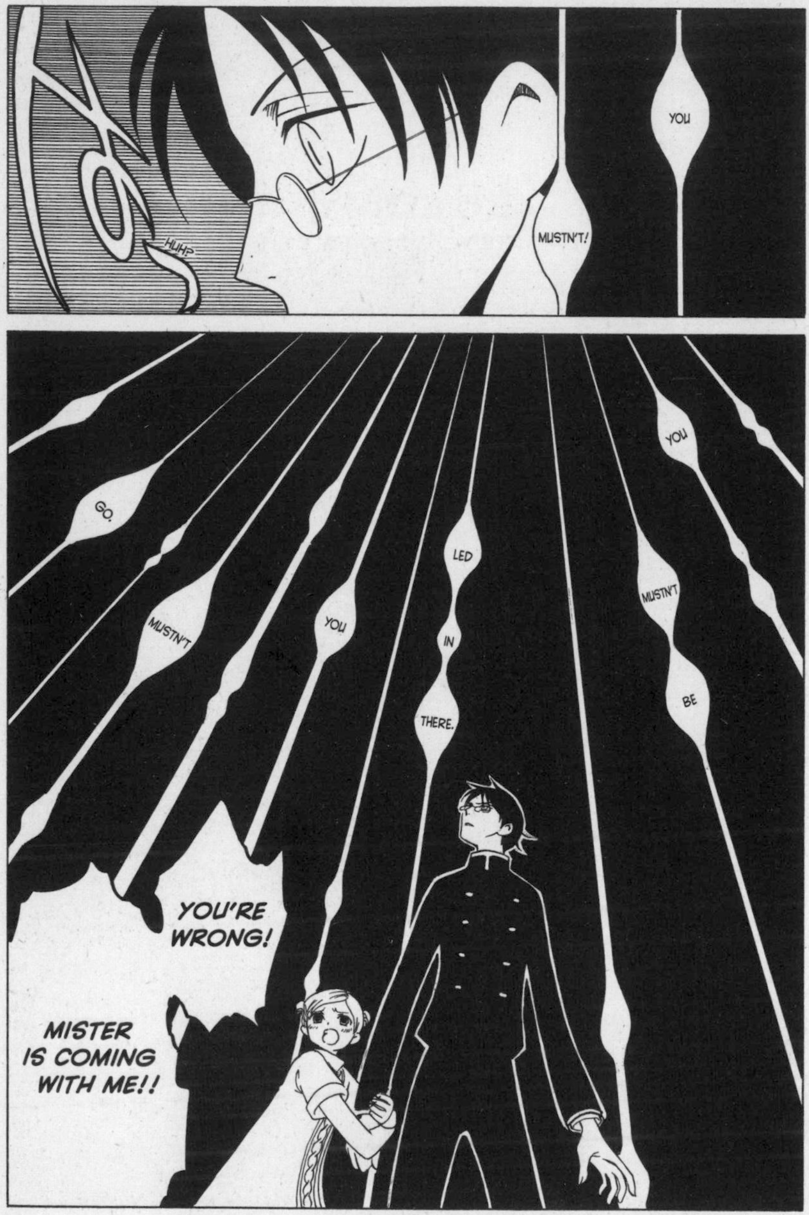
YOU
MUSTN'T!
HUH?
YOU
MUSTN'T
BE
LED
IN
THERE.
YOU
MUSTN'T
GO.
YOU'RE WRONG!
MISTER IS COMING WITH ME!!

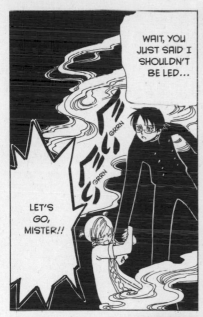

WAIT, YOU JUST SAID I SHOULDN'T BE LED...

GRRN GRRN GRRN

LET'S GO, MISTER!!

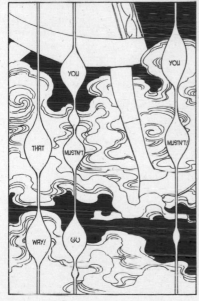

YOU YOU

THAT MUSTN'T MUSTN'T!

WAY! GO

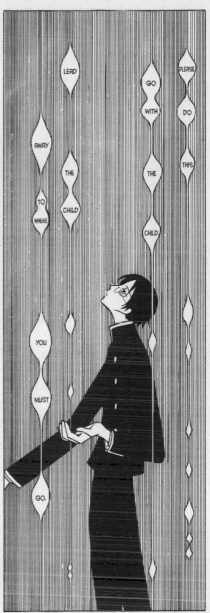

LEAD GO PLEASE

AWAY WITH DO

THE THE THIS.

TO CHILD CHILD.

WHERE

YOU

MUST

GO.

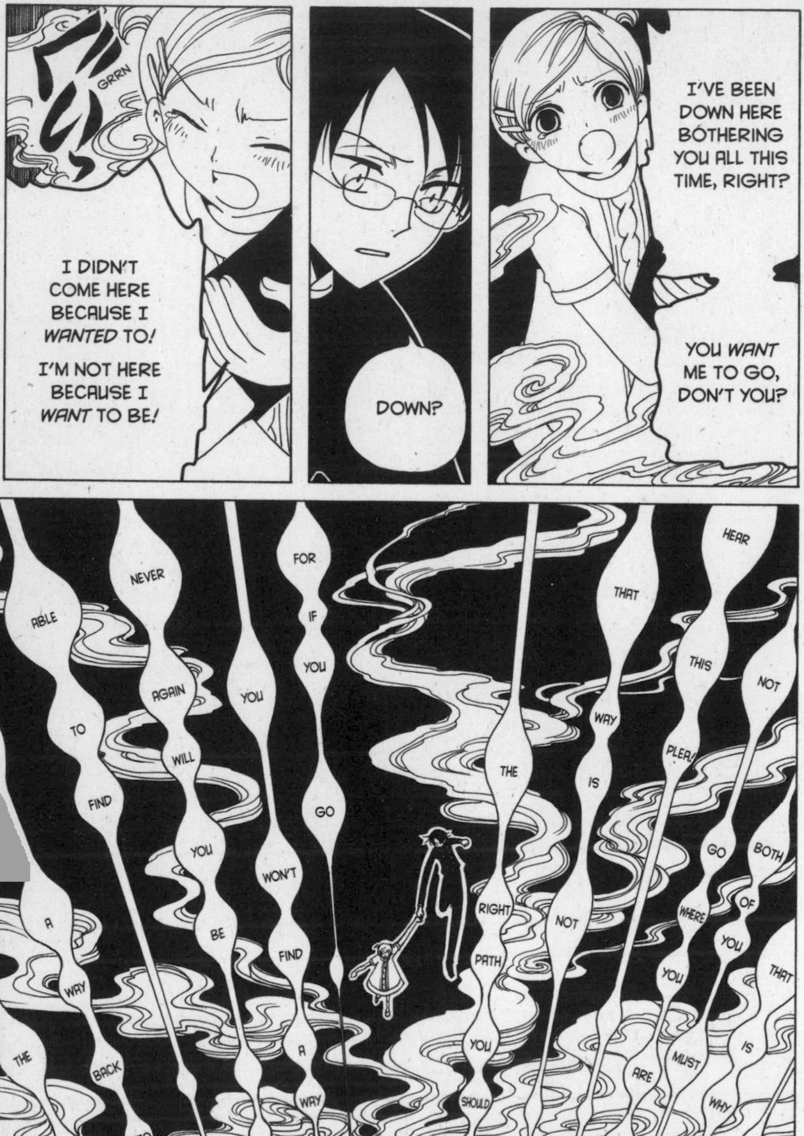
I'VE BEEN DOWN HERE BOTHERING YOU ALL THIS TIME, RIGHT?
YOU WANT ME TO GO, DON'T YOU?
DOWN?
GRRN
I DIDN'T COME HERE BECAUSE I WANTED TO!
I'M NOT HERE BECAUSE I WANT TO BE!
HEAR THIS PLEA!
NOT BOTH OF YOU THAT IS WHY
THAT WAY IS NOT
GO WHERE YOU MUST
ARE GOING
THE RIGHT PATH YOU SHOULD TREAD
FOR IF YOU GO
YOU WON'T FIND A WAY BACK.
NEVER AGAIN WILL YOU BE
ABLE TO FIND A WAY BACK INTO THE LIGHT!

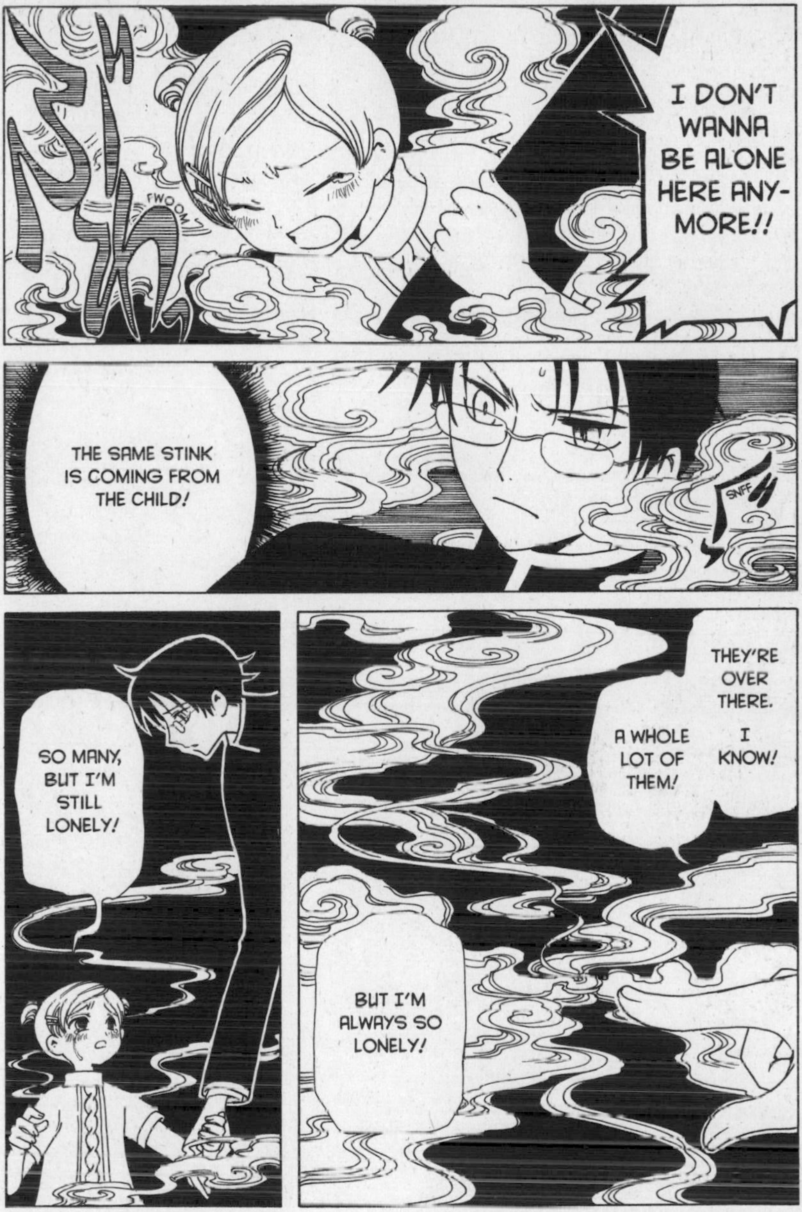
I DON'T WANNA BE ALONE HERE ANYMORE!!
FWOOM
SNFF
THE SAME STINK IS COMING FROM THE CHILD!
THEY'RE OVER THERE.
I KNOW!
A WHOLE LOT OF THEM!
BUT I'M ALWAYS SO LONELY!
SO MANY, BUT I'M STILL LONELY!

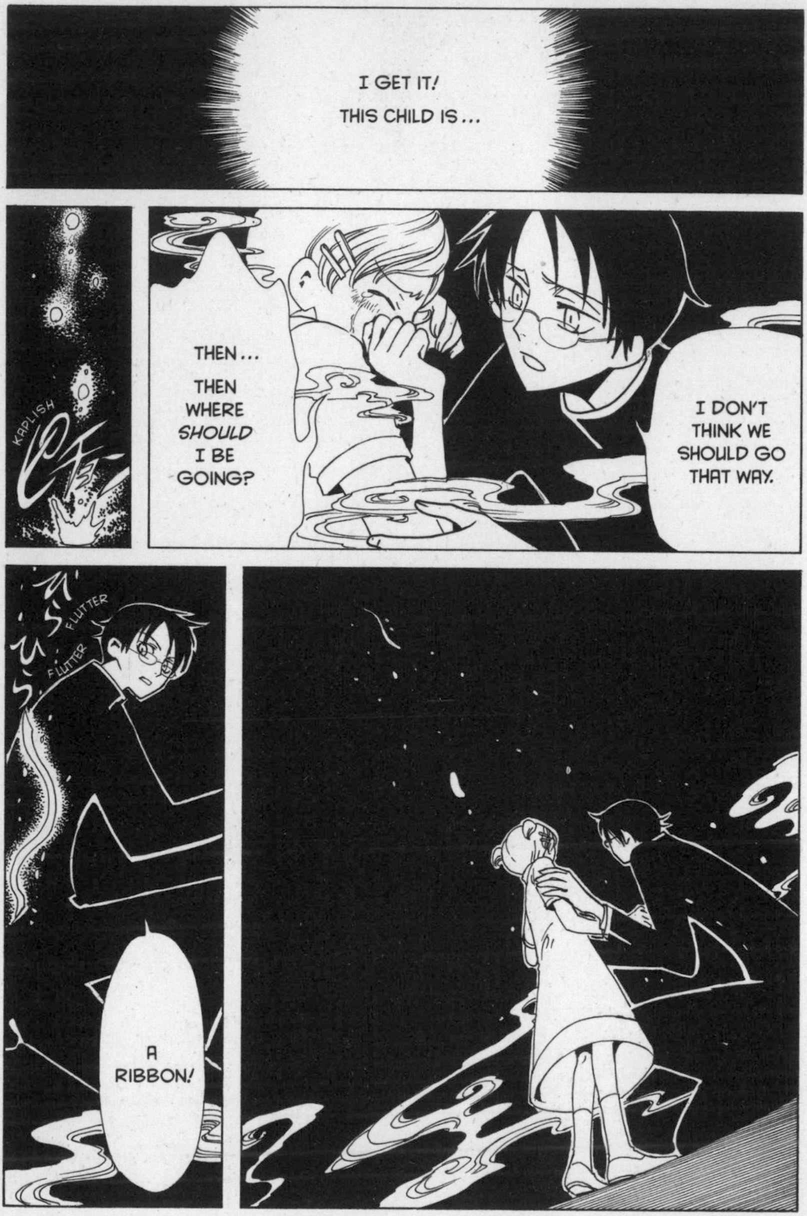
I GET IT!
THIS CHILD IS...
I DON'T THINK WE SHOULD GO THAT WAY.
THEN...
THEN WHERE *SHOULD* I BE GOING?
KAPLISH
FLUTTER
FLUTTER
A RIBBON!

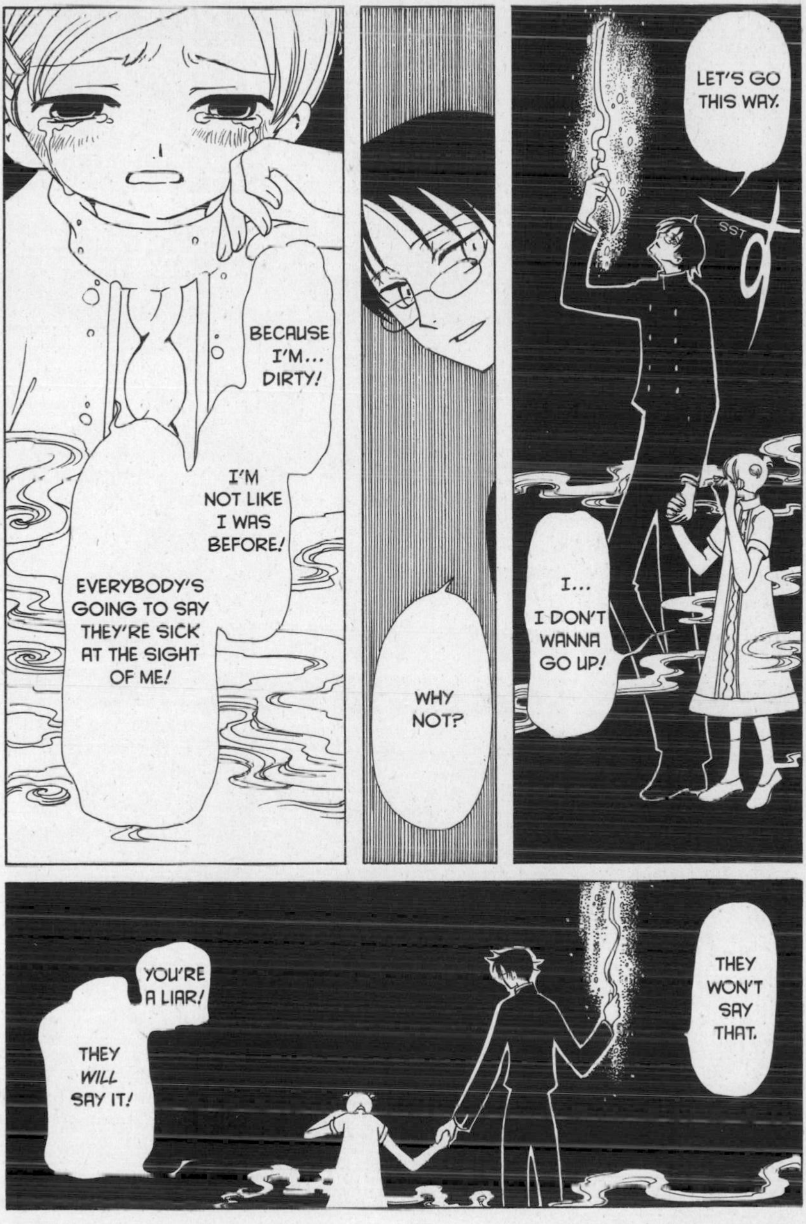
LET'S GO THIS WAY.
SST
I...
I DON'T WANNA GO UP!
WHY NOT?
BECAUSE I'M... DIRTY!
I'M NOT LIKE I WAS BEFORE!
EVERYBODY'S GOING TO SAY THEY'RE SICK AT THE SIGHT OF ME!
THEY WON'T SAY THAT.
YOU'RE A LIAR!
THEY *WILL* SAY IT!

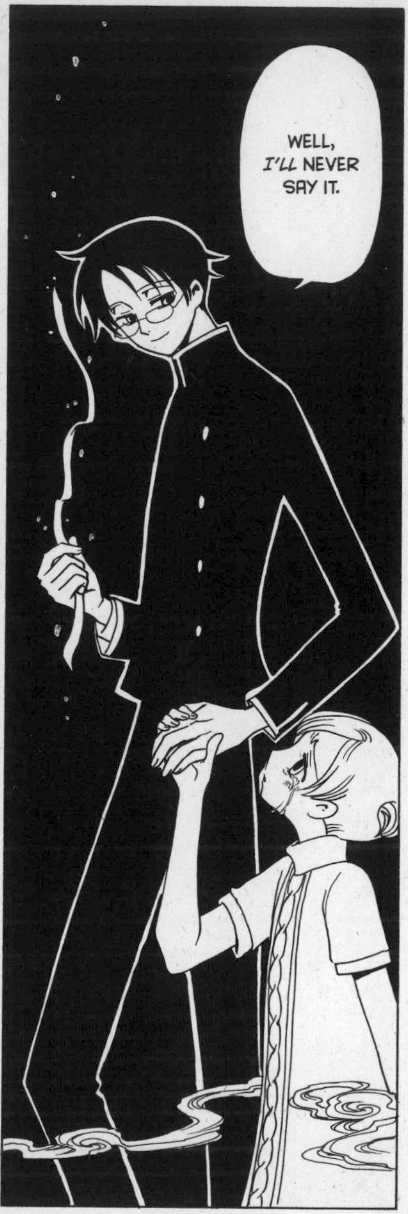
WELL, I'LL NEVER SAY IT.

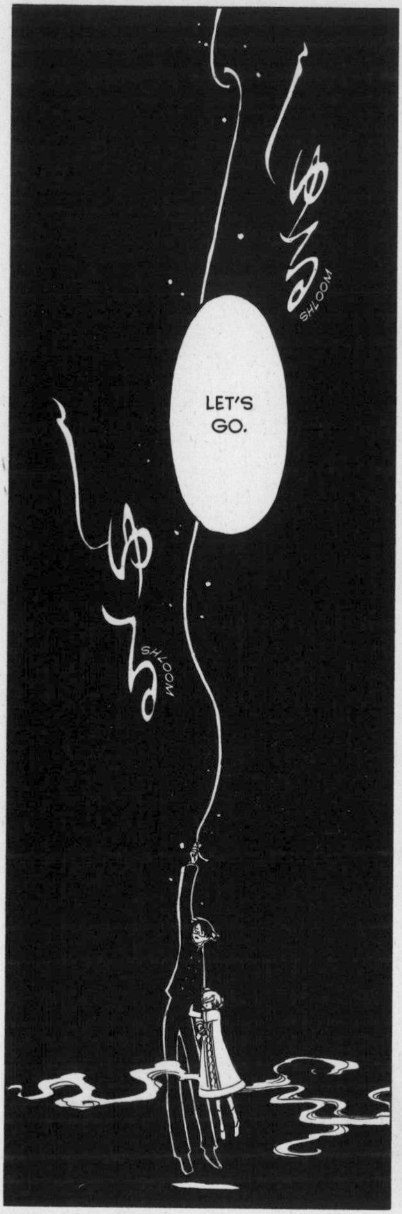
しゅる
SHLOOM
LET'S GO.
しゅる
SHLOOM

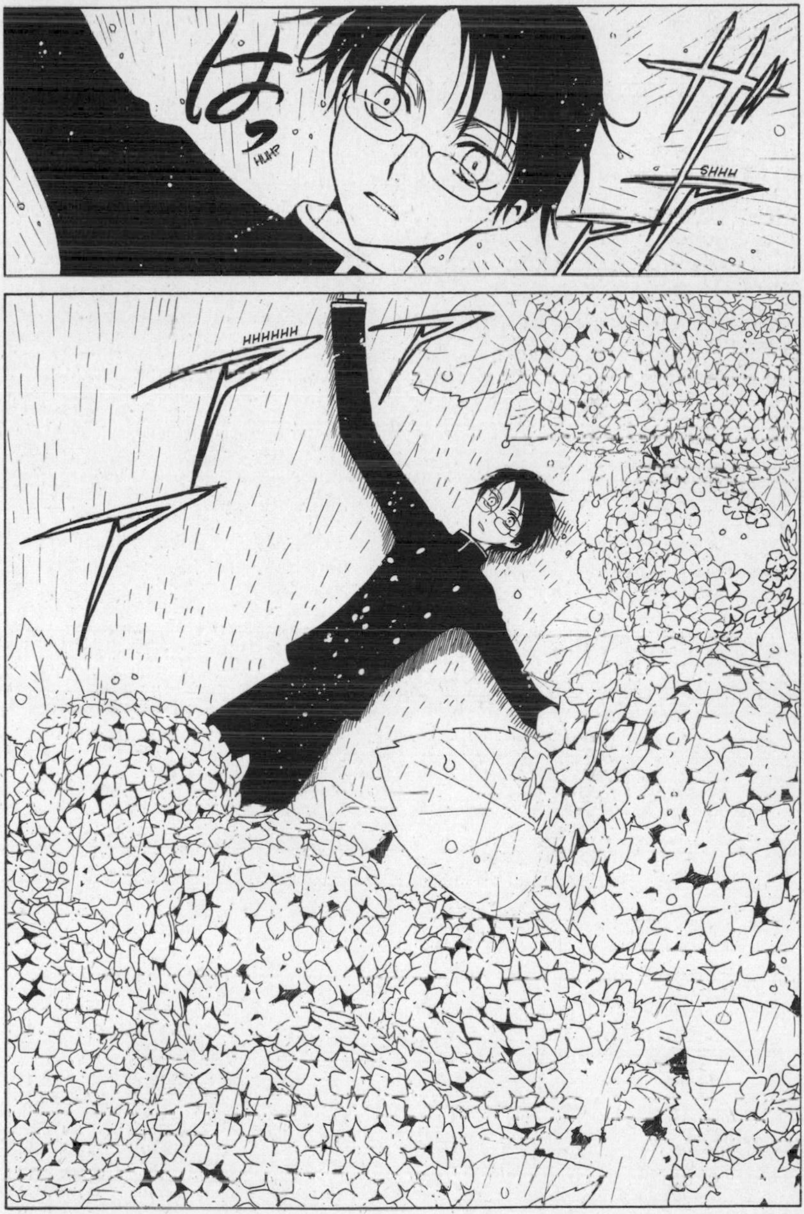
SHHH
はっ
HUMP
HHHHHH

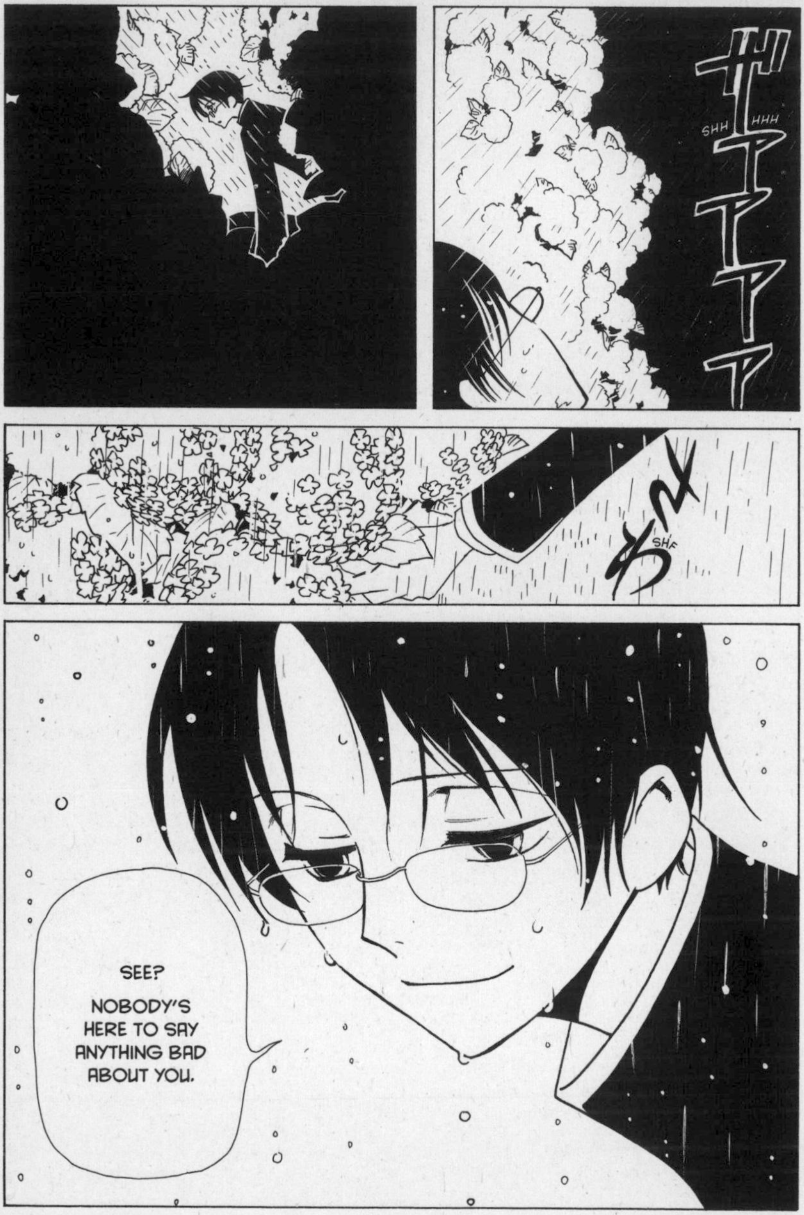
SHH HHH
SHF
SEE? NOBODY'S HERE TO SAY ANYTHING BAD ABOUT YOU.

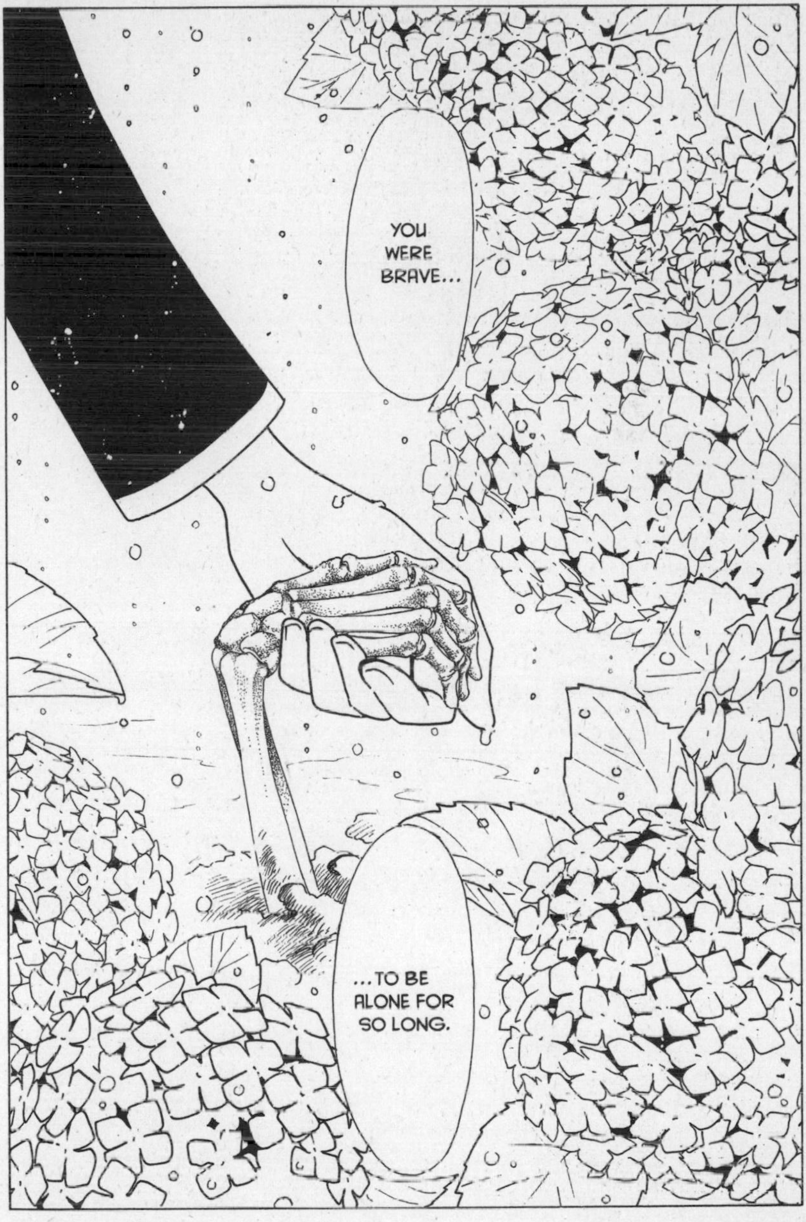
YOU WERE BRAVE...
...TO BE ALONE FOR SO LONG.

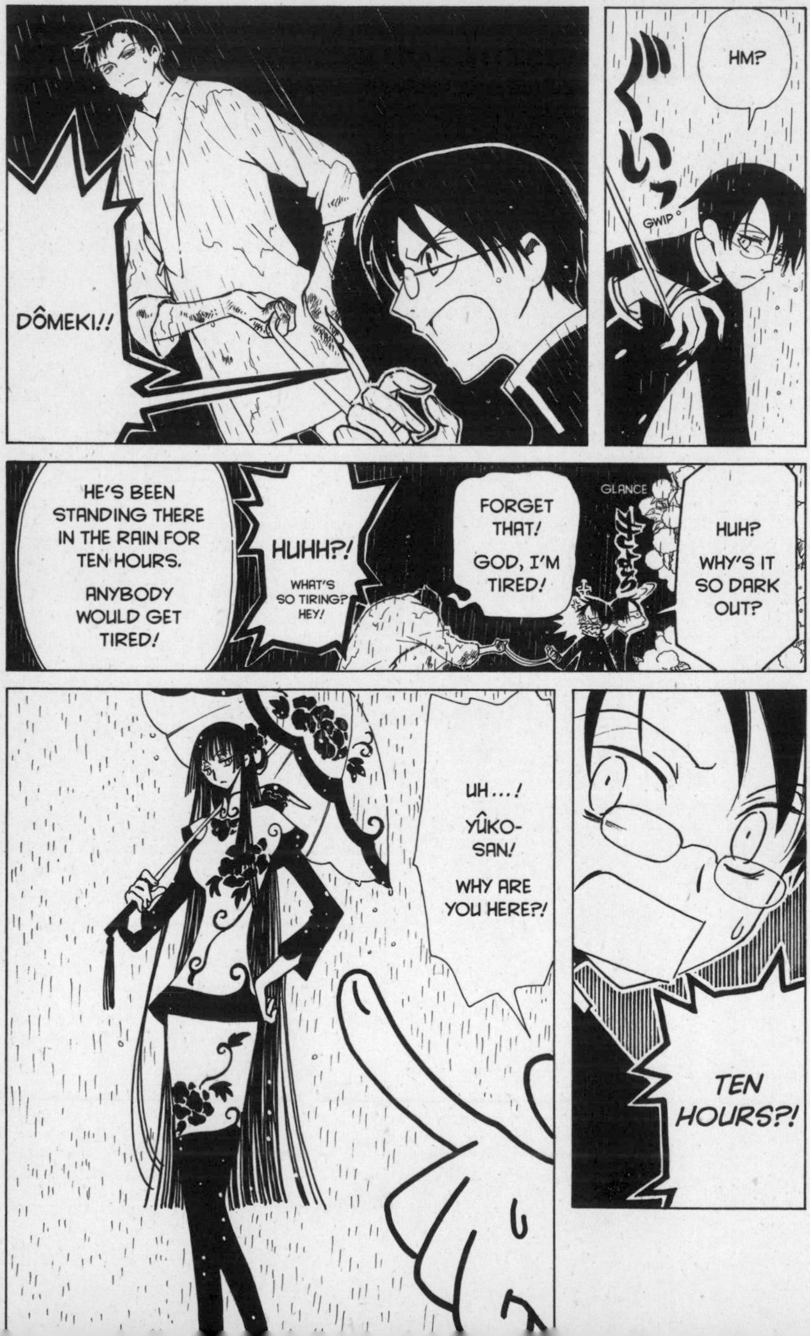
HM?
ぐいっ
GWIP
DÔMEKI!!
HUH? WHY'S IT SO DARK OUT?
GLANCE
FORGET THAT! GOD, I'M TIRED!
HUHH?!
WHAT'S SO TIRING? HEY!
HE'S BEEN STANDING THERE IN THE RAIN FOR TEN HOURS. ANYBODY WOULD GET TIRED!
TEN HOURS?!
UH...! YÛKO-SAN! WHY ARE YOU HERE?!

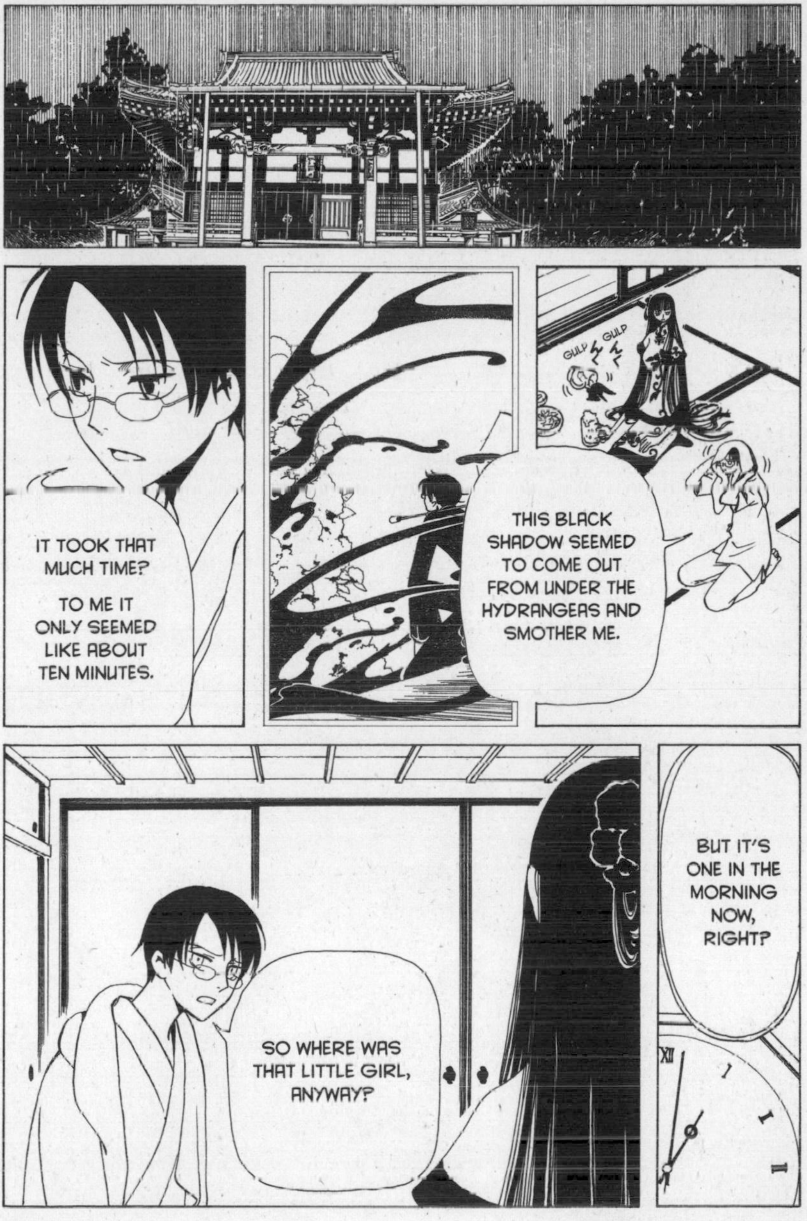
GULP GULP
THIS BLACK SHADOW SEEMED TO COME OUT FROM UNDER THE HYDRANGEAS AND SMOTHER ME.
IT TOOK THAT MUCH TIME?
TO ME IT ONLY SEEMED LIKE ABOUT TEN MINUTES.
BUT IT'S ONE IN THE MORNING NOW, RIGHT?
SO WHERE WAS THAT LITTLE GIRL, ANYWAY?

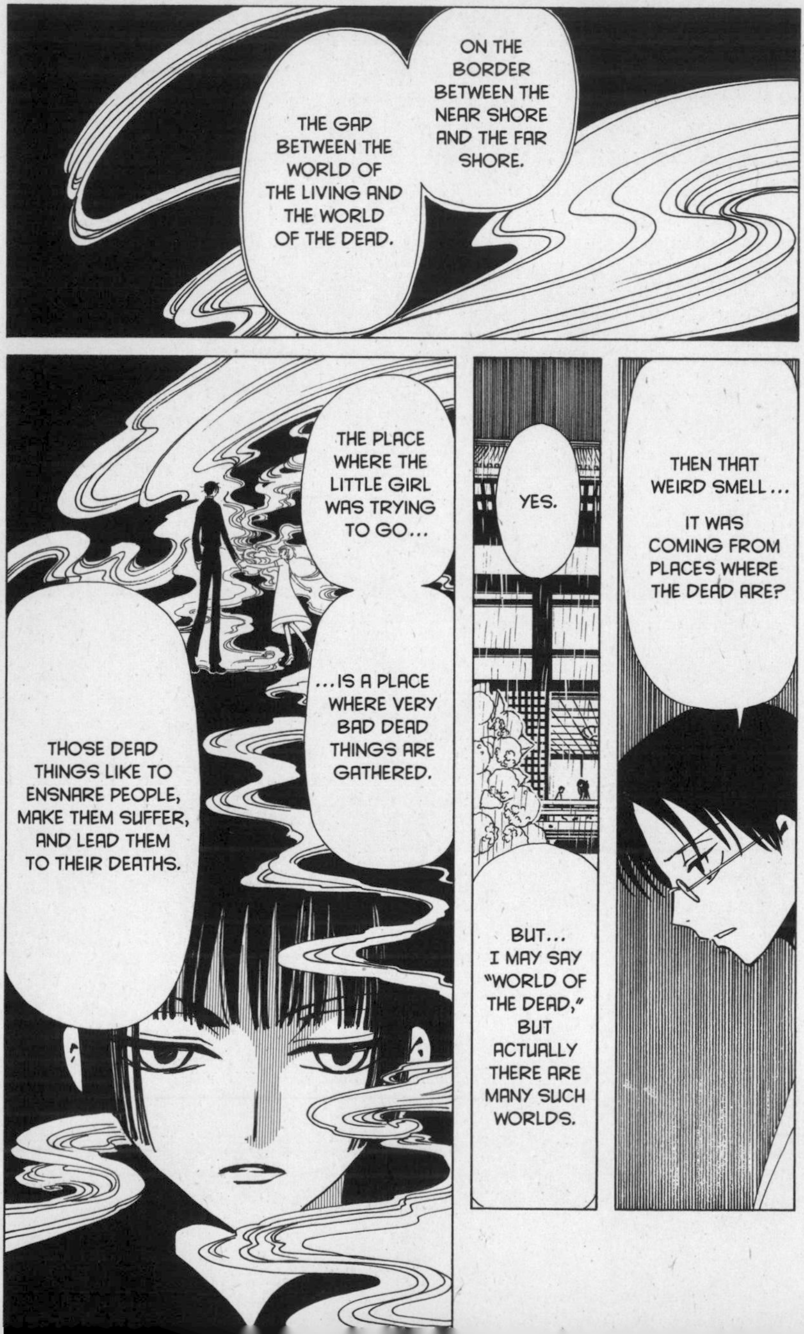
ON THE BORDER BETWEEN THE NEAR SHORE AND THE FAR SHORE.
THE GAP BETWEEN THE WORLD OF THE LIVING AND THE WORLD OF THE DEAD.
THEN THAT WEIRD SMELL... IT WAS COMING FROM PLACES WHERE THE DEAD ARE?
YES.
BUT... I MAY SAY "WORLD OF THE DEAD," BUT ACTUALLY THERE ARE MANY SUCH WORLDS.
THE PLACE WHERE THE LITTLE GIRL WAS TRYING TO GO...
...IS A PLACE WHERE VERY BAD DEAD THINGS ARE GATHERED.
THOSE DEAD THINGS LIKE TO ENSNARE PEOPLE, MAKE THEM SUFFER, AND LEAD THEM TO THEIR DEATHS.

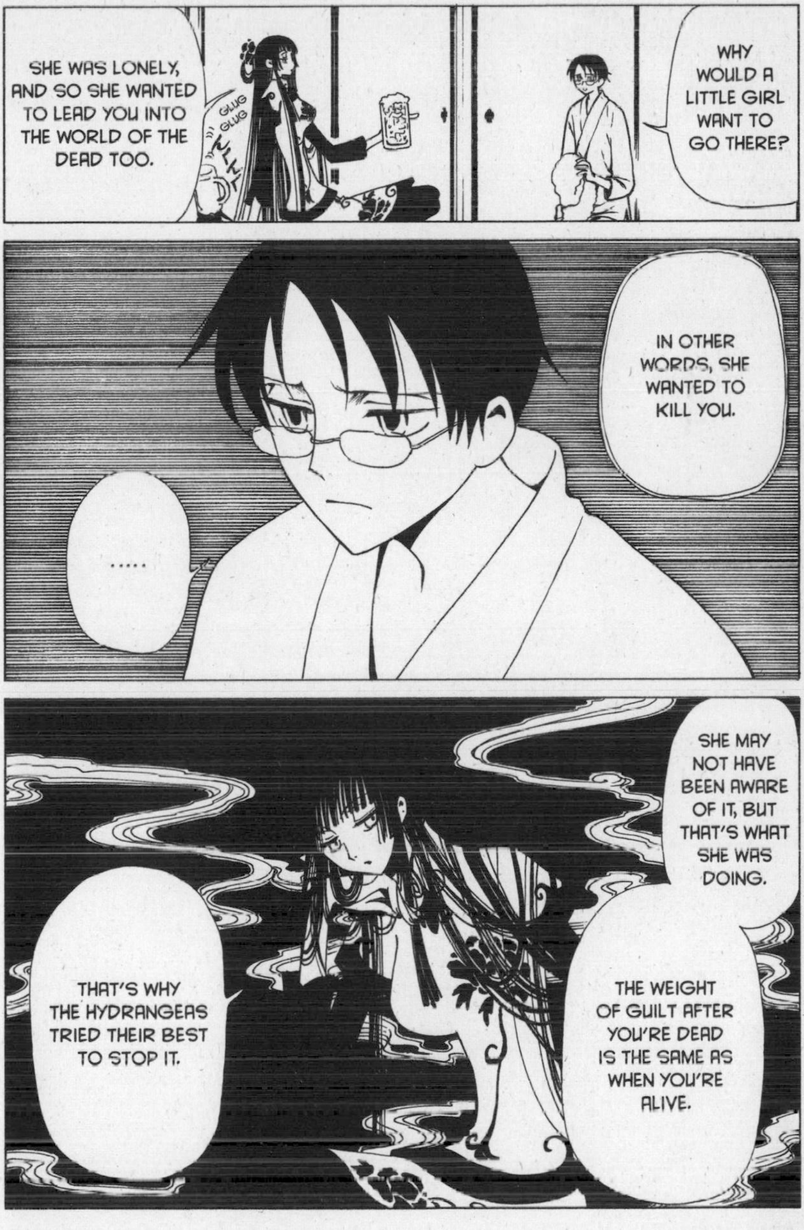
WHY WOULD A LITTLE GIRL WANT TO GO THERE?
SHE WAS LONELY, AND SO SHE WANTED TO LEAD YOU INTO THE WORLD OF THE DEAD TOO.
GLUG GLUG
IN OTHER WORDS, SHE WANTED TO KILL YOU.
.....
SHE MAY NOT HAVE BEEN AWARE OF IT, BUT THAT'S WHAT SHE WAS DOING.
THE WEIGHT OF GUILT AFTER YOU'RE DEAD IS THE SAME AS WHEN YOU'RE ALIVE.
THAT'S WHY THE HYDRANGEAS TRIED THEIR BEST TO STOP IT.

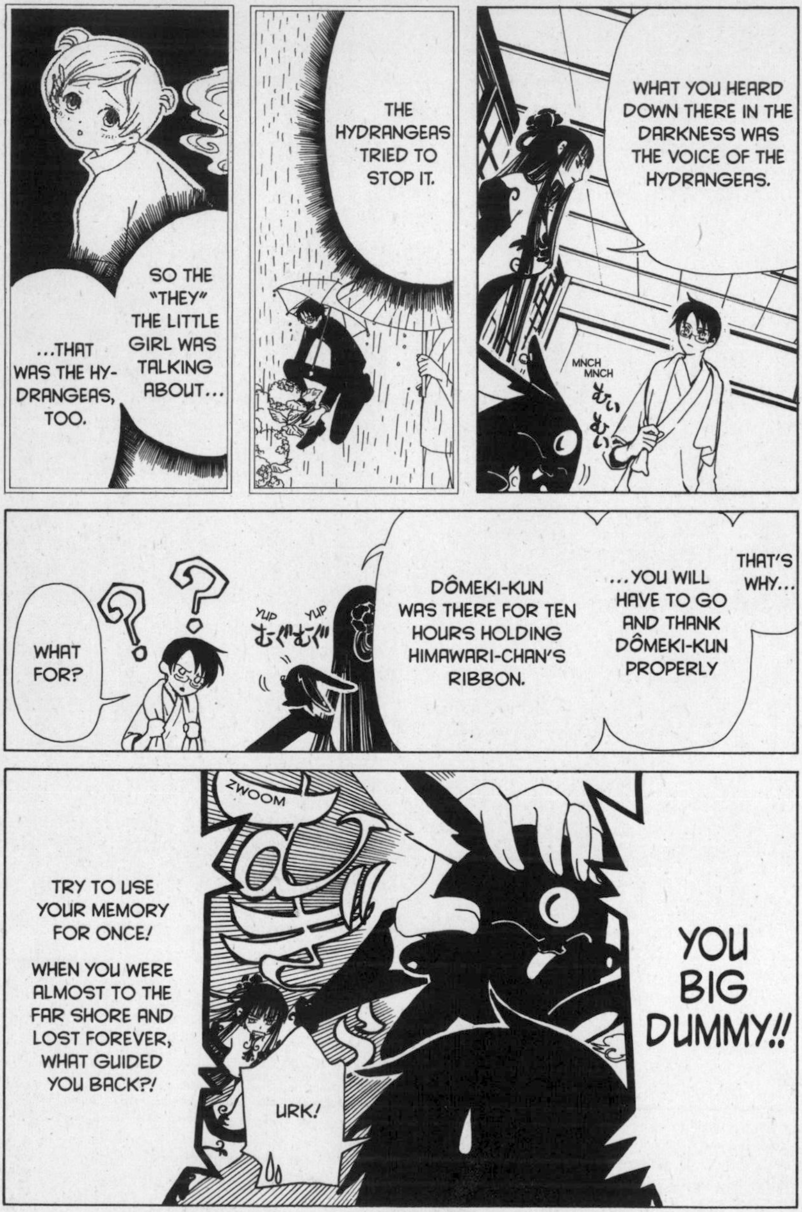
WHAT YOU HEARD DOWN THERE IN THE DARKNESS WAS THE VOICE OF THE HYDRANGEAS.
MNCH MNCH
THE HYDRANGEAS TRIED TO STOP IT.
SO THE "THEY" THE LITTLE GIRL WAS TALKING ABOUT...
...THAT WAS THE HYDRANGEAS, TOO.
THAT'S WHY...
...YOU WILL HAVE TO GO AND THANK DÔMEKI-KUN PROPERLY
DÔMEKI-KUN WAS THERE FOR TEN HOURS HOLDING HIMAWARI-CHAN'S RIBBON.
YUP YUP
WHAT FOR?
YOU BIG DUMMY!!
ZWOOM
TRY TO USE YOUR MEMORY FOR ONCE!
WHEN YOU WERE ALMOST TO THE FAR SHORE AND LOST FOREVER, WHAT GUIDED YOU BACK?!
URK!

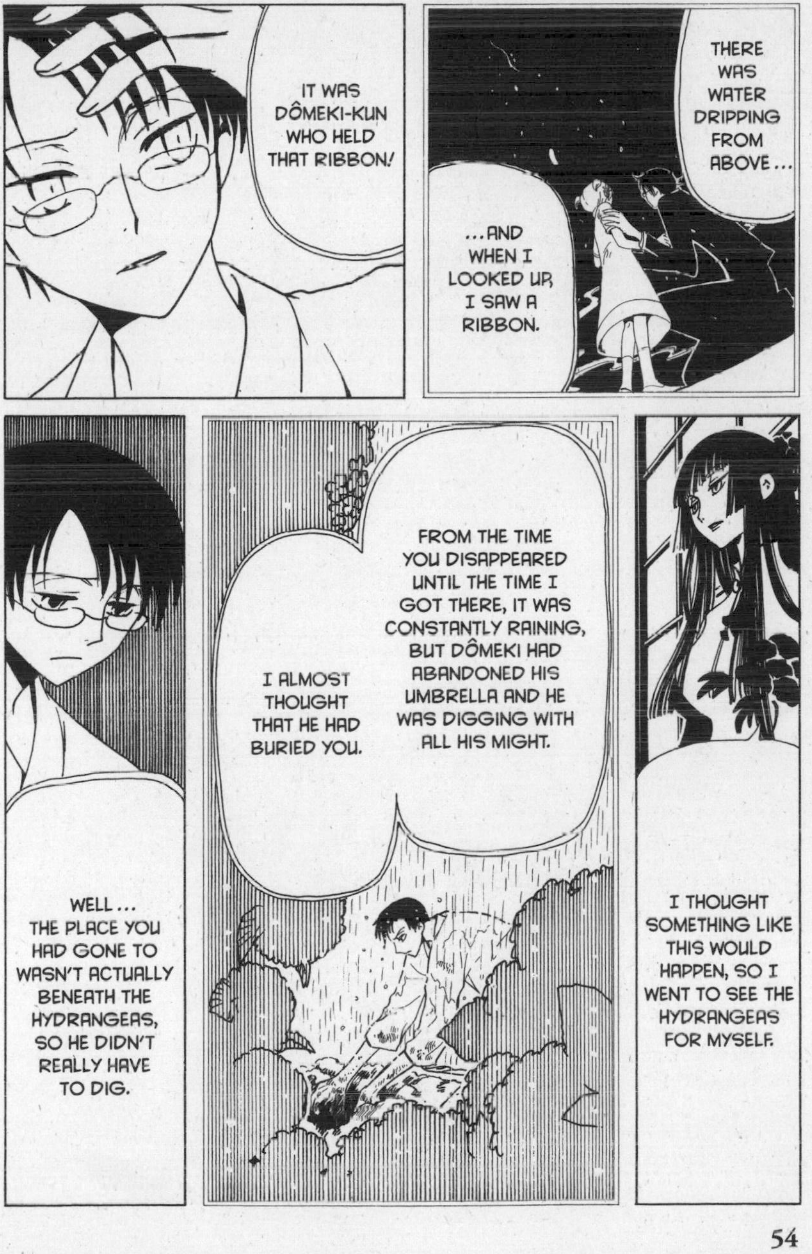
THERE WAS WATER DRIPPING FROM ABOVE...
...AND WHEN I LOOKED UP, I SAW A RIBBON.
IT WAS DÔMEKI-KUN WHO HELD THAT RIBBON!
I THOUGHT SOMETHING LIKE THIS WOULD HAPPEN, SO I WENT TO SEE THE HYDRANGEAS FOR MYSELF.
FROM THE TIME YOU DISAPPEARED UNTIL THE TIME I GOT THERE, IT WAS CONSTANTLY RAINING, BUT DÔMEKI HAD ABANDONED HIS UMBRELLA AND HE WAS DIGGING WITH ALL HIS MIGHT.
I ALMOST THOUGHT THAT HE HAD BURIED YOU.
WELL... THE PLACE YOU HAD GONE TO WASN'T ACTUALLY BENEATH THE HYDRANGEAS, SO HE DIDN'T REALLY HAVE TO DIG.

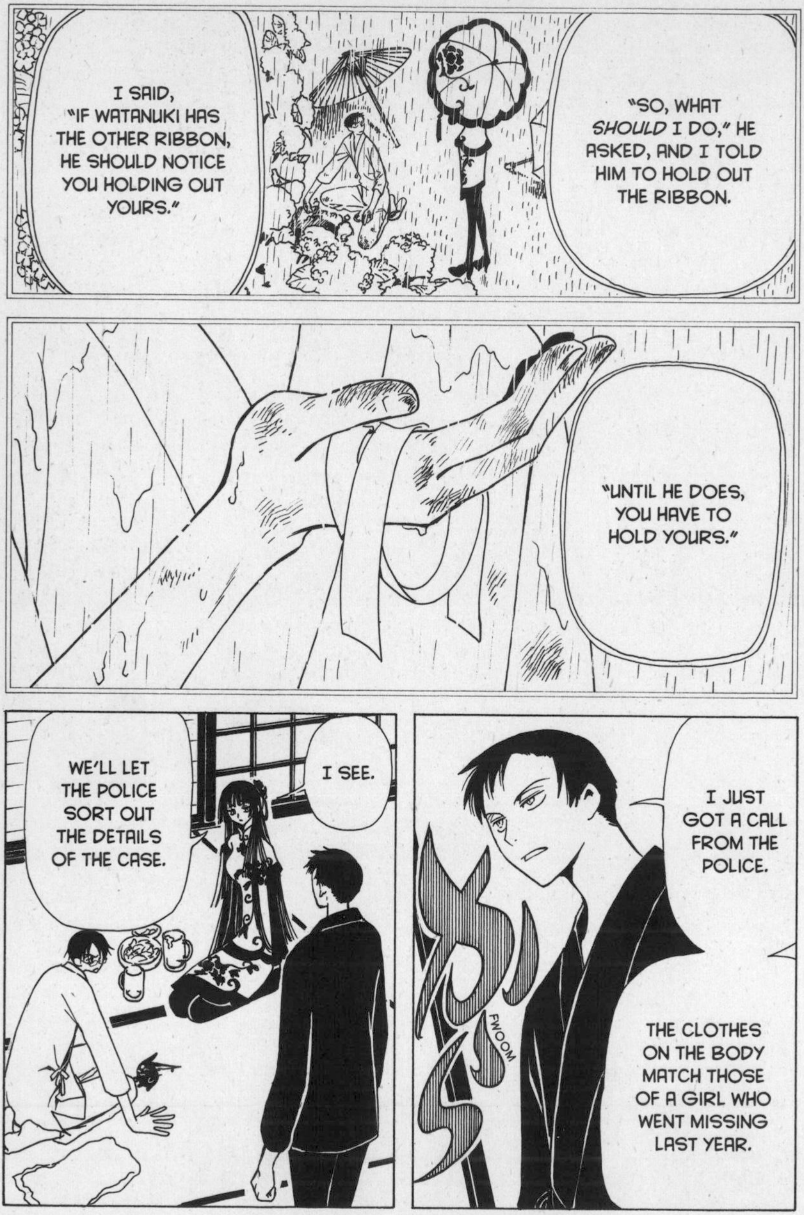
"SO, WHAT *SHOULD* I DO," HE ASKED, AND I TOLD HIM TO HOLD OUT THE RIBBON.
I SAID, "IF WATANUKI HAS THE OTHER RIBBON, HE SHOULD NOTICE YOU HOLDING OUT YOURS."
"UNTIL HE DOES, YOU HAVE TO HOLD YOURS."
I JUST GOT A CALL FROM THE POLICE.
FWOOM
THE CLOTHES ON THE BODY MATCH THOSE OF A GIRL WHO WENT MISSING LAST YEAR.
I SEE.
WE'LL LET THE POLICE SORT OUT THE DETAILS OF THE CASE.

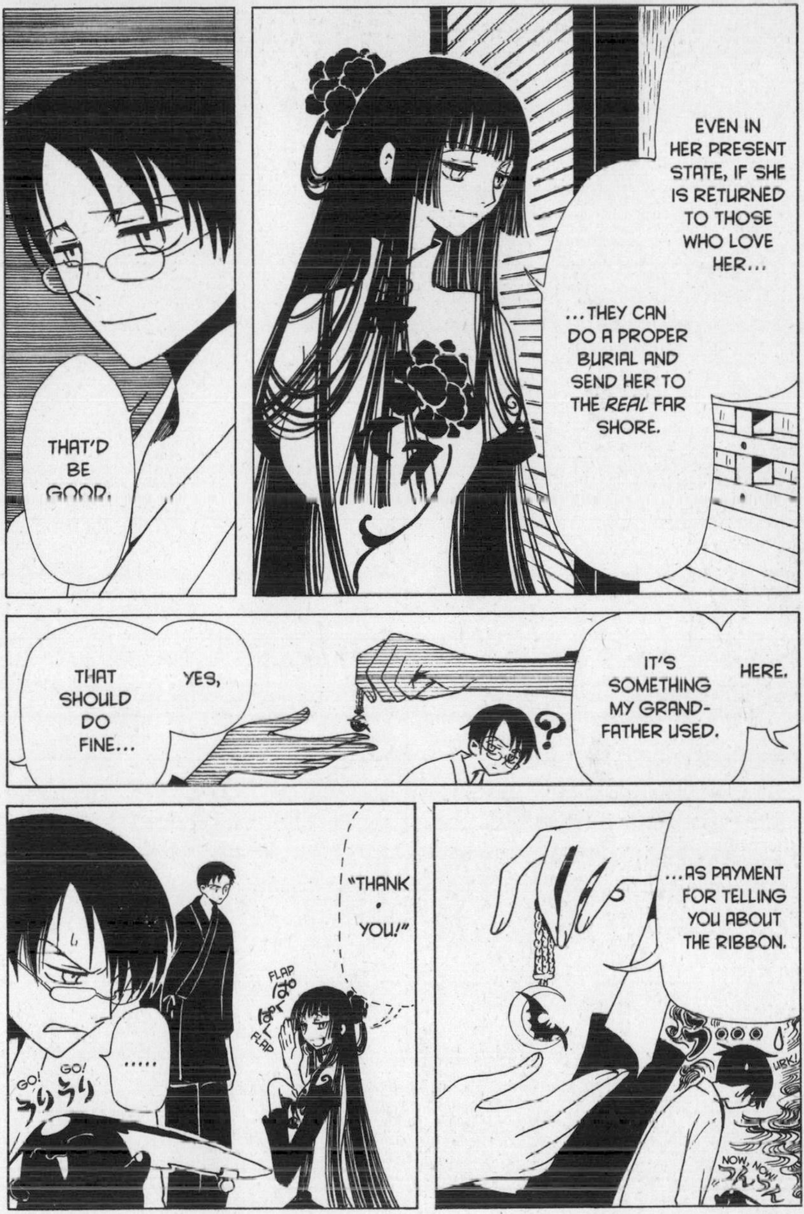
EVEN IN HER PRESENT STATE, IF SHE IS RETURNED TO THOSE WHO LOVE HER...
...THEY CAN DO A PROPER BURIAL AND SEND HER TO THE *REAL* FAR SHORE.
THAT'D BE GOOD.
HERE.
IT'S SOMETHING MY GRAND-FATHER USED.
?
YES,
THAT SHOULD DO FINE...
...AS PAYMENT FOR TELLING YOU ABOUT THE RIBBON.
URK!
NOW, NOW!
"THANK YOU!"
FLAP
FLAP
.....
GO!
GO!

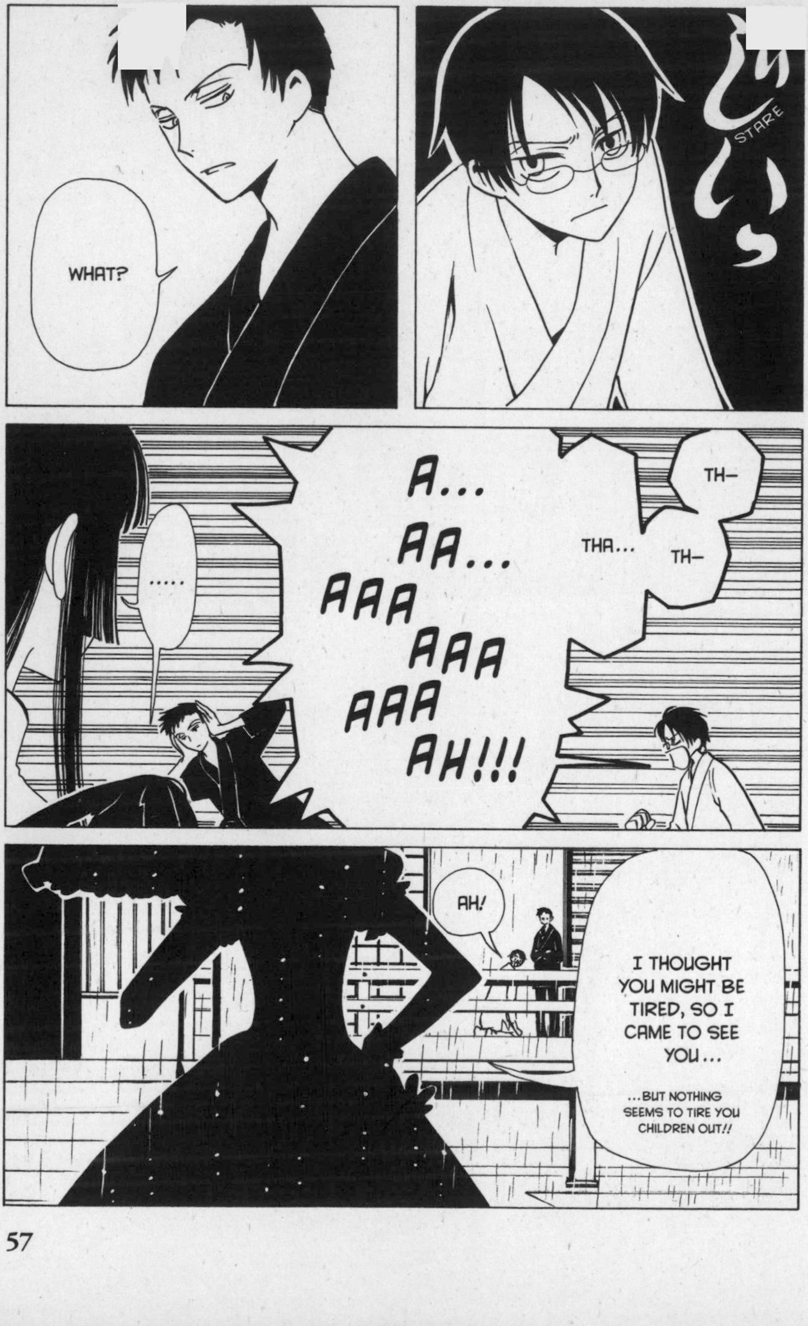
STARE
WHAT?
TH–
TH–
THA...
A... AA... AAA AAA AAA AH!!!
.....
I THOUGHT YOU MIGHT BE TIRED, SO I CAME TO SEE YOU...
...BUT NOTHING SEEMS TO TIRE YOU CHILDREN OUT!!
AH!

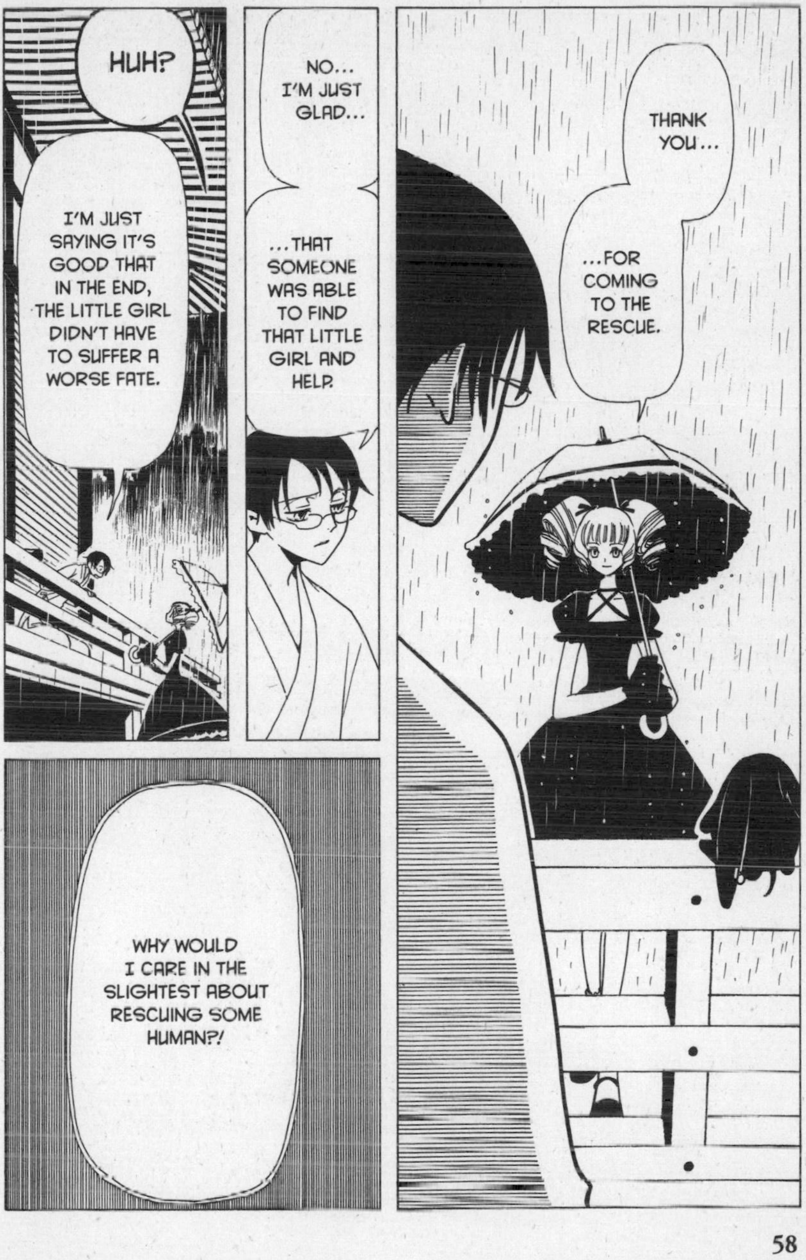
THANK YOU...
...FOR COMING TO THE RESCUE.
NO... I'M JUST GLAD...
...THAT SOMEONE WAS ABLE TO FIND THAT LITTLE GIRL AND HELP.
HUH?
I'M JUST SAYING IT'S GOOD THAT IN THE END, THE LITTLE GIRL DIDN'T HAVE TO SUFFER A WORSE FATE.
WHY WOULD I CARE IN THE SLIGHTEST ABOUT RESCUING SOME HUMAN?!

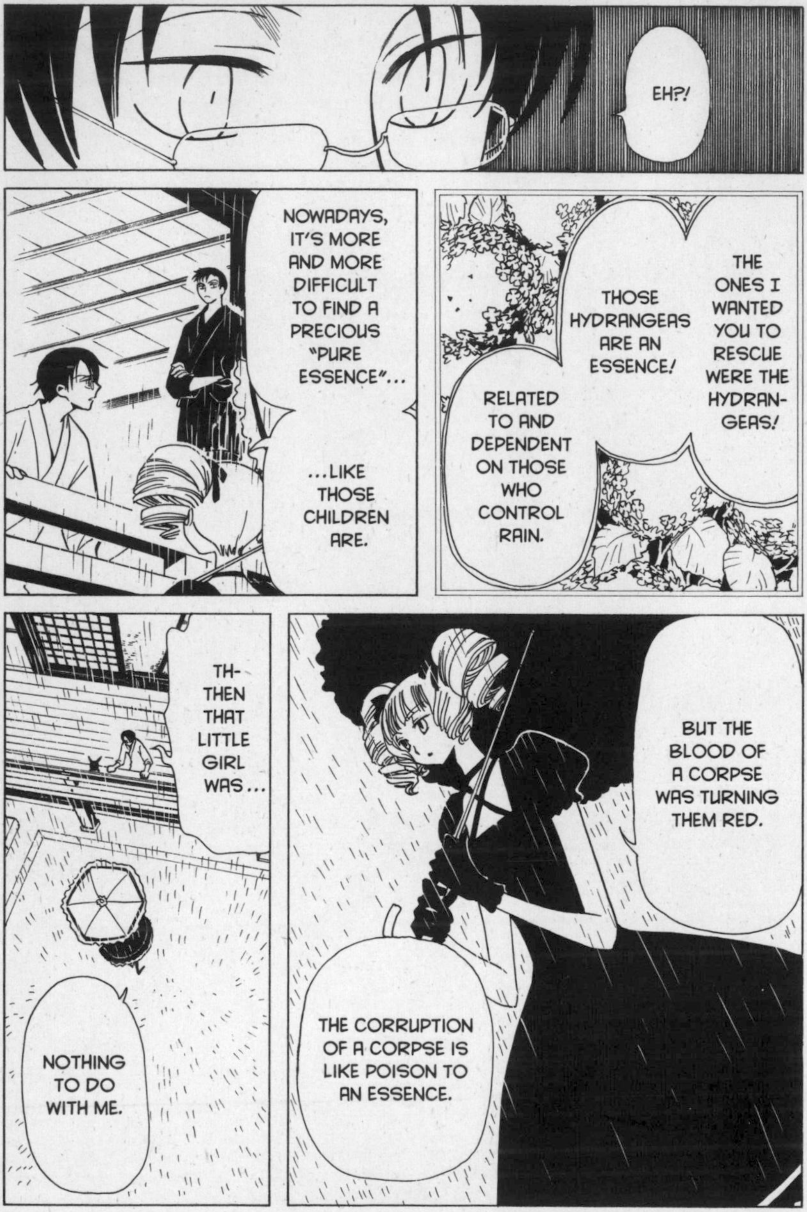
EH?!
THE ONES I WANTED YOU TO RESCUE WERE THE HYDRANGEAS!
THOSE HYDRANGEAS ARE AN ESSENCE!
RELATED TO AND DEPENDENT ON THOSE WHO CONTROL RAIN.
NOWADAYS, IT'S MORE AND MORE DIFFICULT TO FIND A PRECIOUS "PURE ESSENCE"...
...LIKE THOSE CHILDREN ARE.
BUT THE BLOOD OF A CORPSE WAS TURNING THEM RED.
THE CORRUPTION OF A CORPSE IS LIKE POISON TO AN ESSENCE.
TH-THEN THAT LITTLE GIRL WAS...
NOTHING TO DO WITH ME.

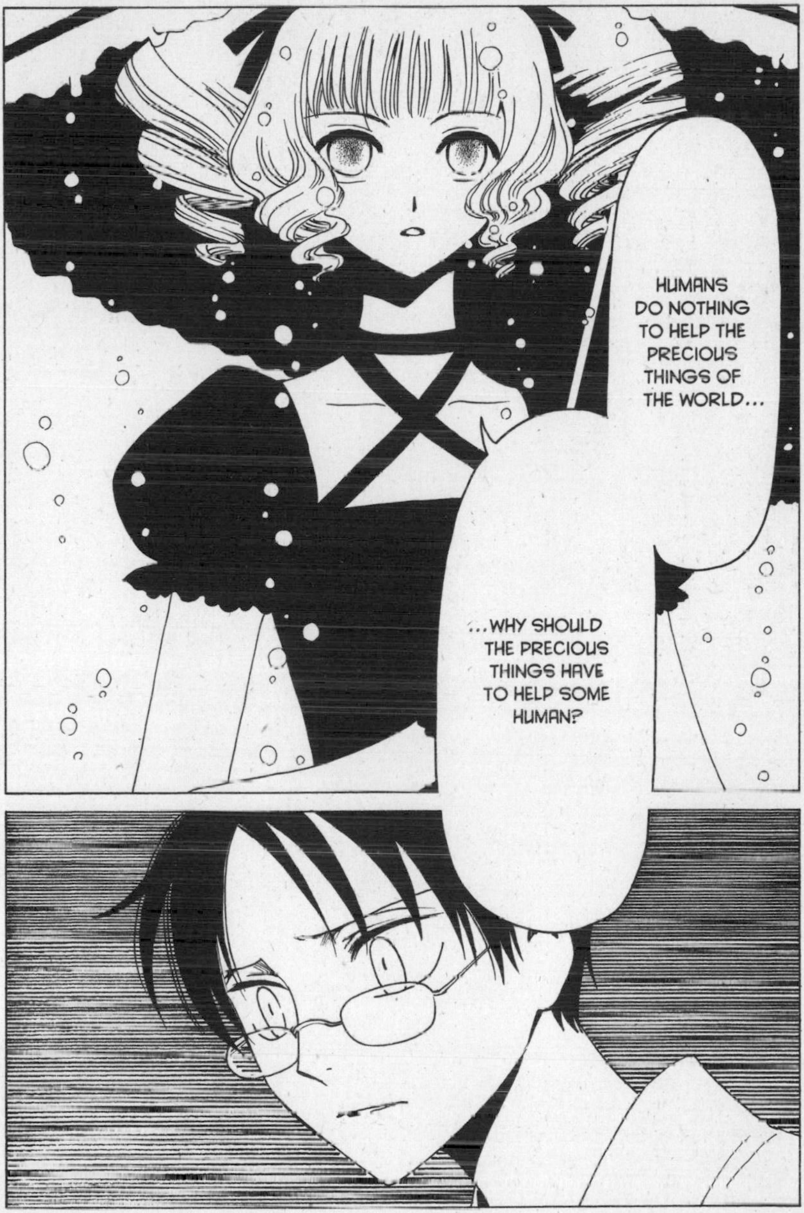
HUMANS DO NOTHING TO HELP THE PRECIOUS THINGS OF THE WORLD...
...WHY SHOULD THE PRECIOUS THINGS HAVE TO HELP SOME HUMAN?

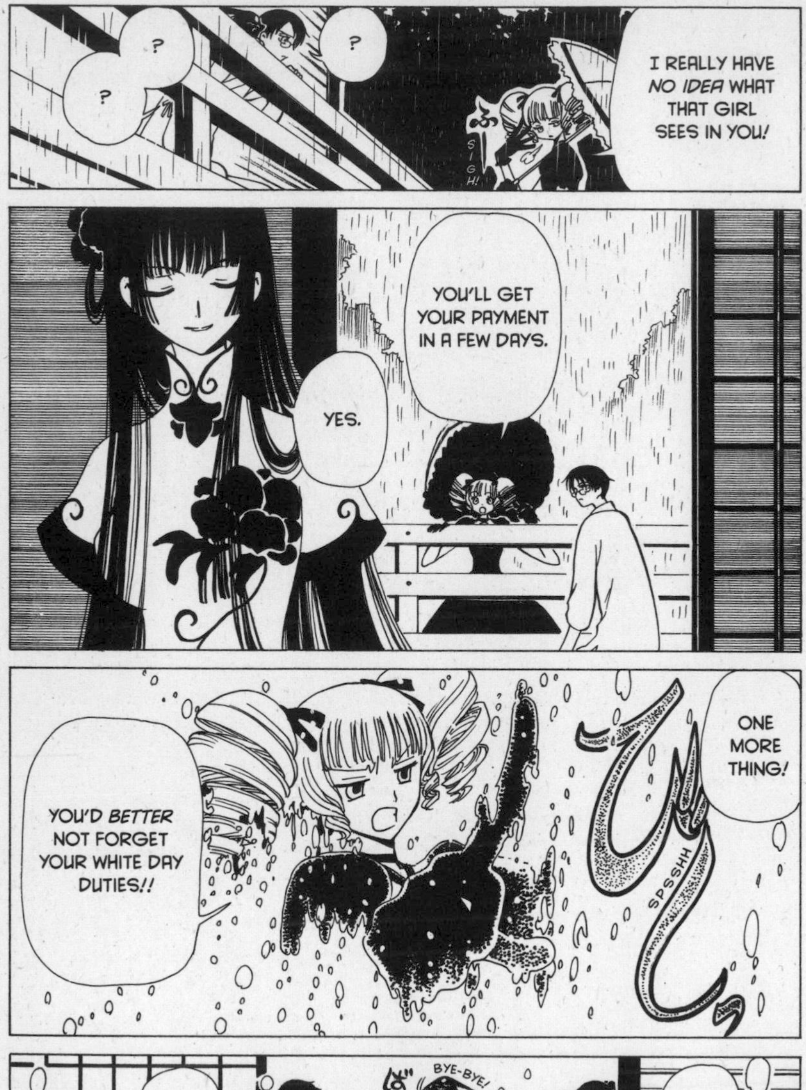
I REALLY HAVE *NO IDEA* WHAT THAT GIRL SEES IN YOU!
ふ
SIGH!
?
?
?
YOU'LL GET YOUR PAYMENT IN A FEW DAYS.
YES.
ONE MORE THING!
SPSSHH
YOU'D *BETTER* NOT FORGET YOUR WHITE DAY DUTIES!!
EH?
ばい
ばい
BYE-BYE!
EH?

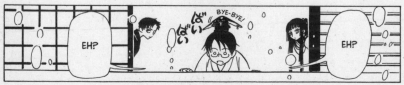

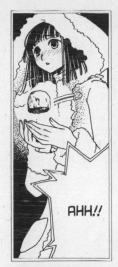

YOU'RE GONNA GET IT!
YOU'RE GONNA GET IT!
STAB
STAB
STAB
I CAN'T FORGIVE *ANYBODY* WHO DOESN'T RETURN A PRESENT FOR WHITE DAY!
I MEAN, WHAT ARE THESE YOUNG PEOPLE COMING TO TODAY?!
HUH?
I CAN'T REMEMBER ANYBODY GIVING...
AHH!!
YOU MEAN THAT COUNTS AS BEING GIVEN A VALENTINE'S DAY CHOCOLATE?
YOU'RE STEPPING ON A POOR GIRL'S HEART!
YÛKO-SAAAAAAN!!
AH HA HA HA HA
HE REALLY *IS* NOBITA!!
I AGREE.

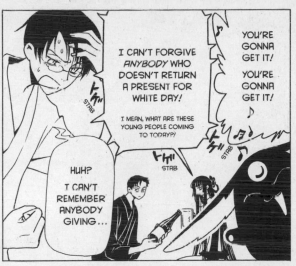

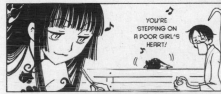

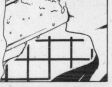

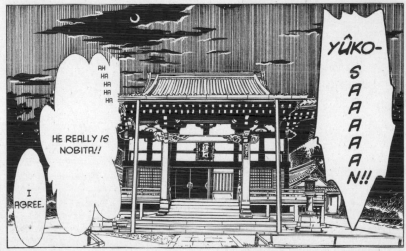

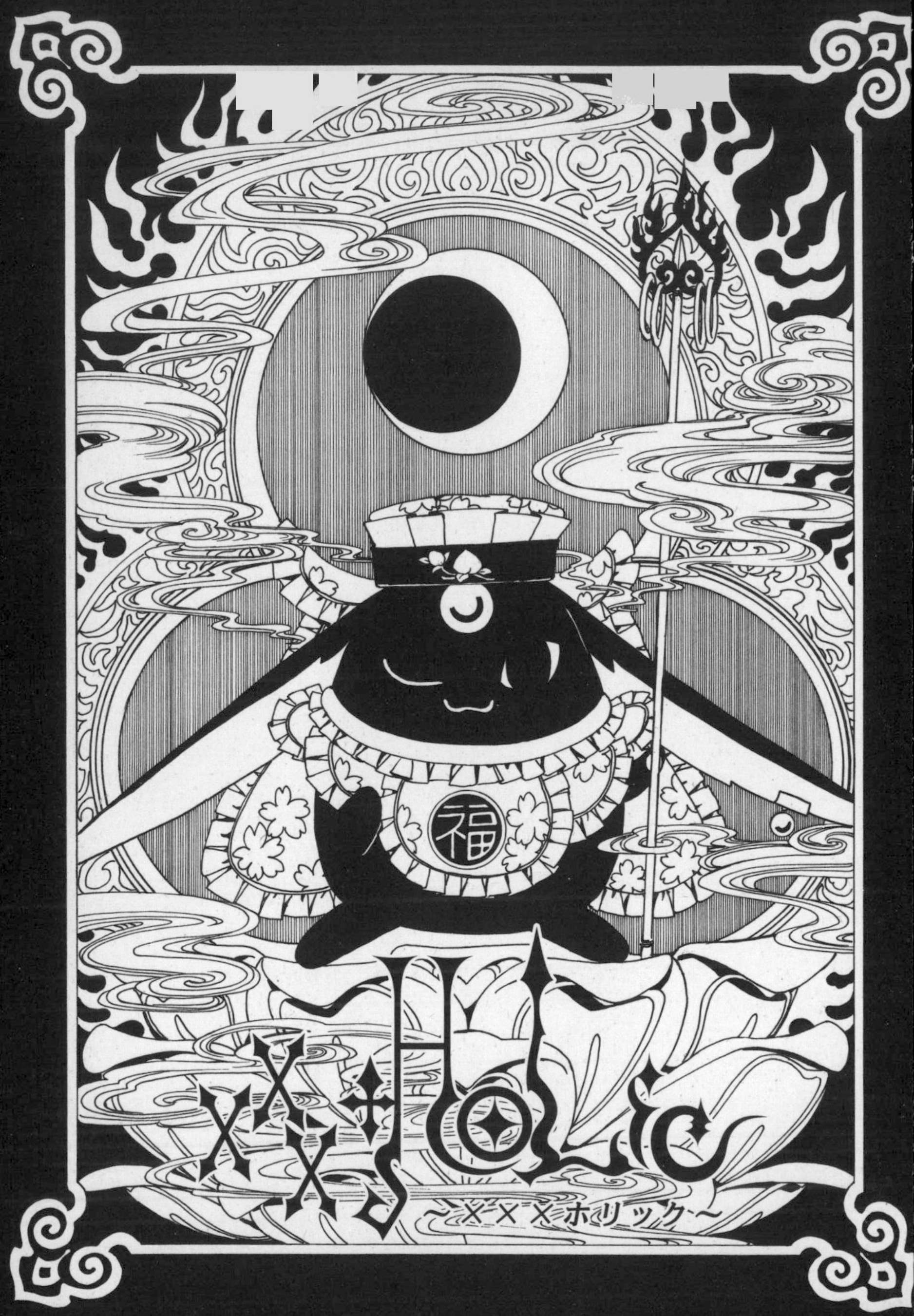
xxxHOLiC
~×××ホリック~

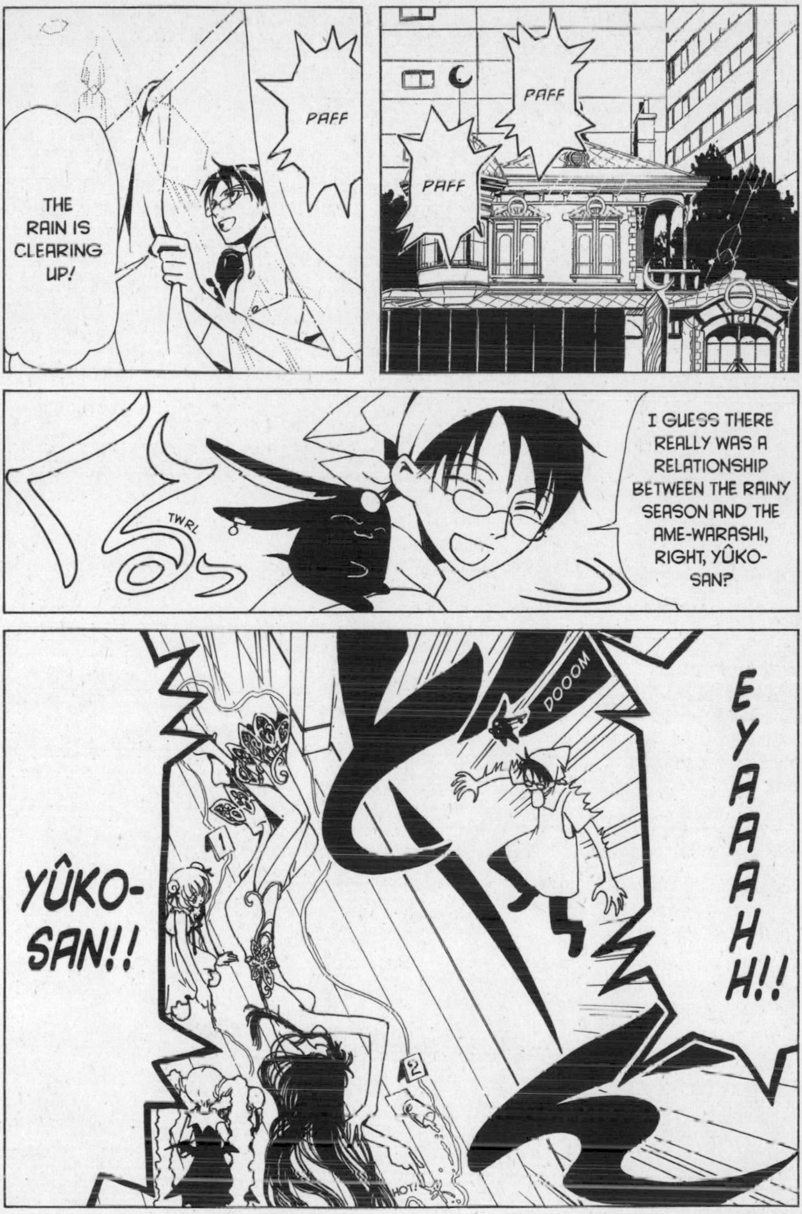
PAFF
PAFF
PAFF
THE RAIN IS CLEARING UP!
I GUESS THERE REALLY WAS A RELATIONSHIP BETWEEN THE RAINY SEASON AND THE AME-WARASHI, RIGHT, YÛKO-SAN?
TWRL
EYAAAAAHH!!
DOOOM
YÛKO-SAN!!
HOT!

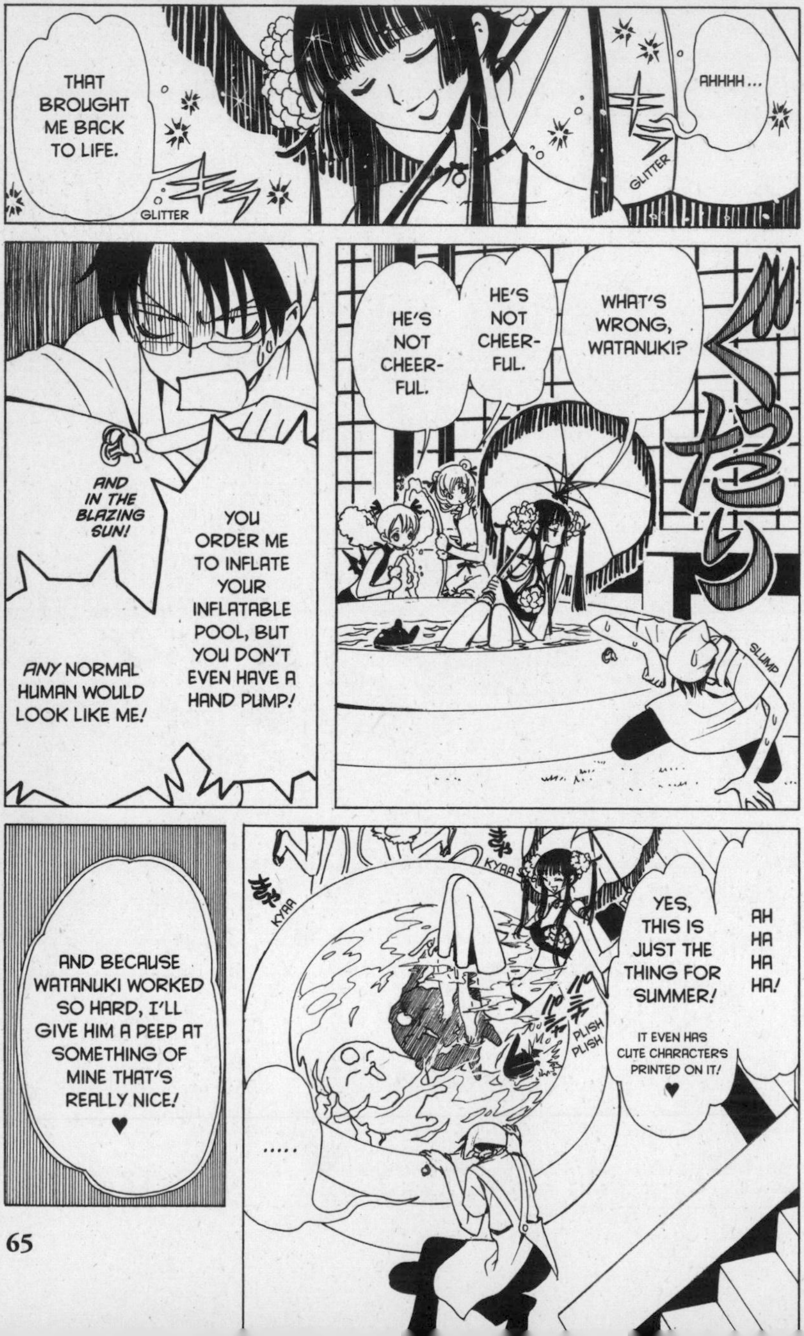
AHHHH...
GLITTER
THAT BROUGHT ME BACK TO LIFE.
GLITTER
WHAT'S WRONG, WATANUKI?
HE'S NOT CHEER-FUL.
HE'S NOT CHEER-FUL.
SLUMP
YOU ORDER ME TO INFLATE YOUR INFLATABLE POOL, BUT YOU DON'T EVEN HAVE A HAND PUMP!
AND IN THE BLAZING SUN!
ANY NORMAL HUMAN WOULD LOOK LIKE ME!
KYAA
AH HA HA HA!
YES, THIS IS JUST THE THING FOR SUMMER!
IT EVEN HAS CUTE CHARACTERS PRINTED ON IT! ♥
PLISH PLISH
KYAA
.....
AND BECAUSE WATANUKI WORKED SO HARD, I'LL GIVE HIM A PEEP AT SOMETHING OF MINE THAT'S REALLY NICE! ♥

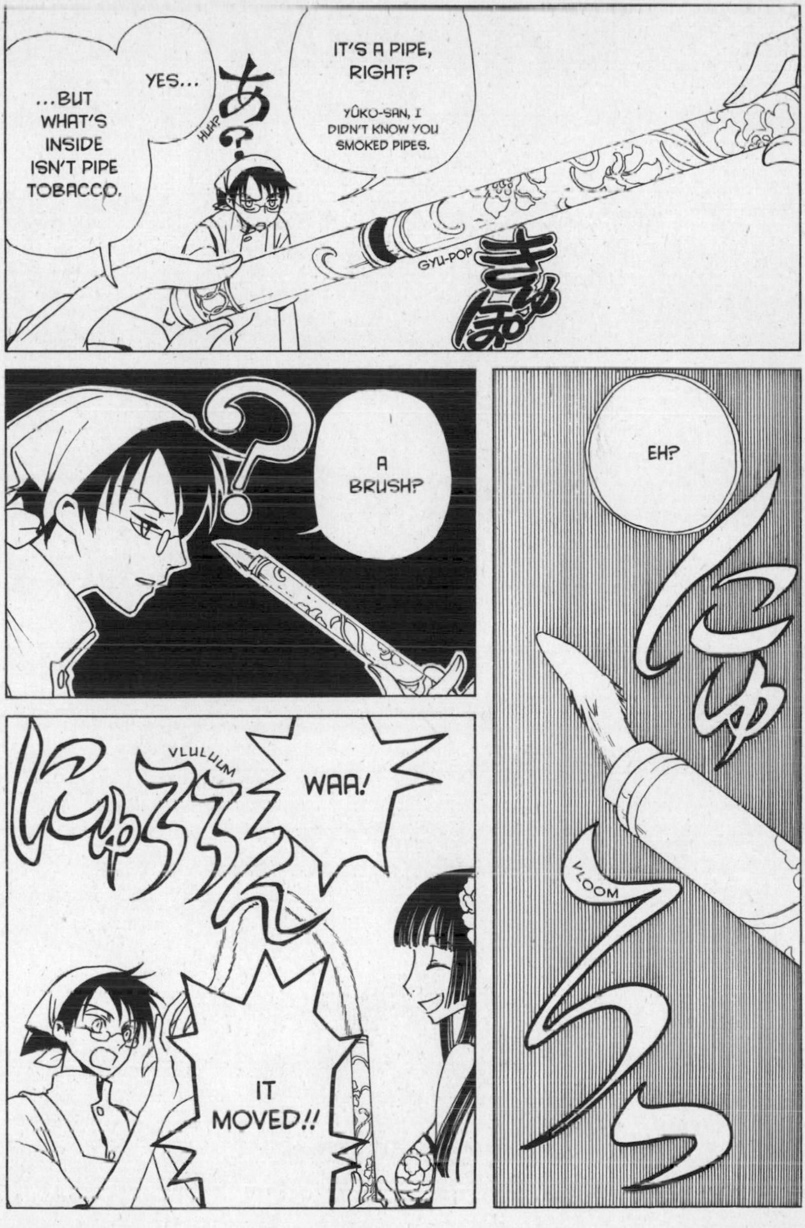
IT'S A PIPE, RIGHT?
YÛKO-SAN, I DIDN'T KNOW YOU SMOKED PIPES.
HUH?
YES...
...BUT WHAT'S INSIDE ISN'T PIPE TOBACCO.
GYU-POP
EH?
VLOOM
A BRUSH?
WAA!
VLULULUM
IT MOVED!!

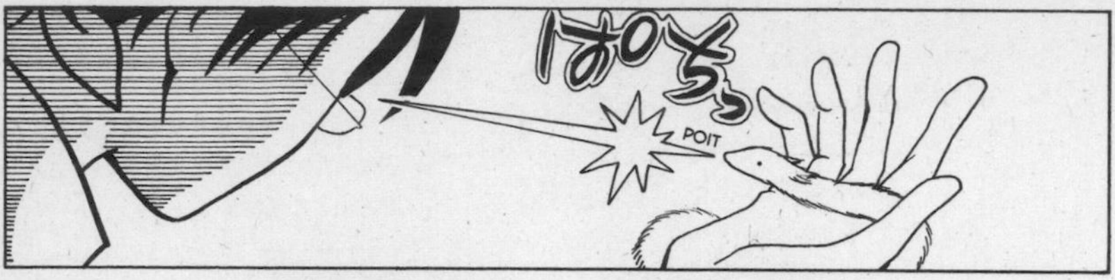
ぱちっ
POIT
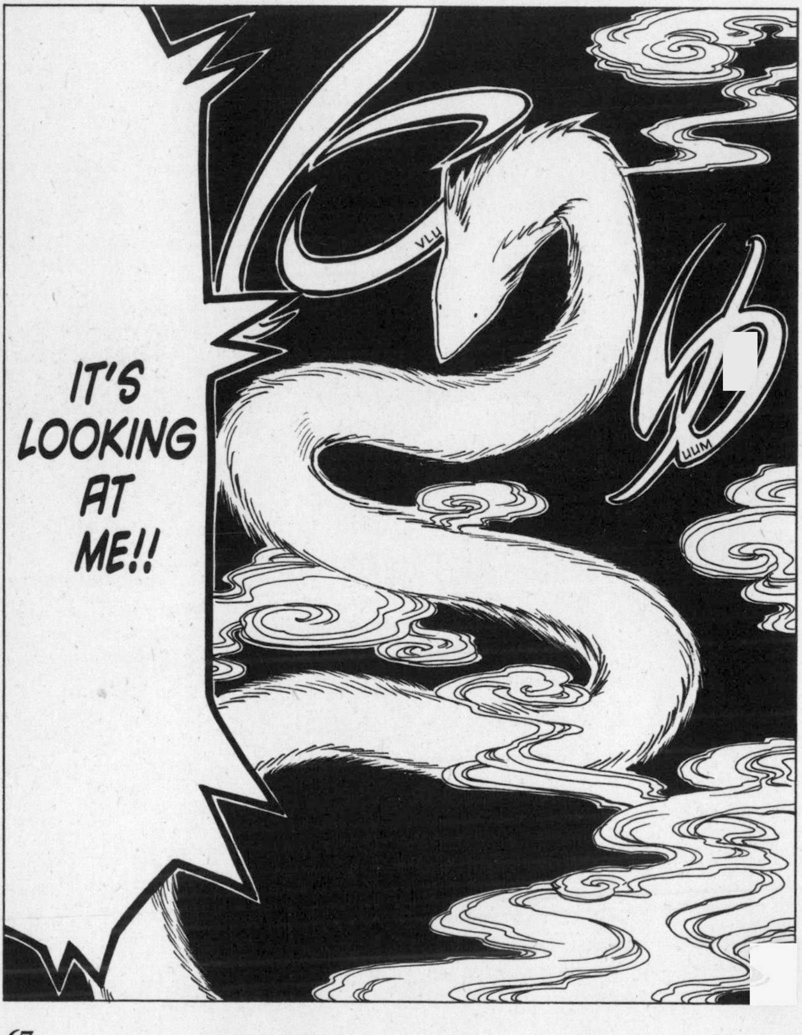
VLU
UUM
IT'S LOOKING AT ME!!

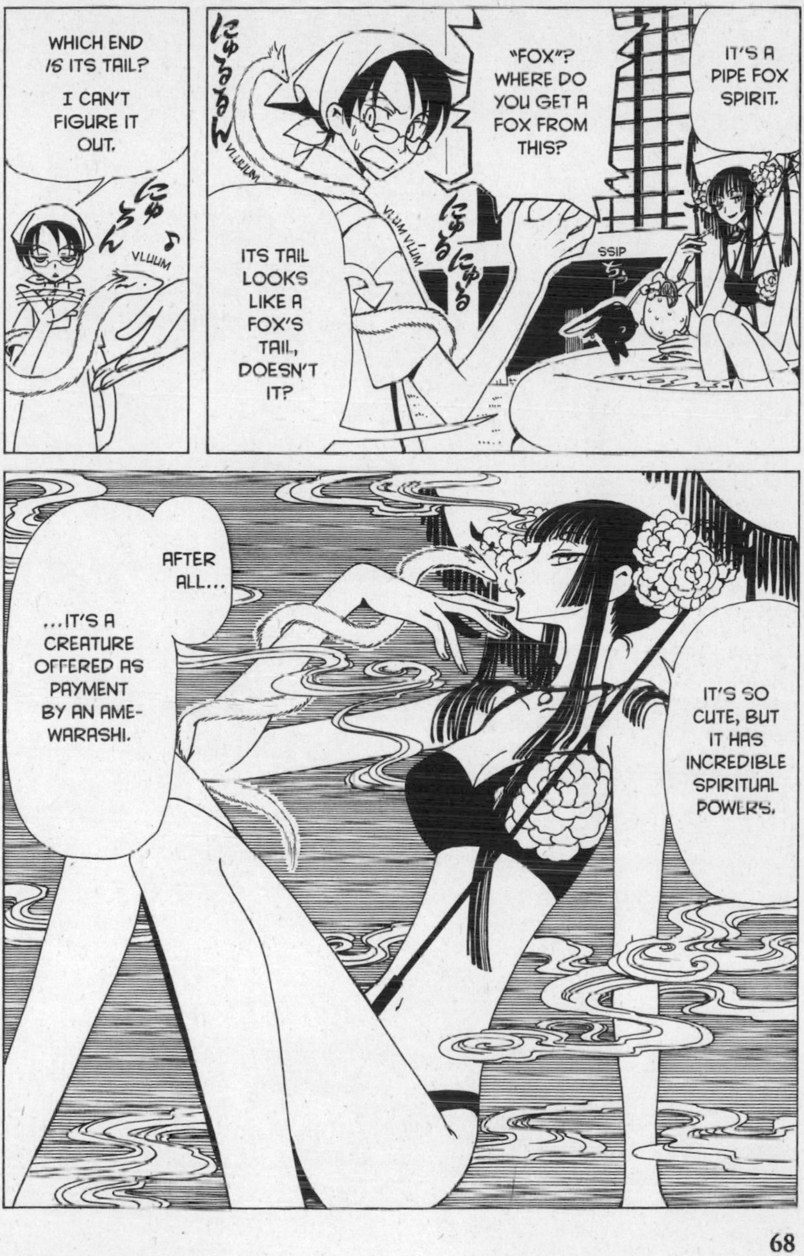
IT'S A PIPE FOX SPIRIT.
SSIP ちゅー
"FOX"? WHERE DO YOU GET A FOX FROM THIS?
にゅるにゅる
VLUUM VLUUM
にゅるるん
VLUUUM
ITS TAIL LOOKS LIKE A FOX'S TAIL, DOESN'T IT?
WHICH END IS ITS TAIL?
I CAN'T FIGURE IT OUT.
にゅるん ♪
VLUUM
IT'S SO CUTE, BUT IT HAS INCREDIBLE SPIRITUAL POWERS.
AFTER ALL...
...IT'S A CREATURE OFFERED AS PAYMENT BY AN AME-WARASHI.

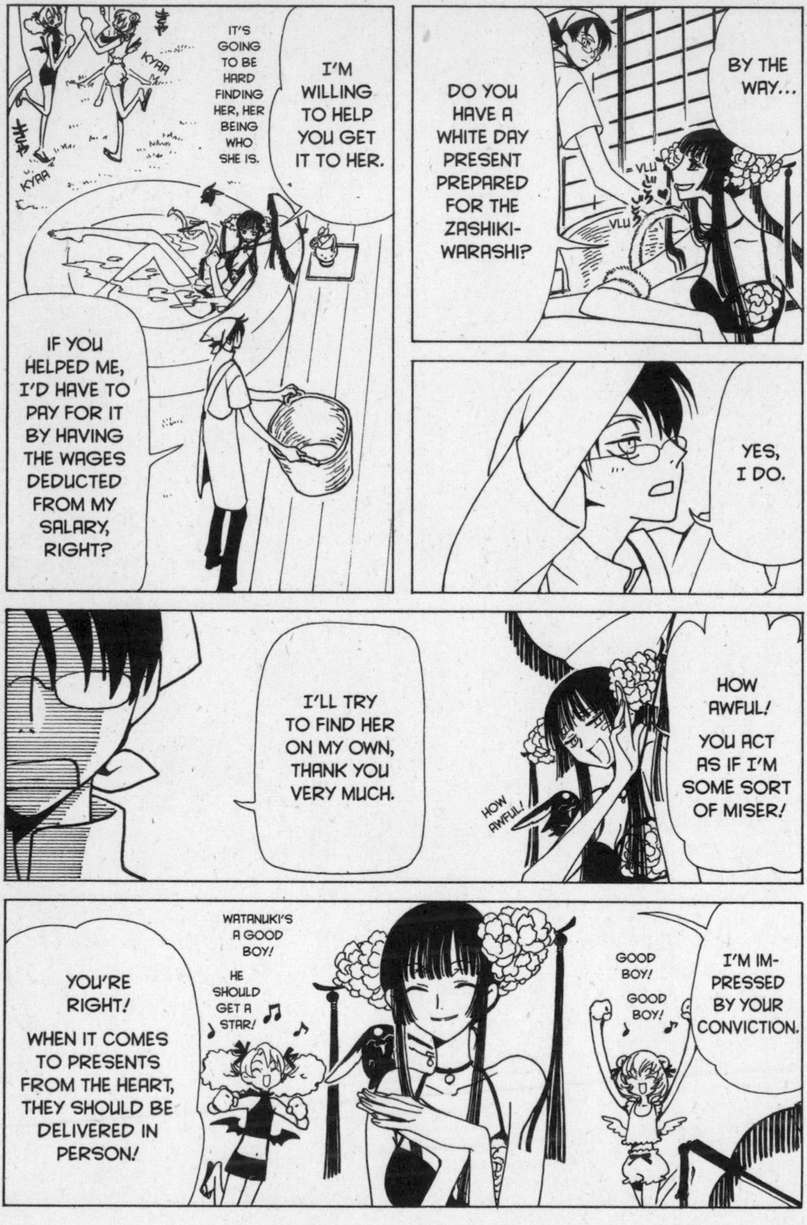
BY THE WAY...
DO YOU HAVE A WHITE DAY PRESENT PREPARED FOR THE ZASHIKI-WARASHI?
VLU VLU
YES, I DO.
I'M WILLING TO HELP YOU GET IT TO HER.
IT'S GOING TO BE HARD FINDING HER, HER BEING WHO SHE IS.
KYAA
KYAA
IF YOU HELPED ME, I'D HAVE TO PAY FOR IT BY HAVING THE WAGES DEDUCTED FROM MY SALARY, RIGHT?
HOW AWFUL!
YOU ACT AS IF I'M SOME SORT OF MISER!
HOW AWFUL!
I'LL TRY TO FIND HER ON MY OWN, THANK YOU VERY MUCH.
I'M IM-PRESSED BY YOUR CONVICTION.
GOOD BOY!
GOOD BOY!
WATANUKI'S A GOOD BOY!
HE SHOULD GET A STAR!
YOU'RE RIGHT!
WHEN IT COMES TO PRESENTS FROM THE HEART, THEY SHOULD BE DELIVERED IN PERSON!

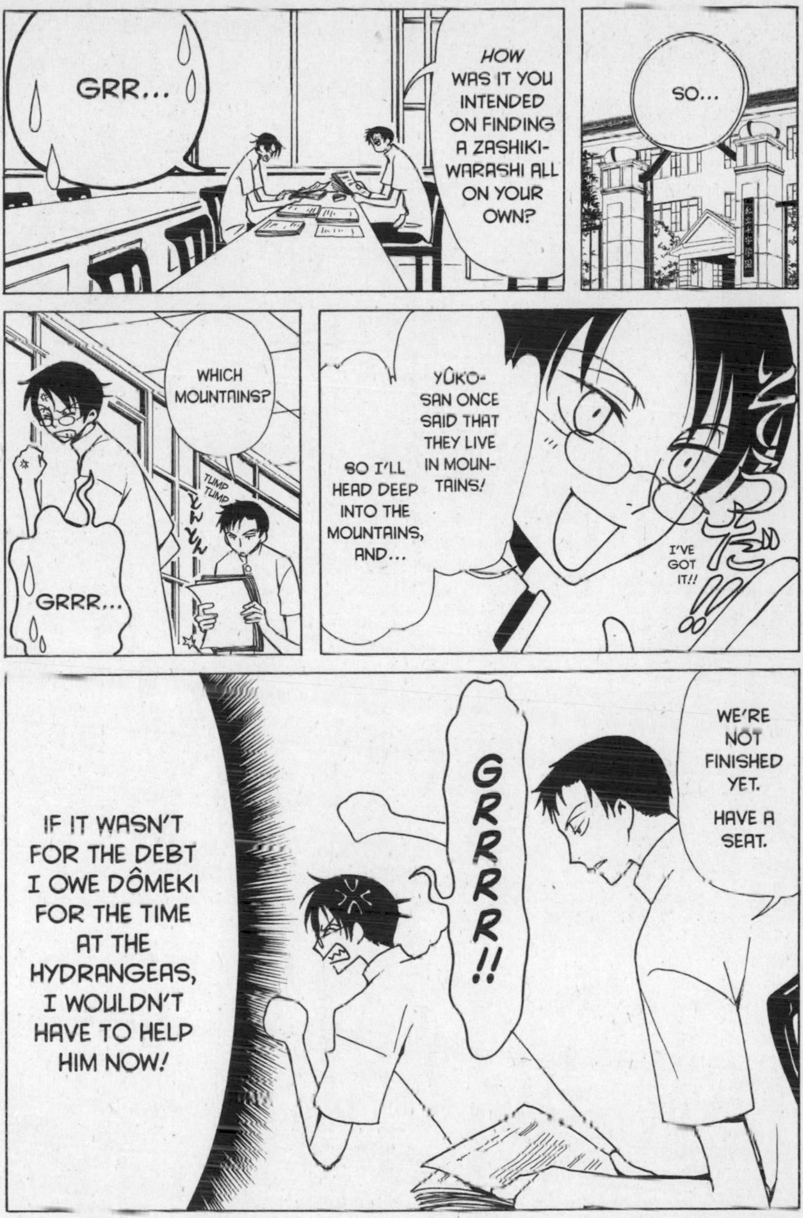
SO...
HOW WAS IT YOU INTENDED ON FINDING A ZASHIKI-WARASHI ALL ON YOUR OWN?
GRR...
I'VE GOT IT!!
YÛKO-SAN ONCE SAID THAT THEY LIVE IN MOUNTAINS!
SO I'LL HEAD DEEP INTO THE MOUNTAINS, AND...
WHICH MOUNTAINS?
TUMP TUMP
GRRR...
WE'RE NOT FINISHED YET.
HAVE A SEAT.
GRRRR!!
IF IT WASN'T FOR THE DEBT I OWE DÔMEKI FOR THE TIME AT THE HYDRANGEAS, I WOULDN'T HAVE TO HELP HIM NOW!

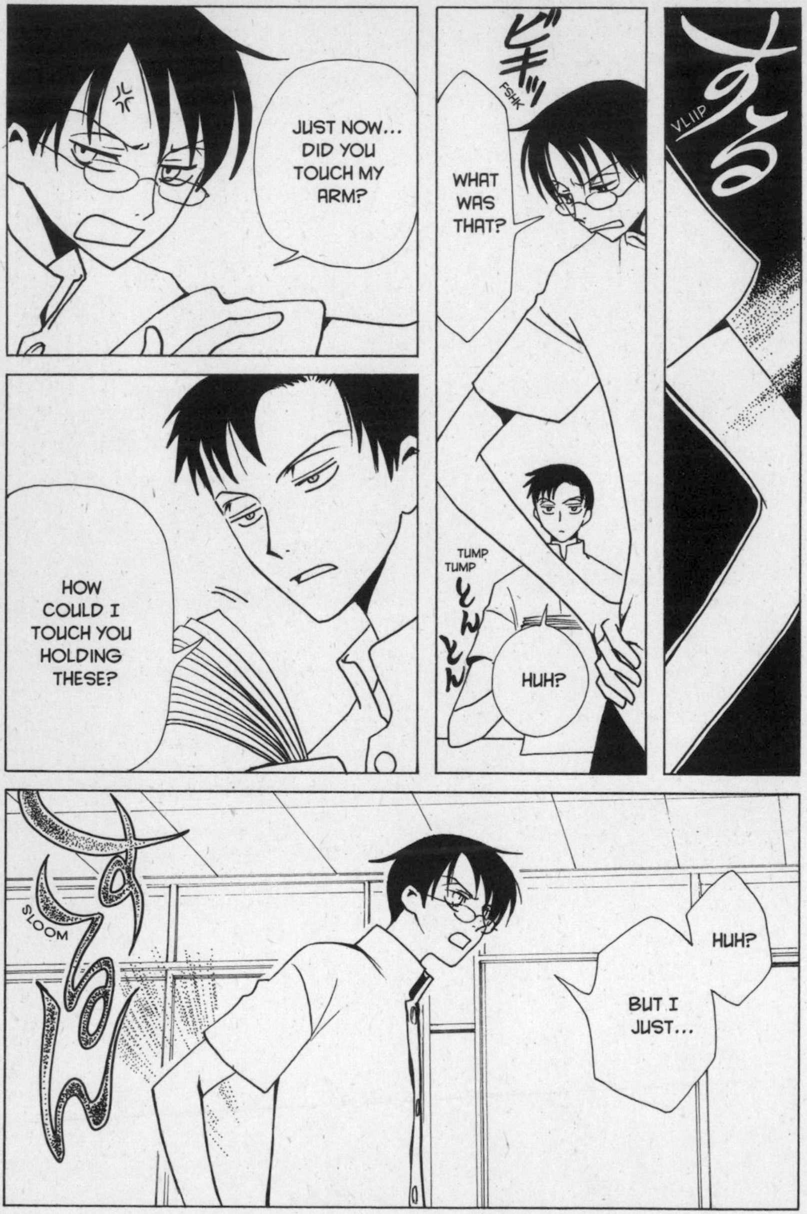
する
VLIIP
FSHK
WHAT WAS THAT?
TUMP TUMP
とんとん
HUH?
JUST NOW... DID YOU TOUCH MY ARM?
HOW COULD I TOUCH YOU HOLDING THESE?
S'LOOM
HUH?
BUT I JUST...

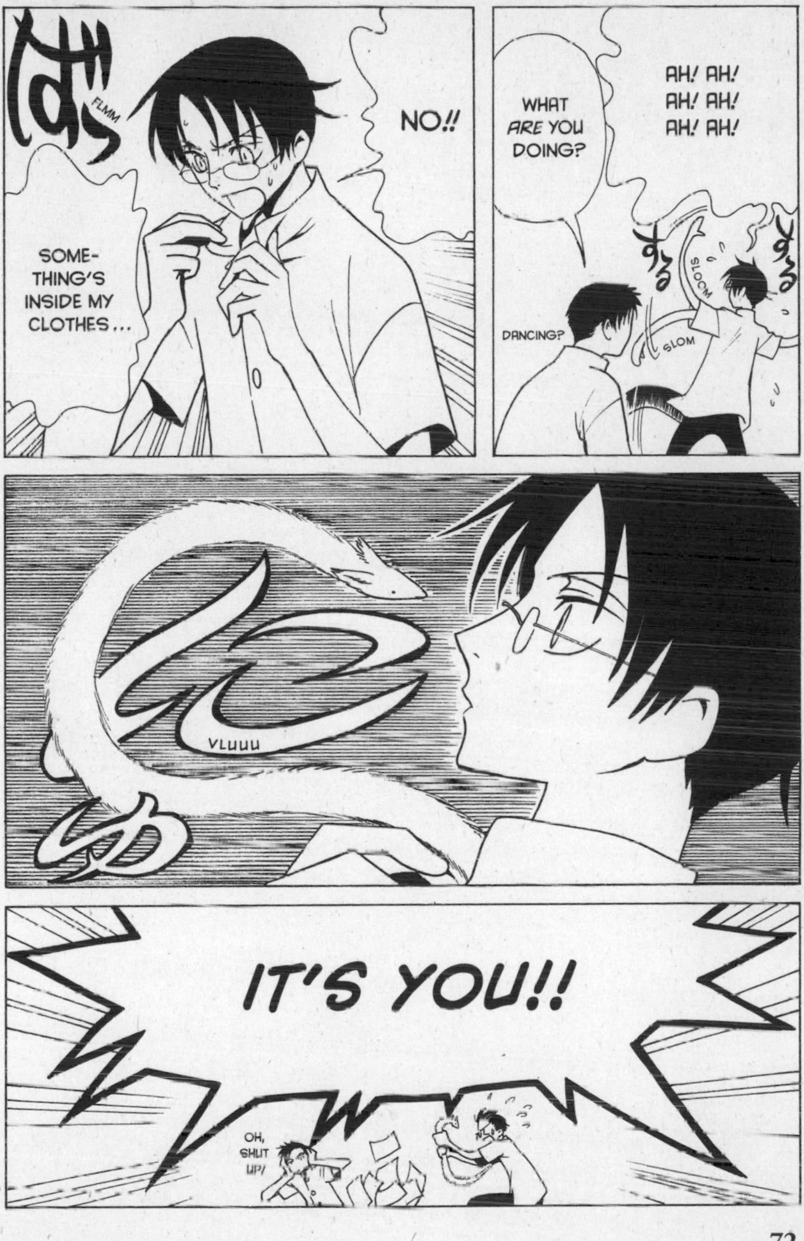
AH! AH! AH! AH! AH! AH!
WHAT ARE YOU DOING?
する
する
SLOOM
SLOM
DANCING?
ばっ
FLMM
NO!!
SOME-THING'S INSIDE MY CLOTHES...
VLUUU
IT'S YOU!!
OH, SHUT UP!

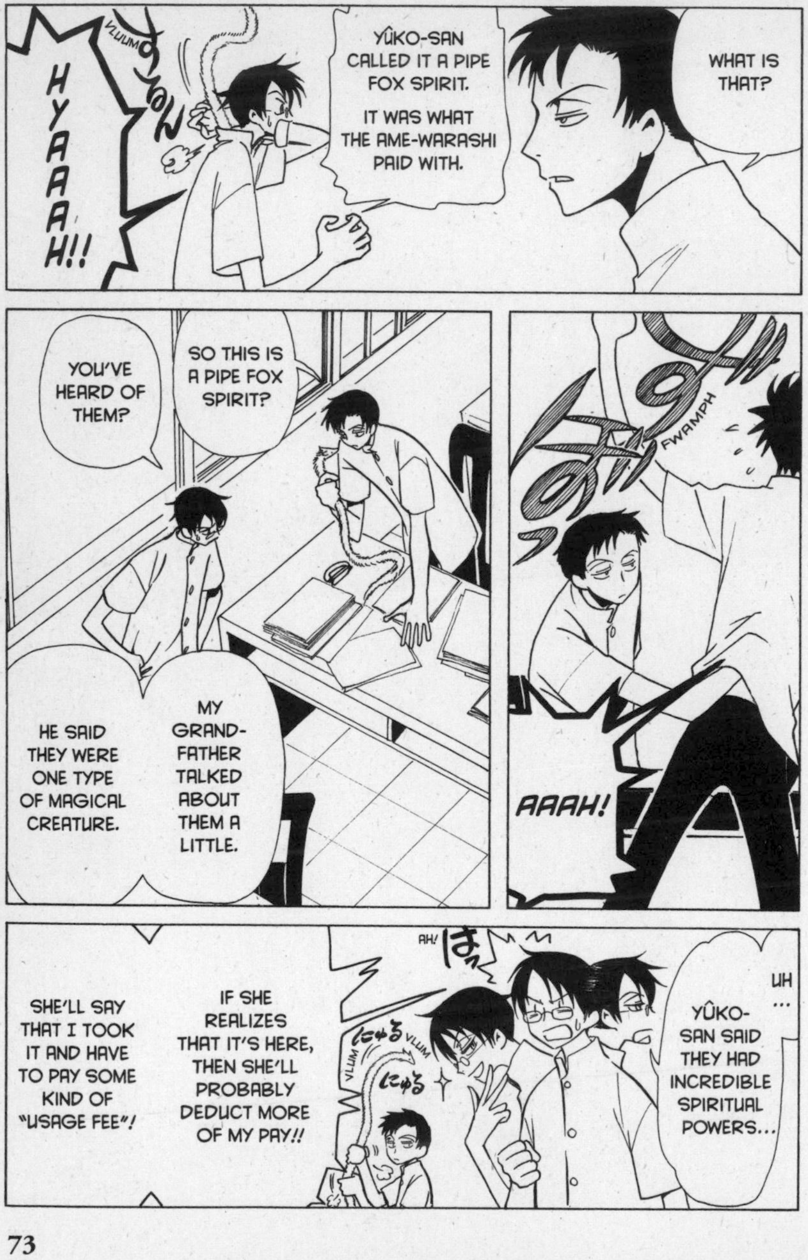
WHAT IS THAT?
YÛKO-SAN CALLED IT A PIPE FOX SPIRIT.
IT WAS WHAT THE AME-WARASHI PAID WITH.
VLUUM
HYAAAAH!!
FWAMPH
AAAH!
SO THIS IS A PIPE FOX SPIRIT?
YOU'VE HEARD OF THEM?
MY GRAND-FATHER TALKED ABOUT THEM A LITTLE.
HE SAID THEY WERE ONE TYPE OF MAGICAL CREATURE.
UH ...
YÛKO-SAN SAID THEY HAD INCREDIBLE SPIRITUAL POWERS...
AH!
VLUUM
VLUUM
IF SHE REALIZES THAT IT'S HERE, THEN SHE'LL PROBABLY DEDUCT MORE OF MY PAY!!
SHE'LL SAY THAT I TOOK IT AND HAVE TO PAY SOME KIND OF "USAGE FEE"!

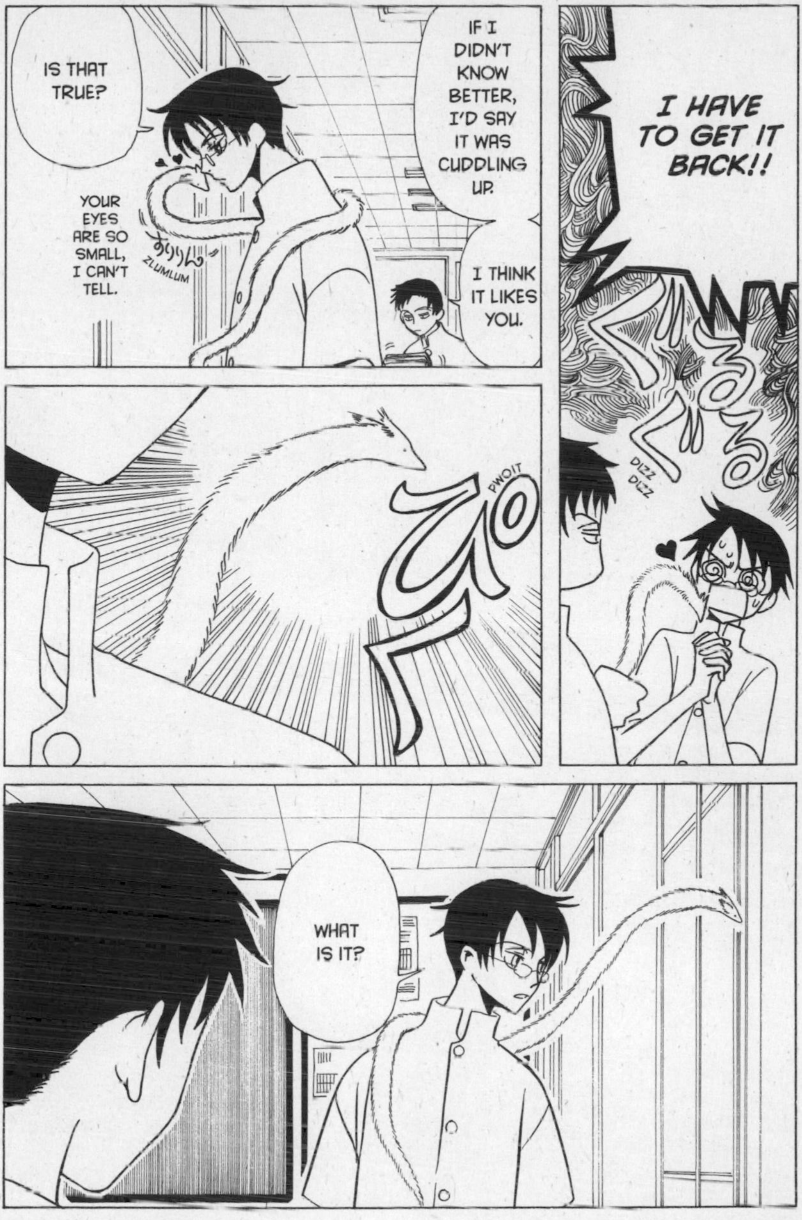
I HAVE TO GET IT BACK!!
DIZZ DIZZ
IF I DIDN'T KNOW BETTER, I'D SAY IT WAS CUDDLING UP.
IS THAT TRUE?
I THINK IT LIKES YOU.
YOUR EYES ARE SO SMALL, I CAN'T TELL.
ZLUMLUM
PWOIT
WHAT IS IT?

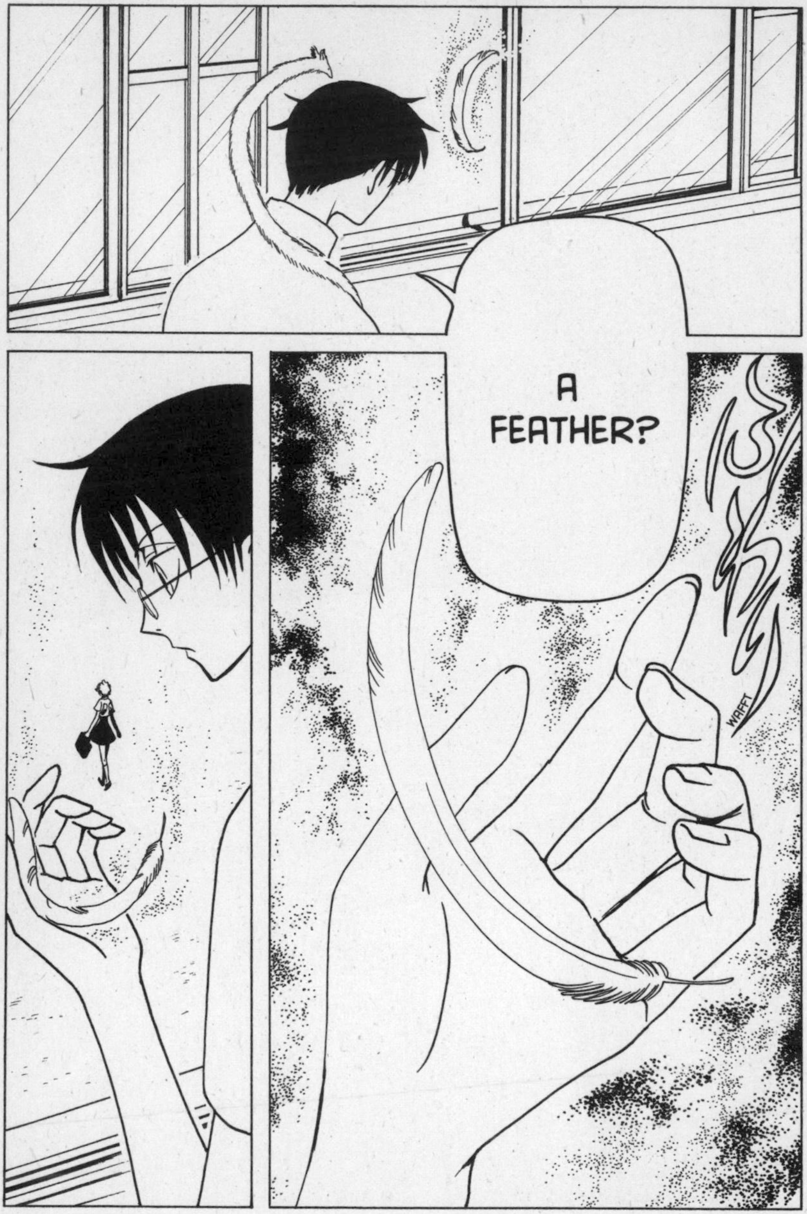
A FEATHER?
WAFFT

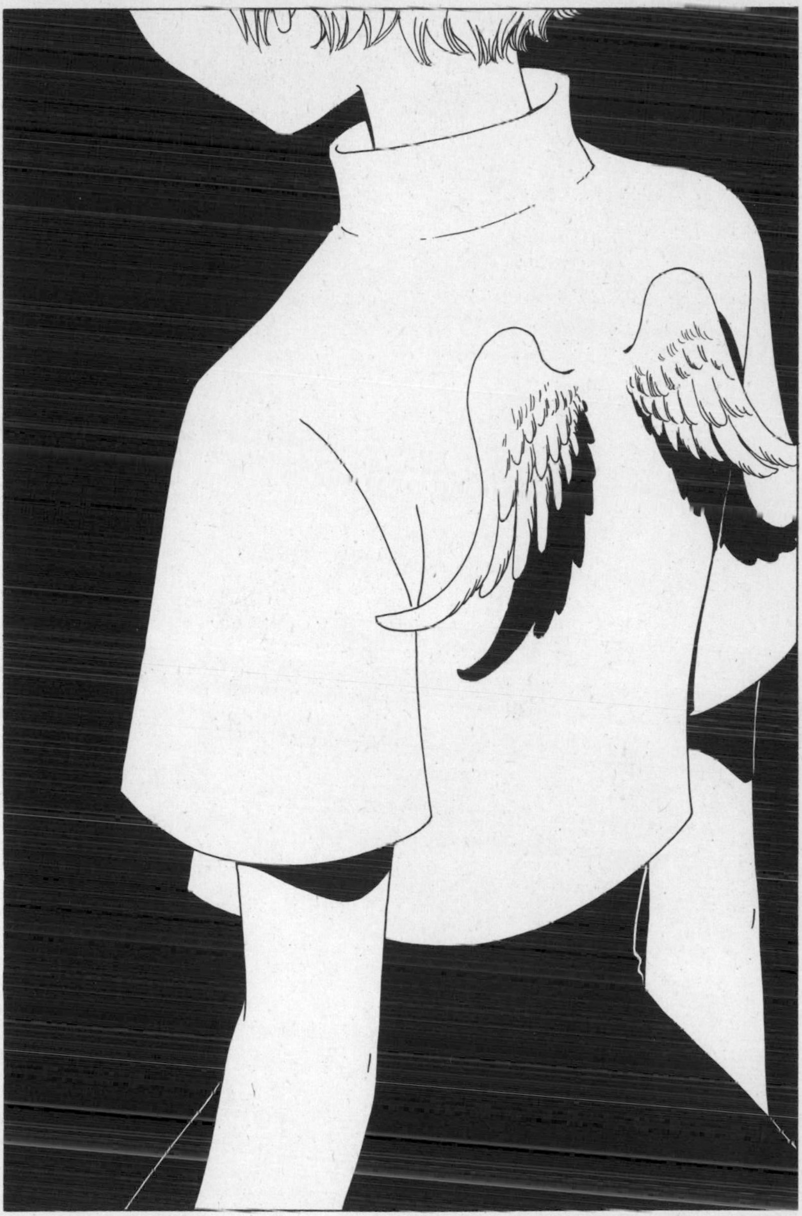

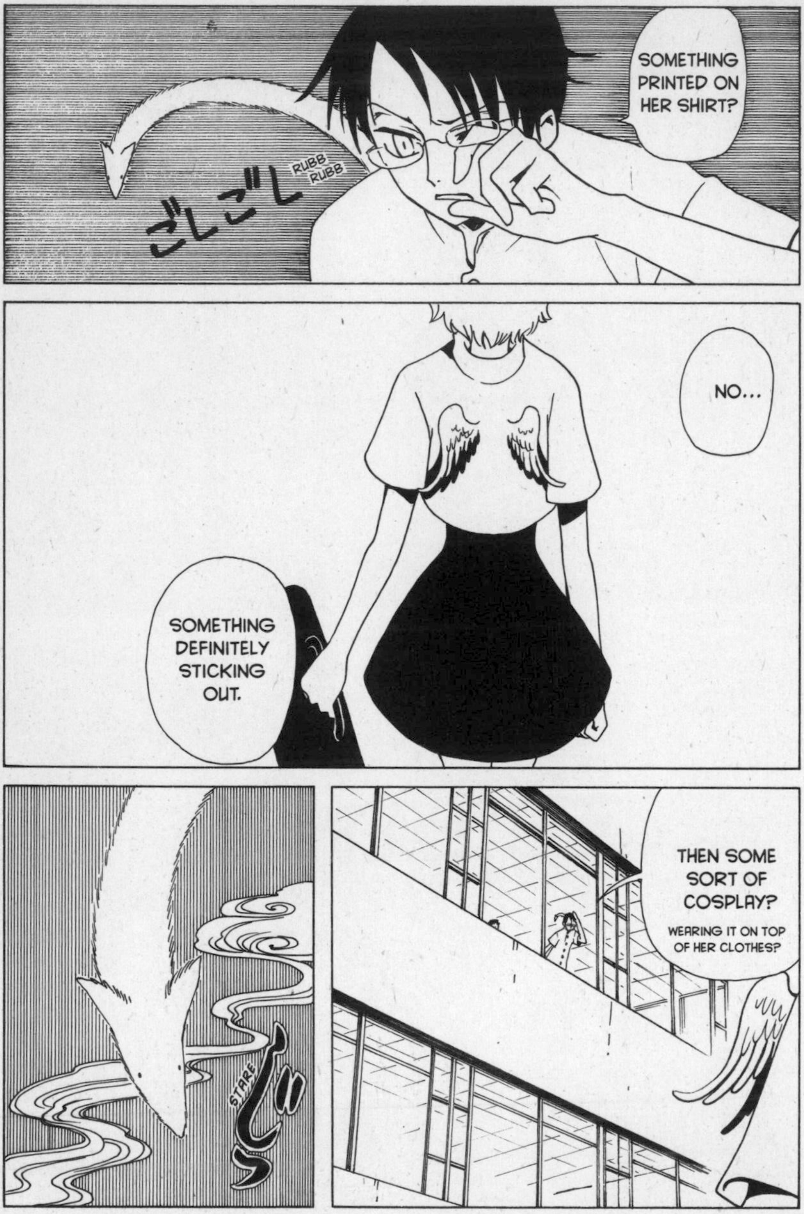
SOMETHING PRINTED ON HER SHIRT?
RUBB RUBB
ごしごし
NO...
SOMETHING DEFINITELY STICKING OUT.
THEN SOME SORT OF COSPLAY?
WEARING IT ON TOP OF HER CLOTHES?
STARE
じー

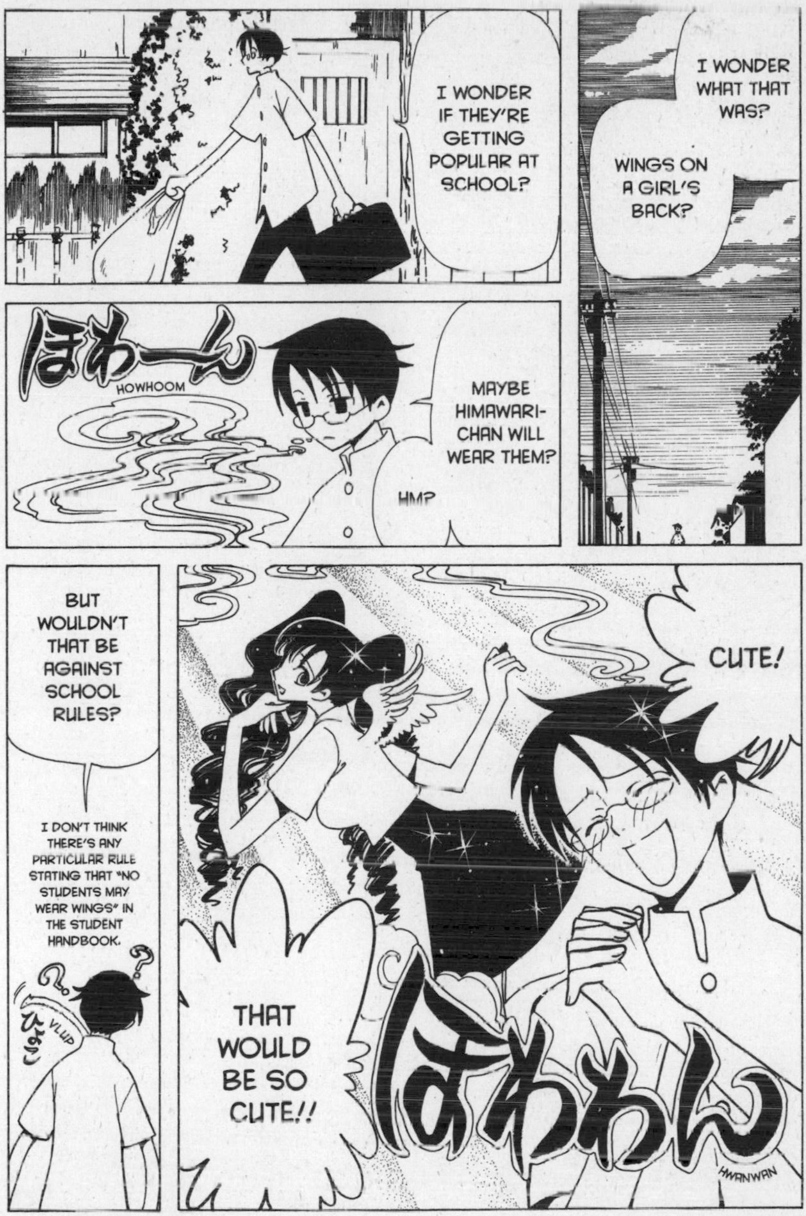
I WONDER WHAT THAT WAS?
WINGS ON A GIRL'S BACK?
I WONDER IF THEY'RE GETTING POPULAR AT SCHOOL?
MAYBE HIMAWARI-CHAN WILL WEAR THEM?
ほわーん
HOWHOOM
HM?
CUTE!
THAT WOULD BE SO CUTE!!
はわわん
HWANWAN
BUT WOULDN'T THAT BE AGAINST SCHOOL RULES?
I DON'T THINK THERE'S ANY PARTICULAR RULE STATING THAT "NO STUDENTS MAY WEAR WINGS" IN THE STUDENT HANDBOOK.
VLLIP

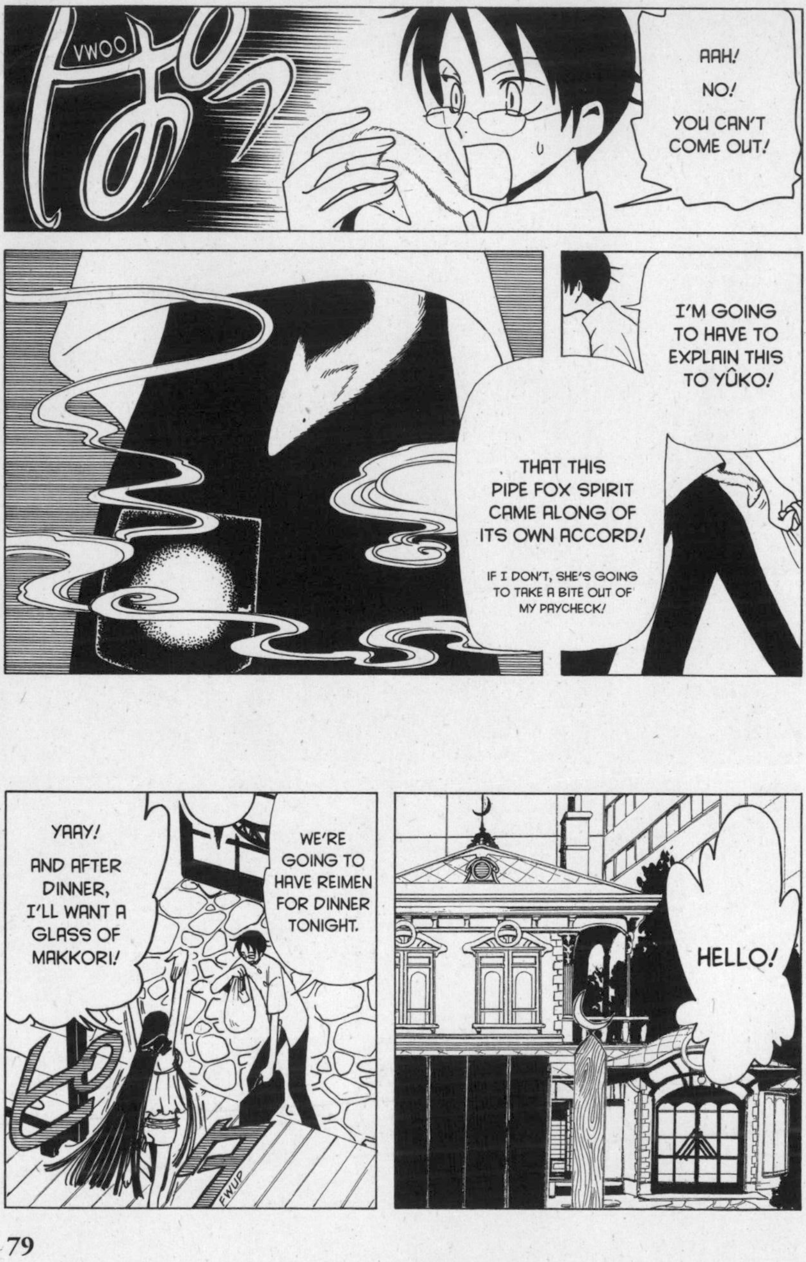
VWOO
AAH!
NO!
YOU CAN'T COME OUT!
I'M GOING TO HAVE TO EXPLAIN THIS TO YÛKO!
THAT THIS PIPE FOX SPIRIT CAME ALONG OF ITS OWN ACCORD!
IF I DON'T, SHE'S GOING TO TAKE A BITE OUT OF MY PAYCHECK!
HELLO!
WE'RE GOING TO HAVE REIMEN FOR DINNER TONIGHT.
YAAY!
AND AFTER DINNER, I'LL WANT A GLASS OF MAKKORI!
FWUP

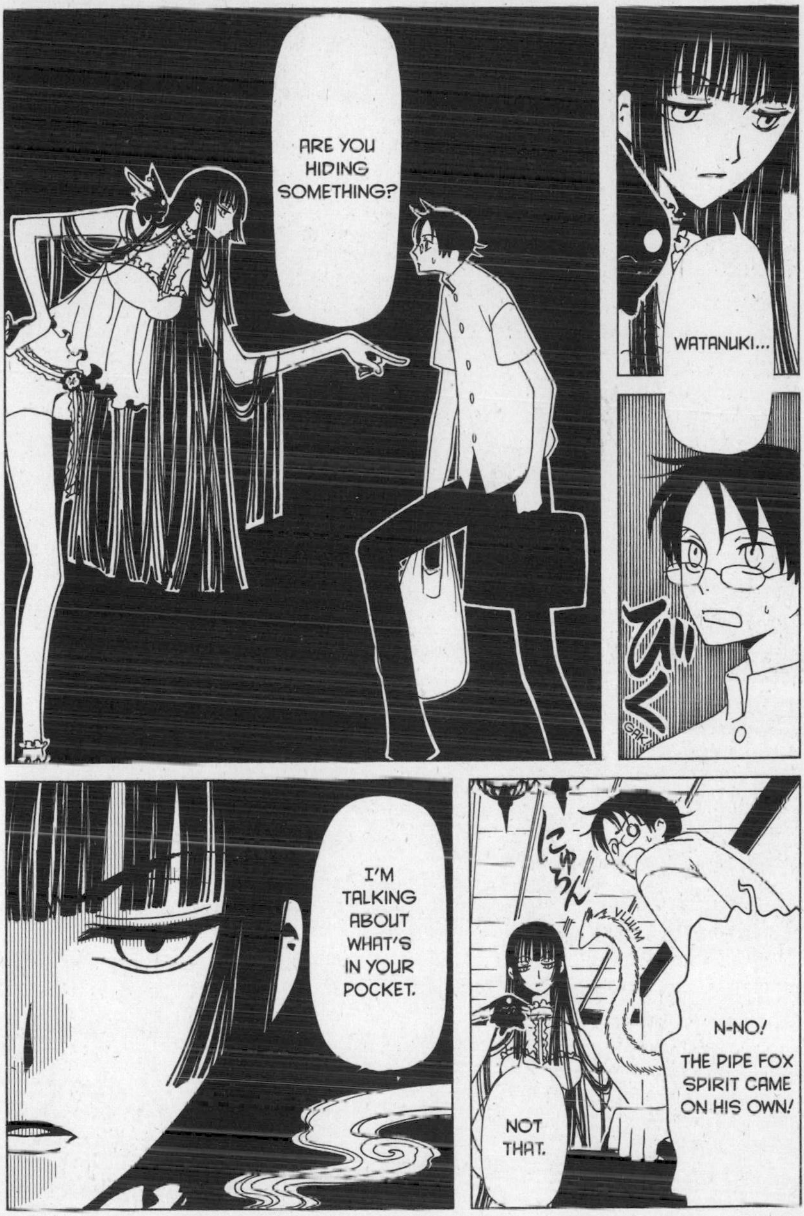
WATANUKI...
びく
GAK
ARE YOU HIDING SOMETHING?
にゅるん
VLLLM
N-NO! THE PIPE FOX SPIRIT CAME ON HIS OWN!
NOT THAT.
I'M TALKING ABOUT WHAT'S IN YOUR POCKET.

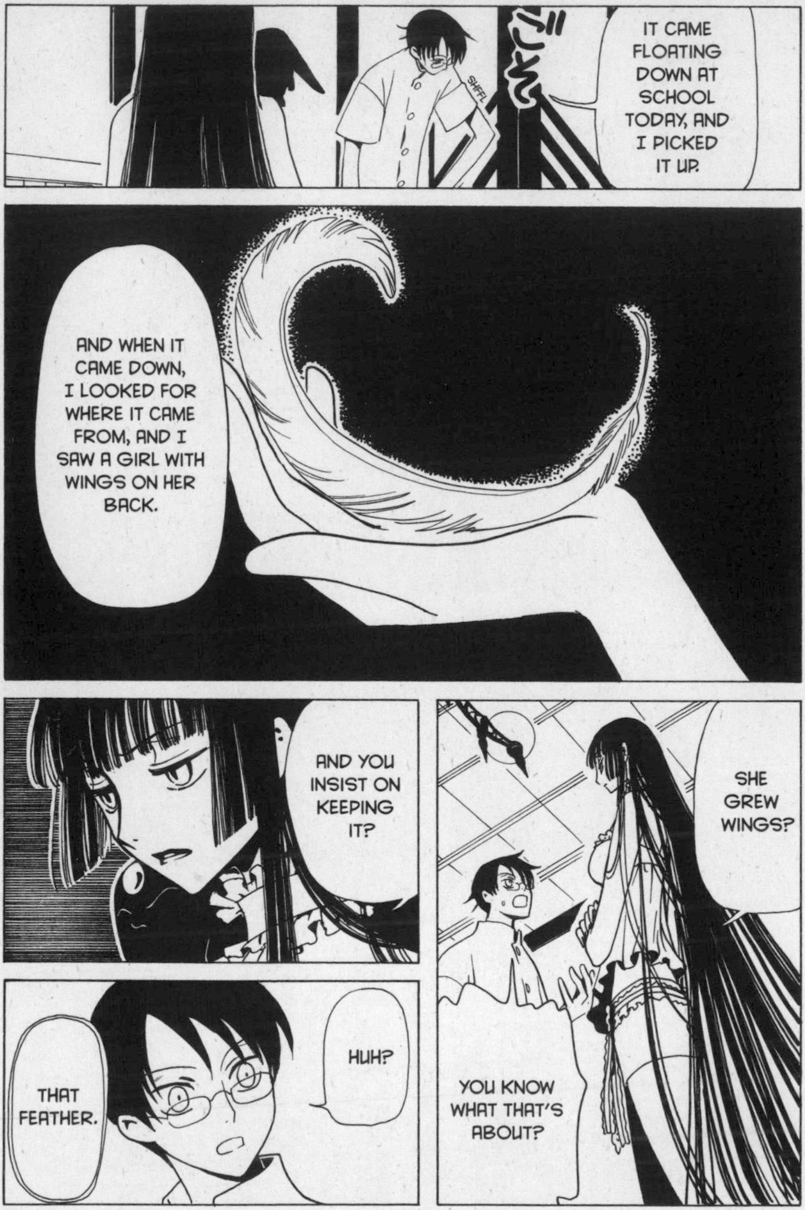
IT CAME FLOATING DOWN AT SCHOOL TODAY, AND I PICKED IT UP.
ごそ
SHFFL
AND WHEN IT CAME DOWN, I LOOKED FOR WHERE IT CAME FROM, AND I SAW A GIRL WITH WINGS ON HER BACK.
SHE GREW WINGS?
YOU KNOW WHAT THAT'S ABOUT?
AND YOU INSIST ON KEEPING IT?
HUH?
THAT FEATHER.

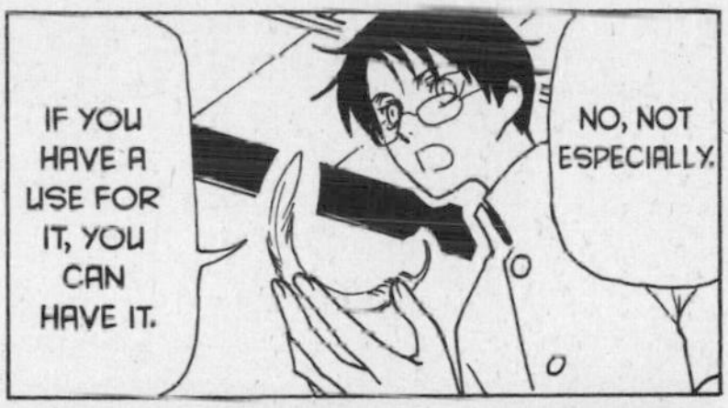
NO, NOT ESPECIALLY.
IF YOU HAVE A USE FOR IT, YOU CAN HAVE IT.
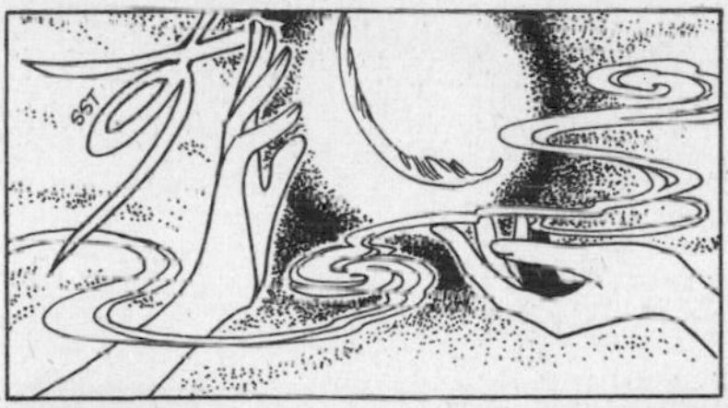
SST
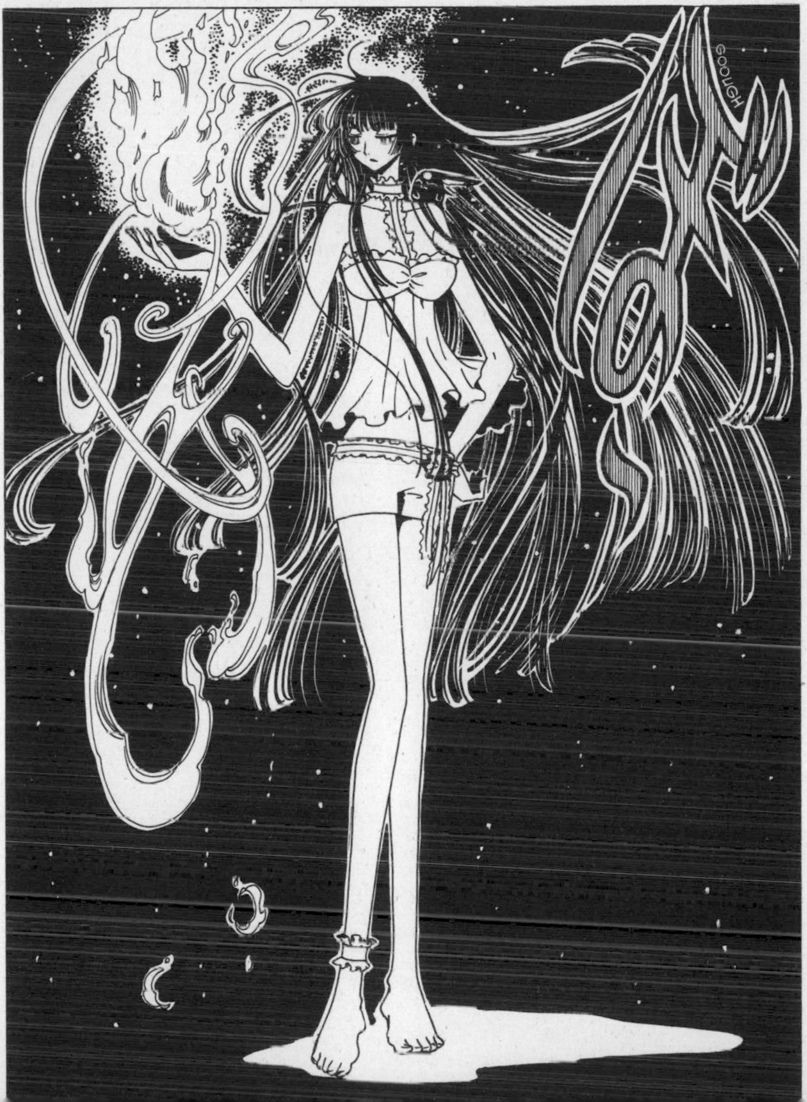
GOOUGH

BE VERY CAREFUL.
BEING "GAME" IS VERY DANGEROUS.

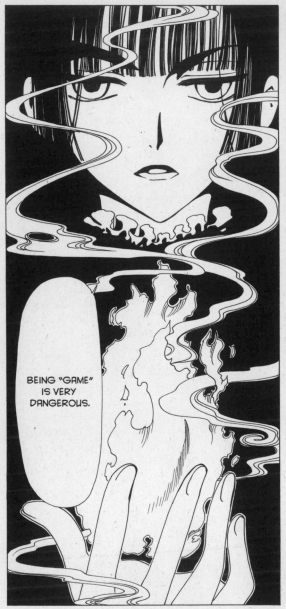

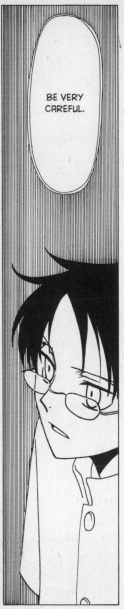

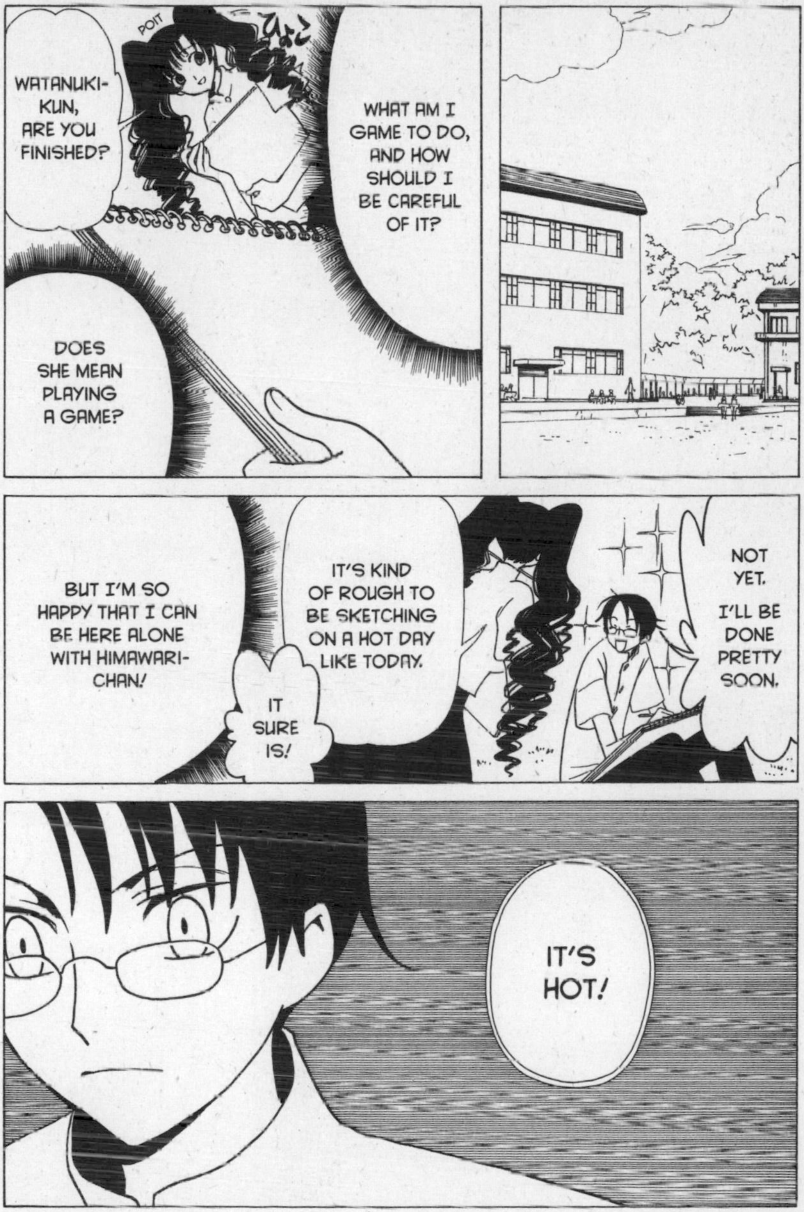
WHAT AM I GAME TO DO, AND HOW SHOULD I BE CAREFUL OF IT?
POIT
WATANUKI-KUN, ARE YOU FINISHED?
DOES SHE MEAN PLAYING A GAME?
NOT YET.
I'LL BE DONE PRETTY SOON.
IT'S KIND OF ROUGH TO BE SKETCHING ON A HOT DAY LIKE TODAY.
IT SURE IS!
BUT I'M SO HAPPY THAT I CAN BE HERE ALONE WITH HIMAWARI-CHAN!
IT'S HOT!

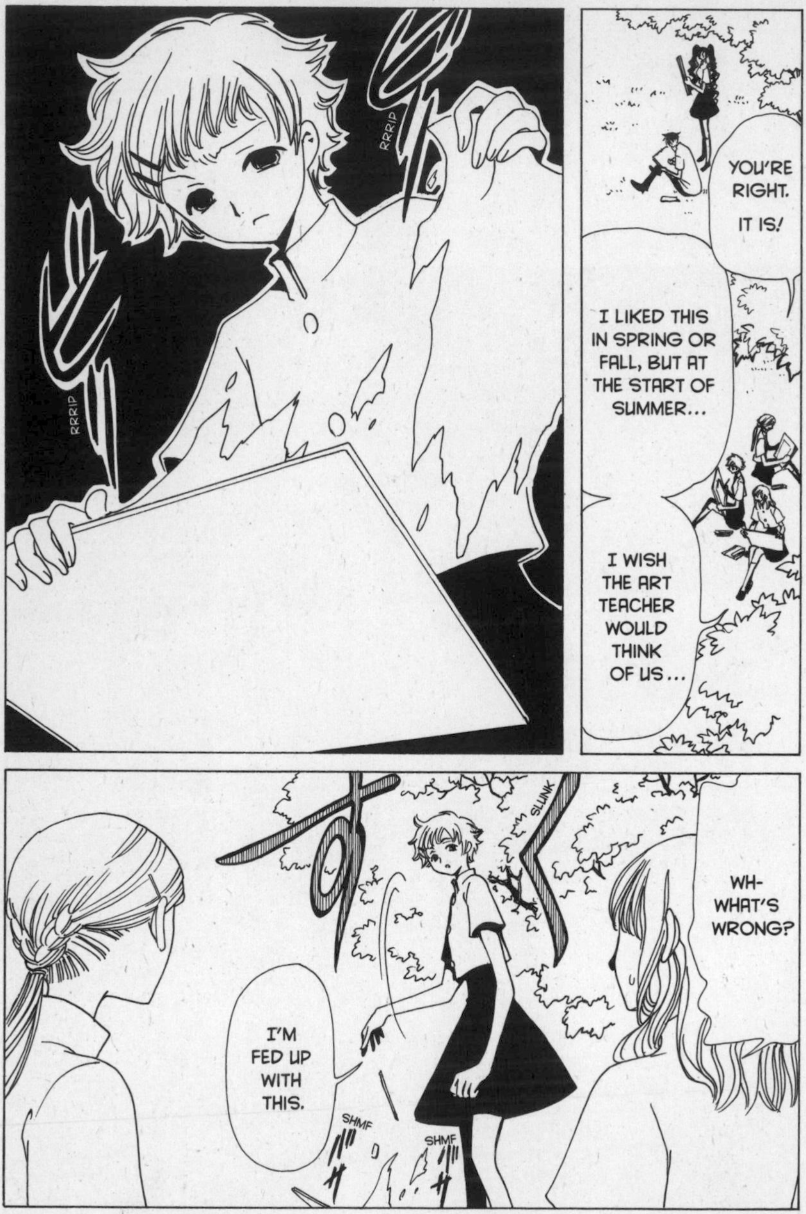
YOU'RE RIGHT. IT IS!
I LIKED THIS IN SPRING OR FALL, BUT AT THE START OF SUMMER...
I WISH THE ART TEACHER WOULD THINK OF US...
RRRIP
RRRIP
WH- WHAT'S WRONG?
SLUNK
I'M FED UP WITH THIS.
SHMF
SHMF

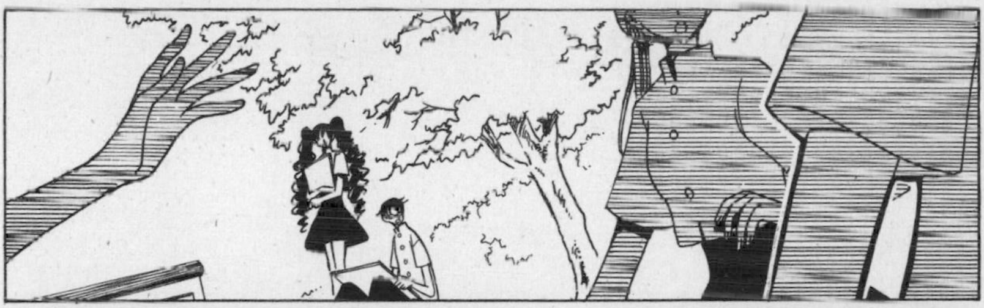
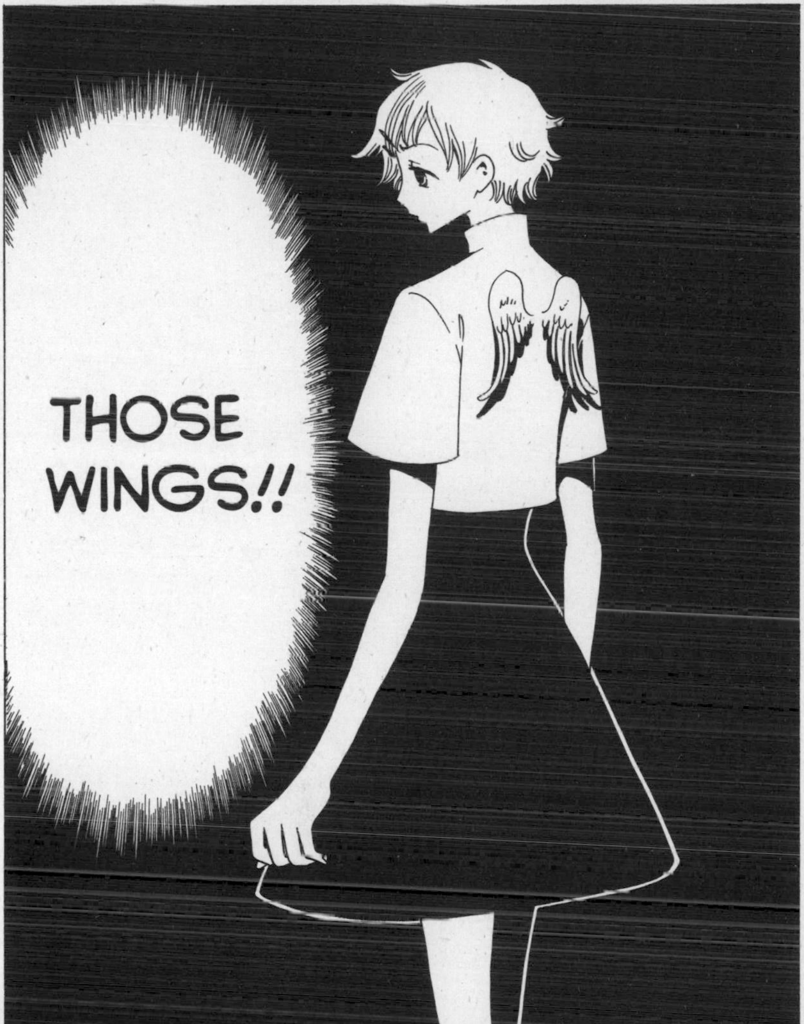
THOSE WINGS!!

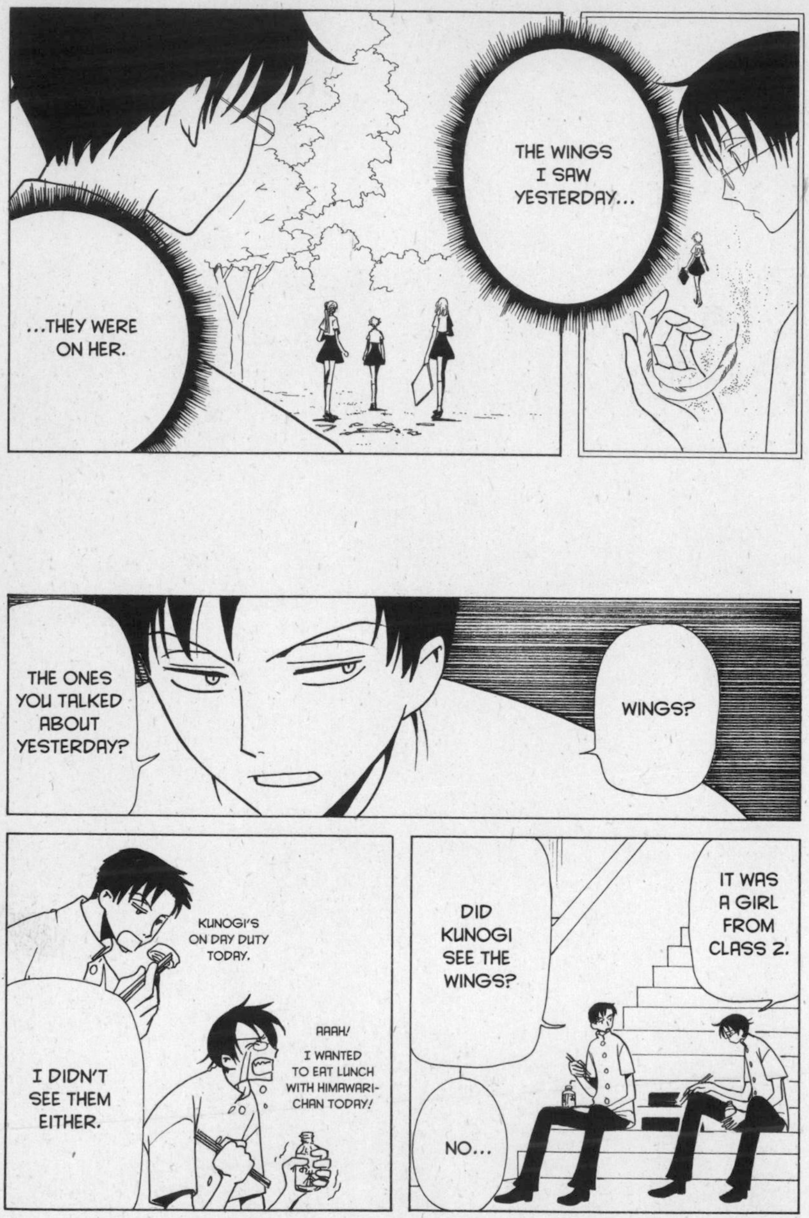
THE WINGS I SAW YESTERDAY...
...THEY WERE ON HER.
WINGS?
THE ONES YOU TALKED ABOUT YESTERDAY?
IT WAS A GIRL FROM CLASS 2.
DID KUNOGI SEE THE WINGS?
NO...
KUNOGI'S ON DAY DUTY TODAY.
AAAH! I WANTED TO EAT LUNCH WITH HIMAWARI-CHAN TODAY!
I DIDN'T SEE THEM EITHER.

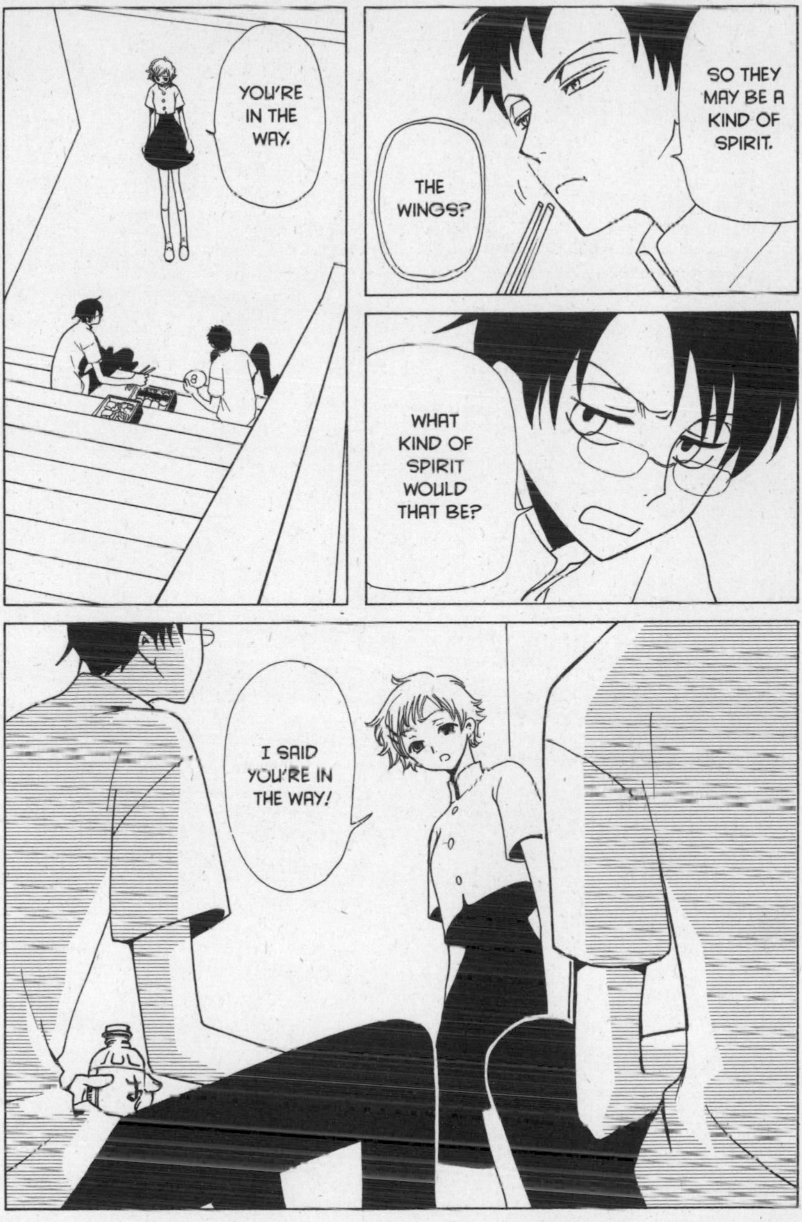
SO THEY MAY BE A KIND OF SPIRIT.
THE WINGS?
WHAT KIND OF SPIRIT WOULD THAT BE?
YOU'RE IN THE WAY.
I SAID YOU'RE IN THE WAY!

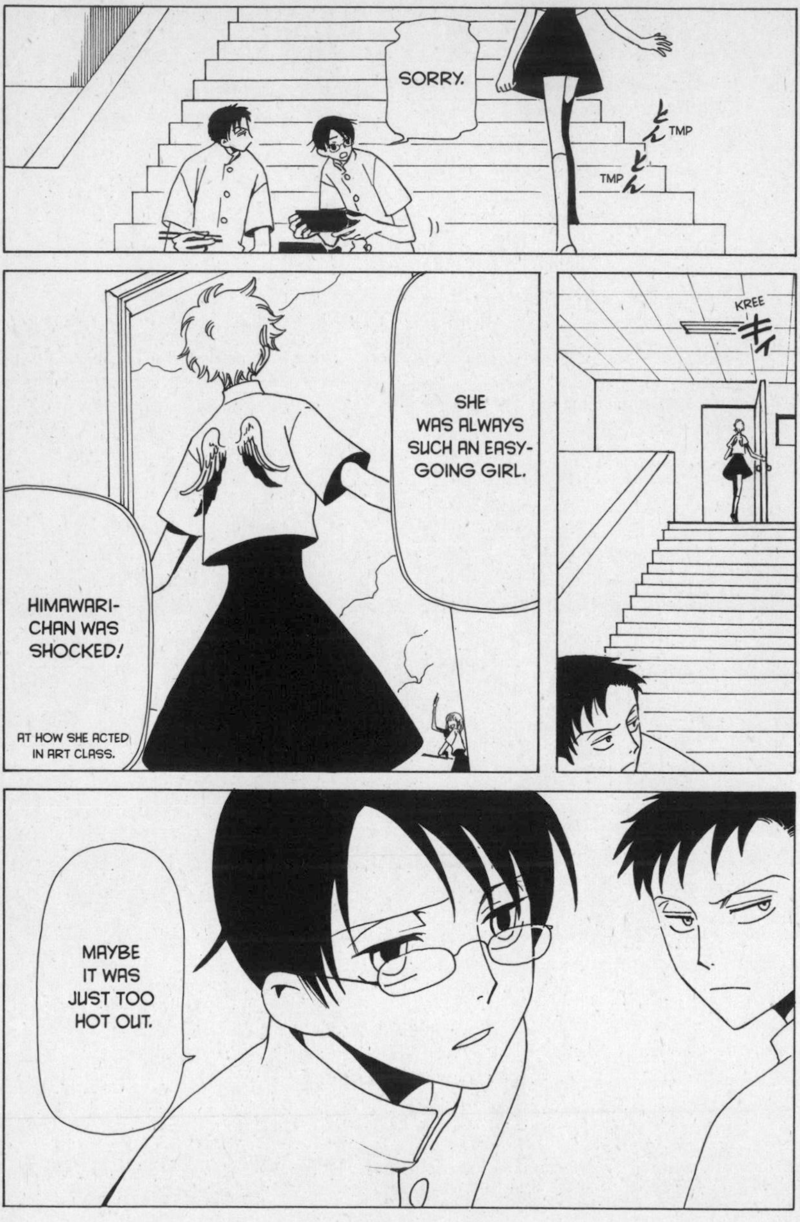
SORRY.
とん TMP
とん TMP
KREE キィ
SHE WAS ALWAYS SUCH AN EASY-GOING GIRL.
HIMAWARI-CHAN WAS SHOCKED!
AT HOW SHE ACTED IN ART CLASS.
MAYBE IT WAS JUST TOO HOT OUT.

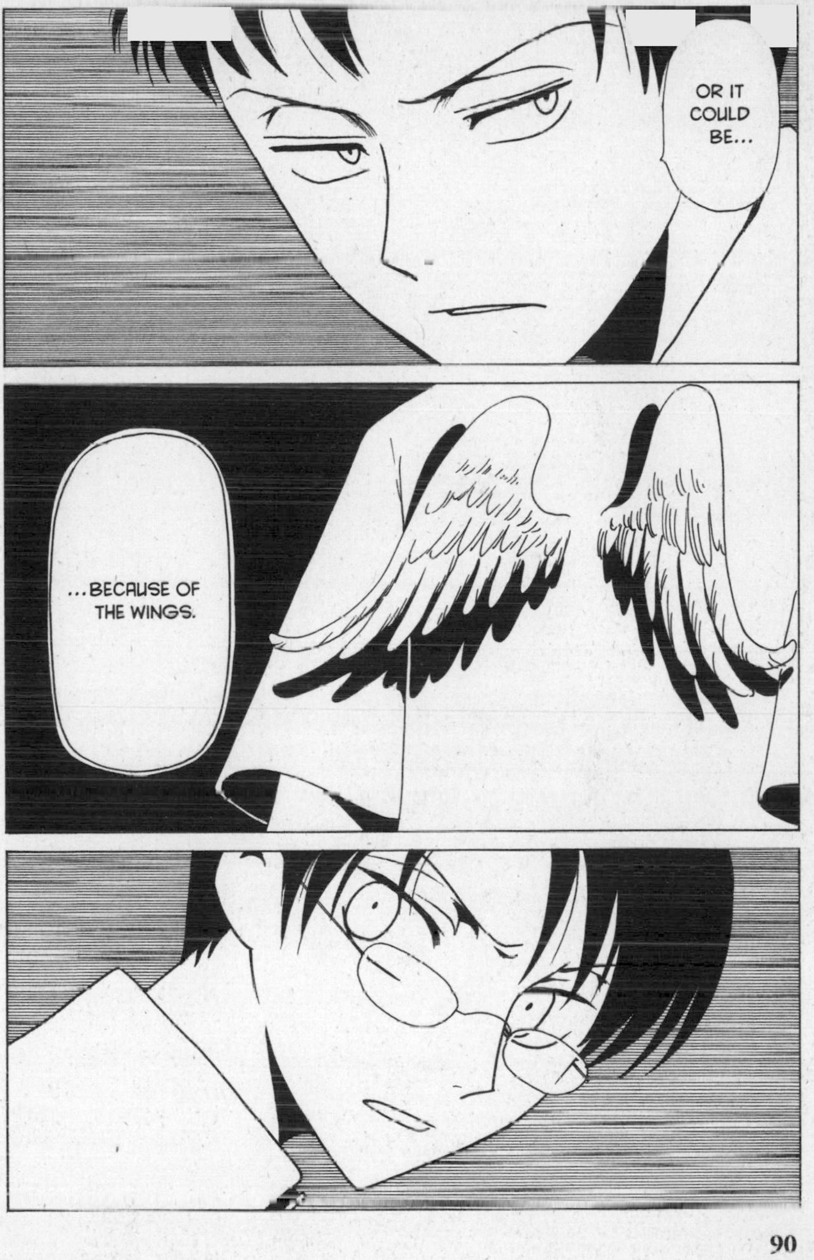
OR IT COULD BE...
...BECAUSE OF THE WINGS.

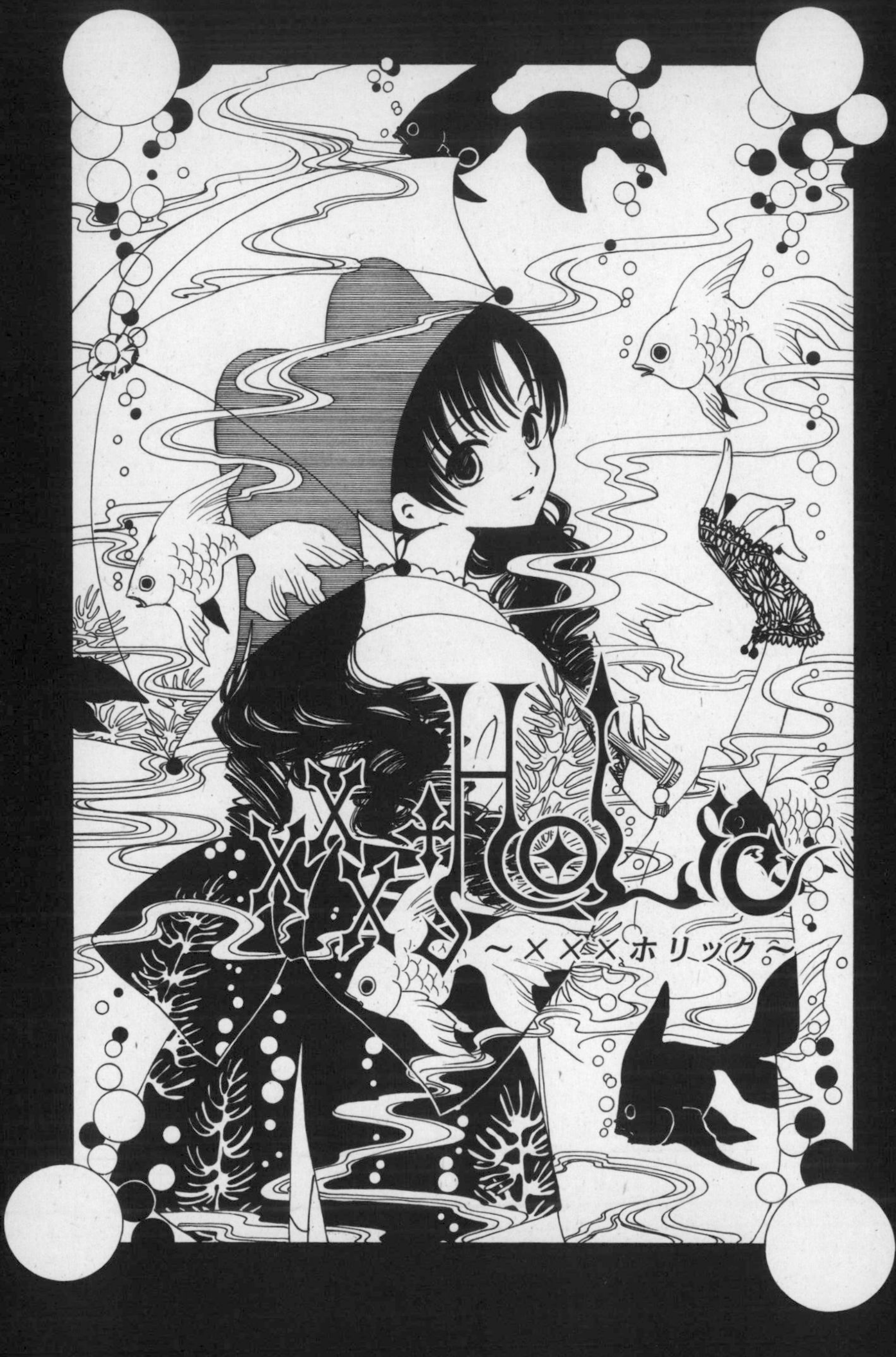
xxxHOLiC
~×××ホリック~

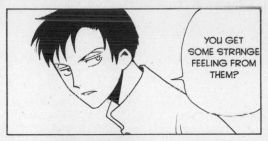

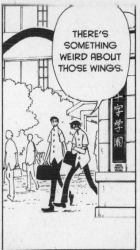

THERE'S SOMETHING WEIRD ABOUT THOSE WINGS.
YOU GET SOME STRANGE FEELING FROM THEM?
NO. NOTHING AT ALL.
BUT YOU REMEMBER WHEN I FOUND A FEATHER...
...WHEN I WAS HELPING YOU IN THE LIBRARY YESTERDAY?
WHEN YÛKO-SAN NOTICED IT...
...SHE SAID TO ME...
..."BE VERY CAREFUL.
BEING 'GAME' IS VERY DANGEROUS."

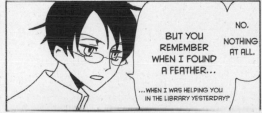

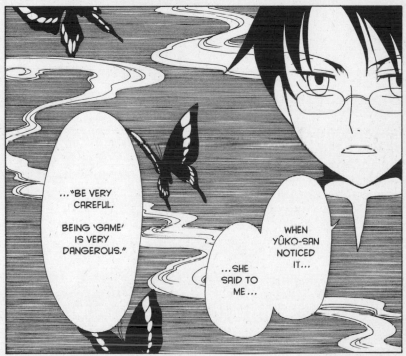

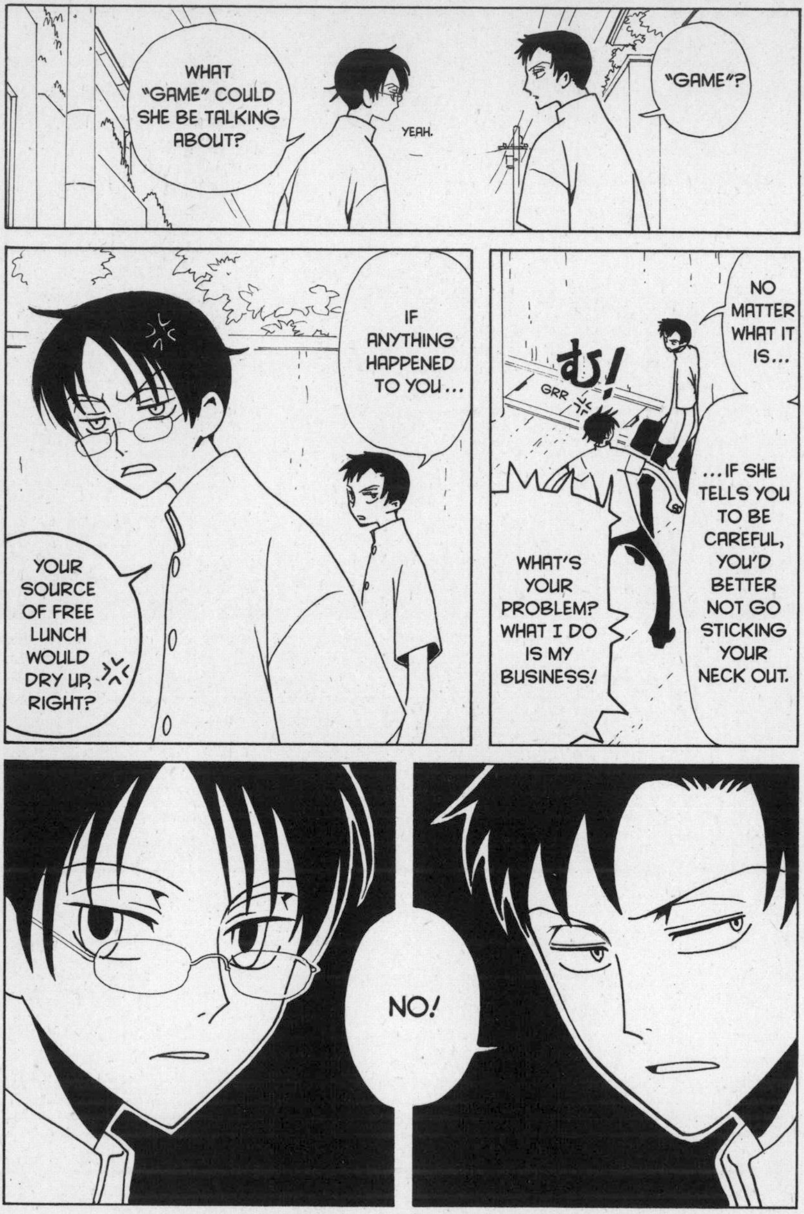
"GAME"?
YEAH.
WHAT "GAME" COULD SHE BE TALKING ABOUT?
NO MATTER WHAT IT IS...
...IF SHE TELLS YOU TO BE CAREFUL, YOU'D BETTER NOT GO STICKING YOUR NECK OUT.
む!
GRR
WHAT'S YOUR PROBLEM? WHAT I DO IS MY BUSINESS!
IF ANYTHING HAPPENED TO YOU...
YOUR SOURCE OF FREE LUNCH WOULD DRY UP, RIGHT?
NO!

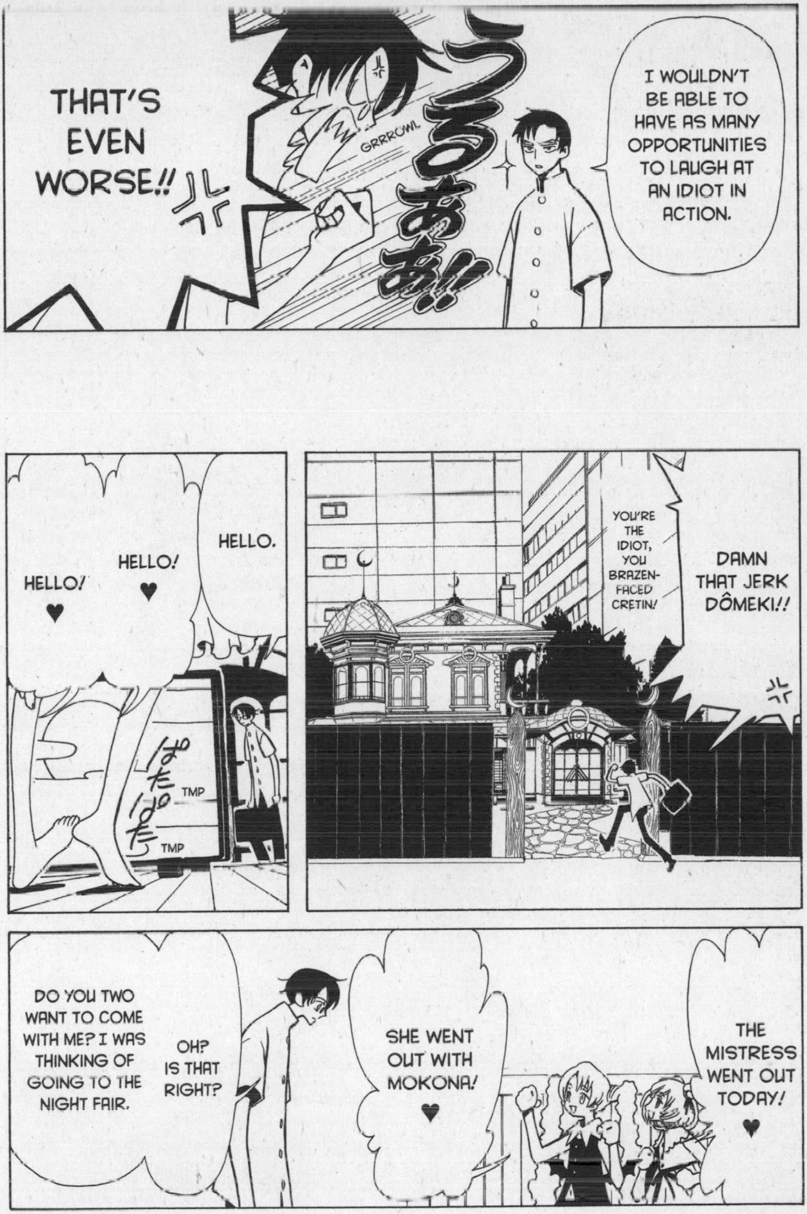
I WOULDN'T BE ABLE TO HAVE AS MANY OPPORTUNITIES TO LAUGH AT AN IDIOT IN ACTION.
うるああ!!
GRRROWL
THAT'S EVEN WORSE!!
DAMN THAT JERK DÔMEKI!!
YOU'RE THE IDIOT, YOU BRAZEN-FACED CRETIN!
HELLO.
HELLO! ♥
HELLO! ♥
ぱたぱた
TMP
TMP
THE MISTRESS WENT OUT TODAY! ♥
SHE WENT OUT WITH MOKONA! ♥
OH? IS THAT RIGHT?
DO YOU TWO WANT TO COME WITH ME? I WAS THINKING OF GOING TO THE NIGHT FAIR.

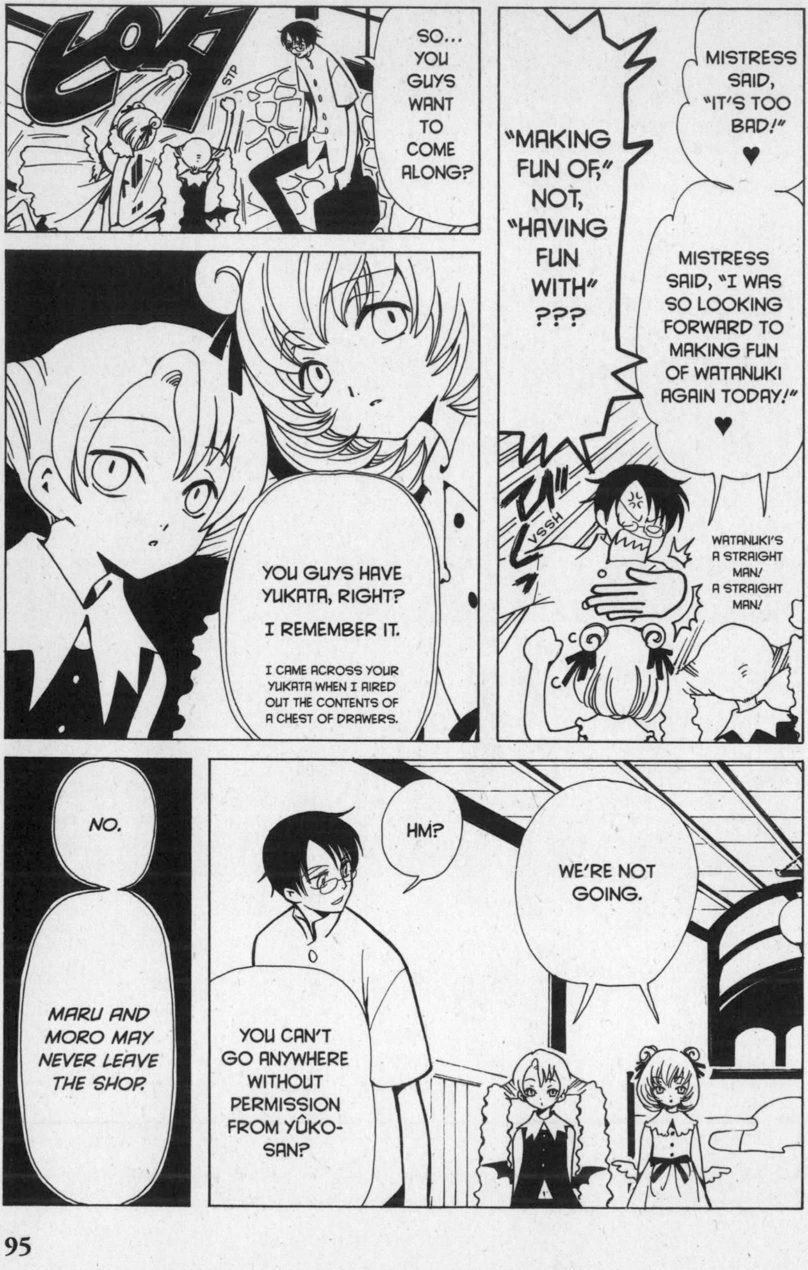
MISTRESS SAID, "IT'S TOO BAD!" ♥
MISTRESS SAID, "I WAS SO LOOKING FORWARD TO MAKING FUN OF WATANUKI AGAIN TODAY!" ♥
"MAKING FUN OF," NOT, "HAVING FUN WITH" ???
VSSH
WATANUKI'S A STRAIGHT MAN! A STRAIGHT MAN!
STP
SO... YOU GUYS WANT TO COME ALONG?
YOU GUYS HAVE YUKATA, RIGHT?
I REMEMBER IT.
I CAME ACROSS YOUR YUKATA WHEN I AIRED OUT THE CONTENTS OF A CHEST OF DRAWERS.
WE'RE NOT GOING.
HM?
YOU CAN'T GO ANYWHERE WITHOUT PERMISSION FROM YÛKO-SAN?
NO.
MARU AND MORO MAY NEVER LEAVE THE SHOP.

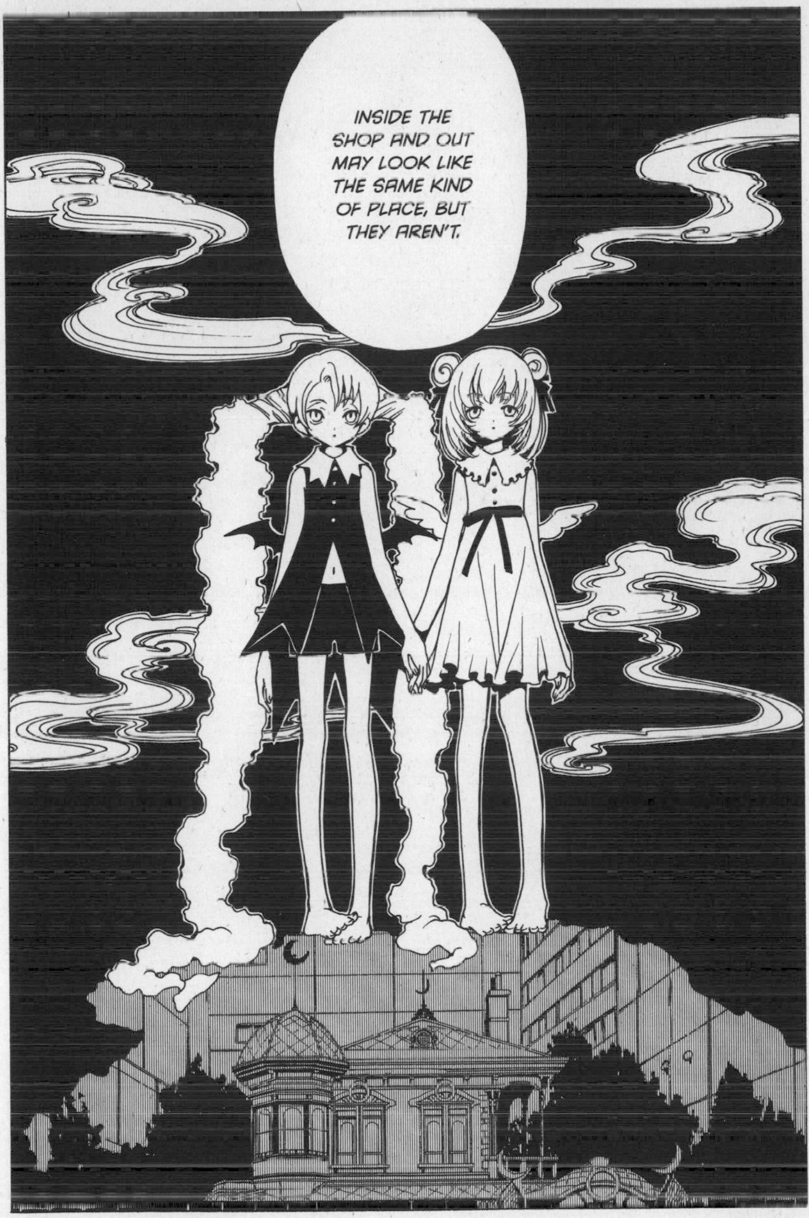
INSIDE THE SHOP AND OUT MAY LOOK LIKE THE SAME KIND OF PLACE, BUT THEY AREN'T.

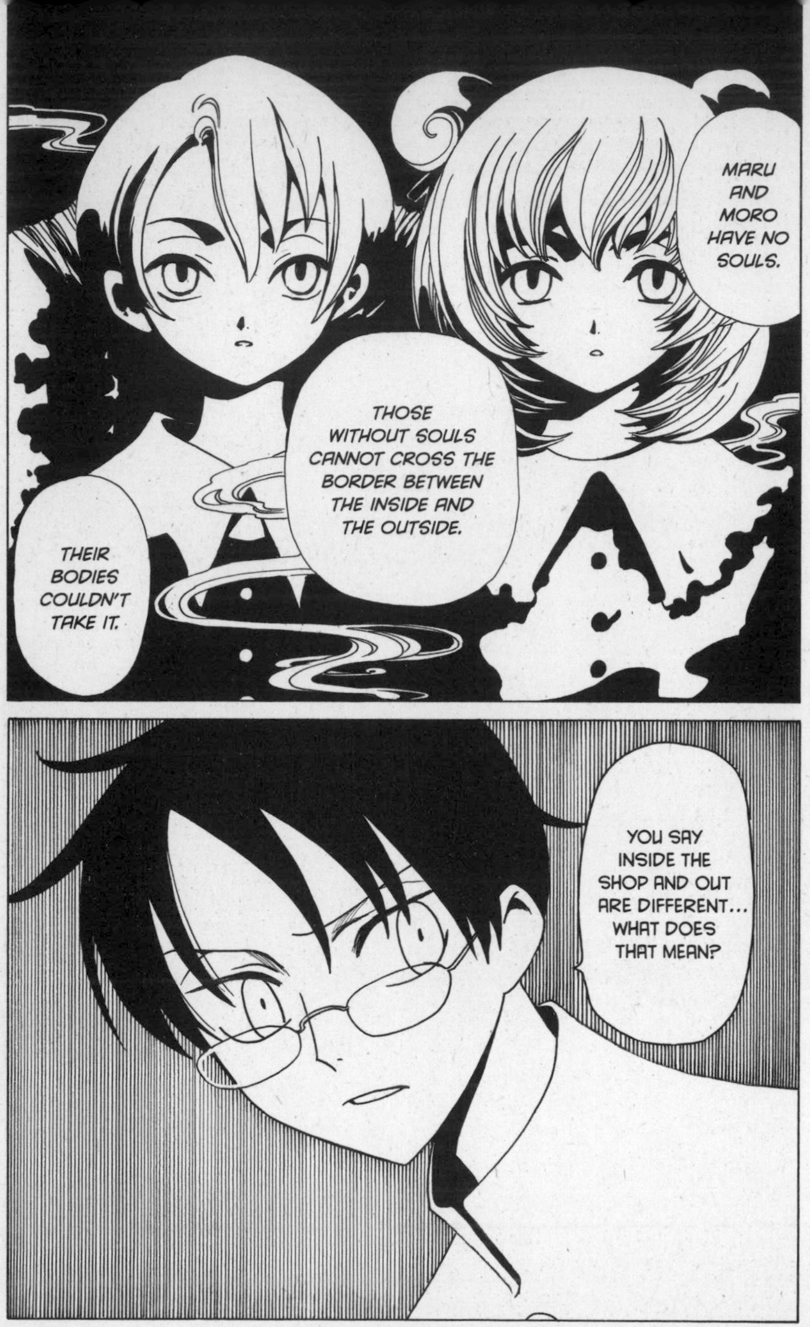
MARU AND MORO HAVE NO SOULS.
THOSE WITHOUT SOULS CANNOT CROSS THE BORDER BETWEEN THE INSIDE AND THE OUTSIDE.
THEIR BODIES COULDN'T TAKE IT.
YOU SAY INSIDE THE SHOP AND OUT ARE DIFFERENT... WHAT DOES THAT MEAN?

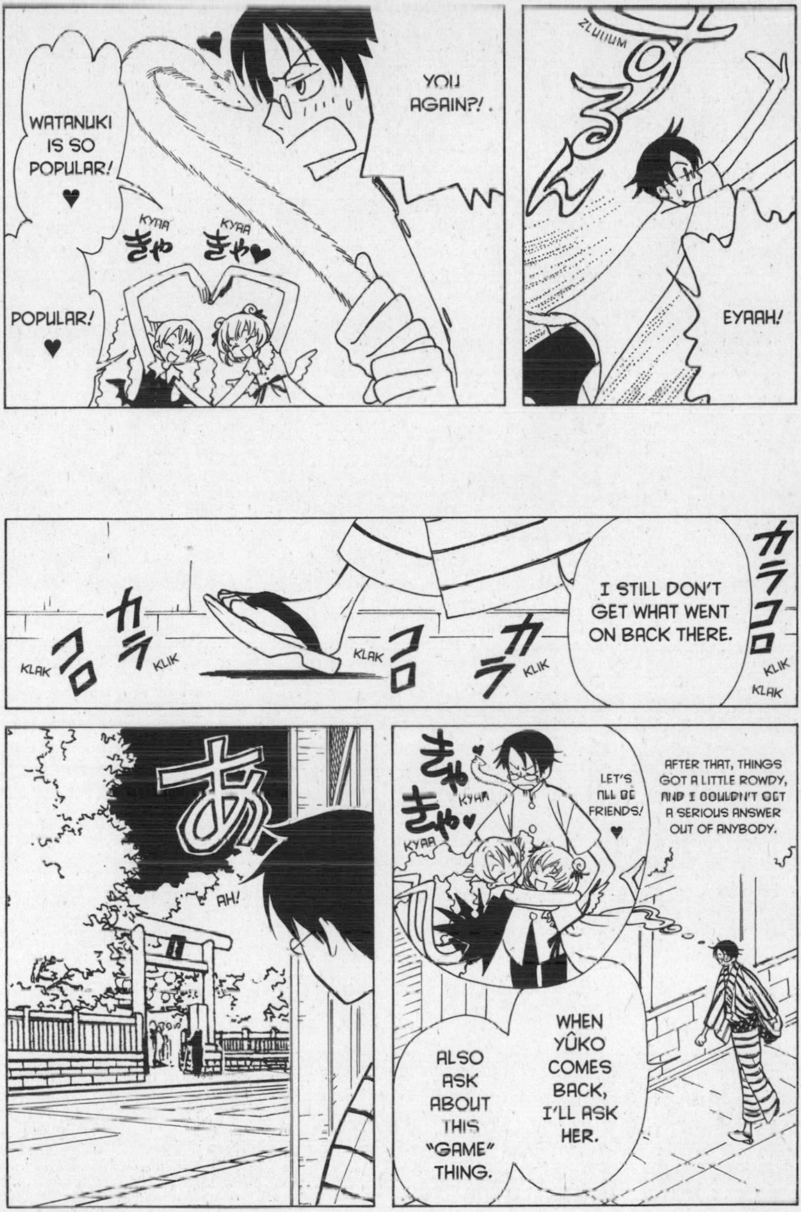
ZLUUUM
EYAAH!
YOU AGAIN?!
WATANUKI IS SO POPULAR! ♥
KYAA きゃ
KYAA きゃ♥
POPULAR! ♥
カラコロ
KLIK KLAK
I STILL DON'T GET WHAT WENT ON BACK THERE.
カラ KLIK
コロ KLAK
カラ KLIK
コロ KLAK
AFTER THAT, THINGS GOT A LITTLE ROWDY, AND I COULDN'T GET A SERIOUS ANSWER OUT OF ANYBODY.
LET'S ALL BE FRIENDS! ♥
きゃ KYAA
きゃ♥ KYAA
WHEN YÛKO COMES BACK, I'LL ASK HER.
ALSO ASK ABOUT THIS "GAME" THING.
あ
AH!

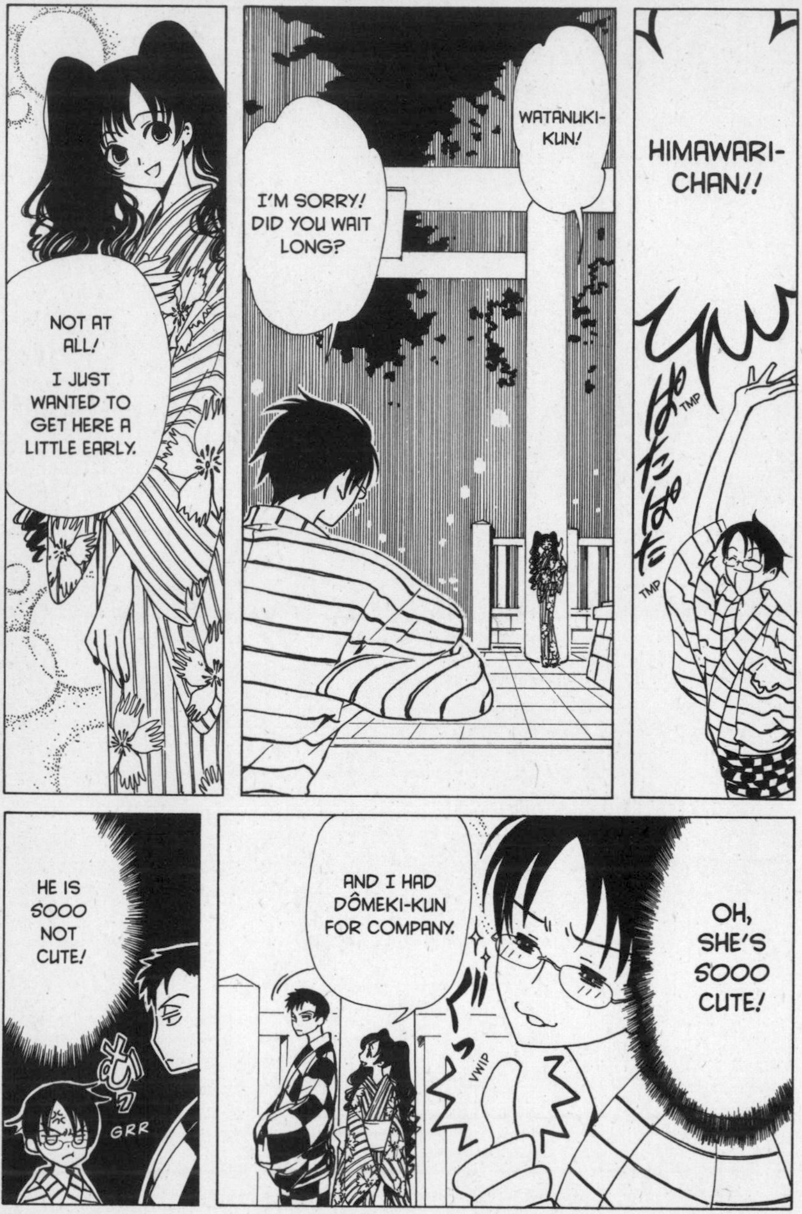
HIMAWARI-CHAN!!
ぱたぱた
TMP
TMP
WATANUKI-KUN!
I'M SORRY! DID YOU WAIT LONG?
NOT AT ALL!
I JUST WANTED TO GET HERE A LITTLE EARLY.
OH, SHE'S SOOO CUTE!
AND I HAD DÔMEKI-KUN FOR COMPANY.
VWIP
HE IS SOOO NOT CUTE!
むっ
GRR

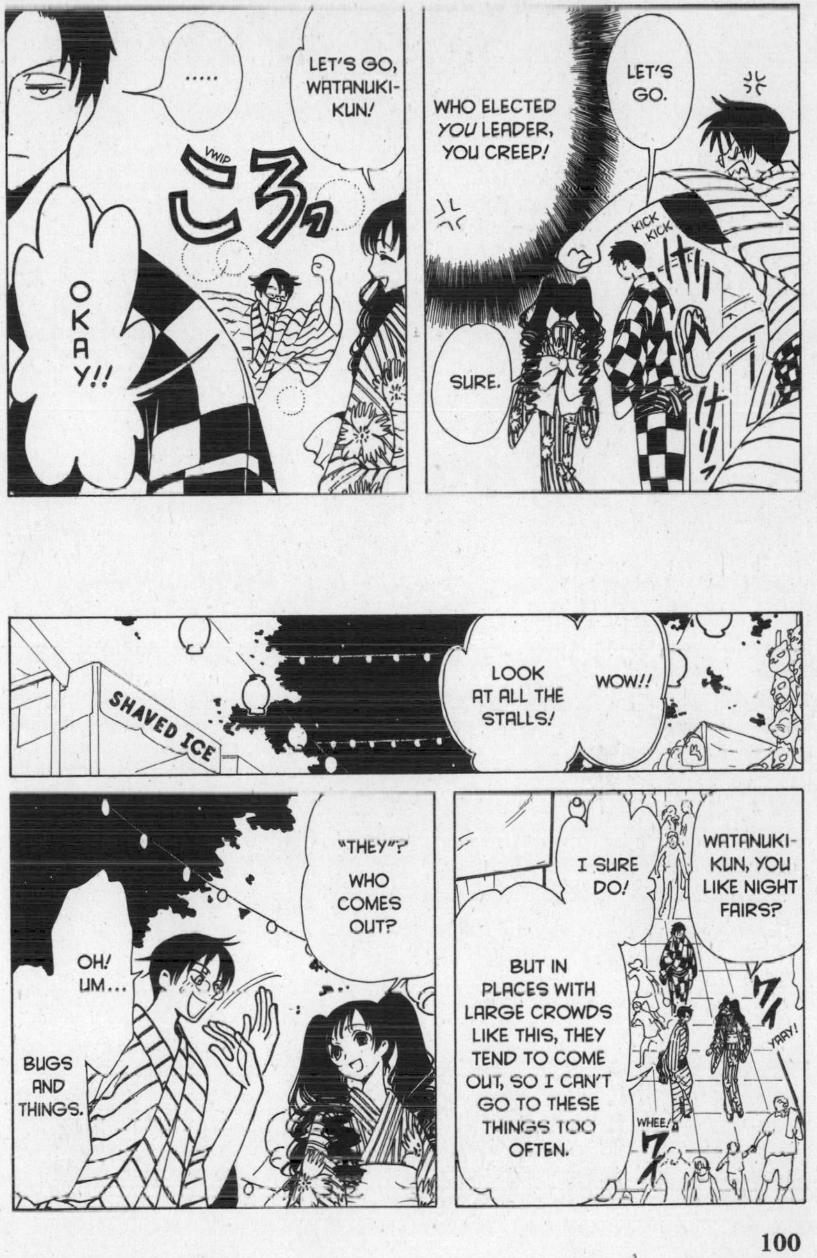
LET'S GO.
WHO ELECTED YOU LEADER, YOU CREEP!
KICK KICK
SURE.
LET'S GO, WATANUKI-KUN!
.....
VWIP
OKAY!!
WOW!!
LOOK AT ALL THE STALLS!
SHAVED ICE
WATANUKI-KUN, YOU LIKE NIGHT FAIRS?
I SURE DO!
BUT IN PLACES WITH LARGE CROWDS LIKE THIS, THEY TEND TO COME OUT, SO I CAN'T GO TO THESE THINGS TOO OFTEN.
YAAY!
WHEE!
"THEY"?
WHO COMES OUT?
OH! UM...
BUGS AND THINGS.

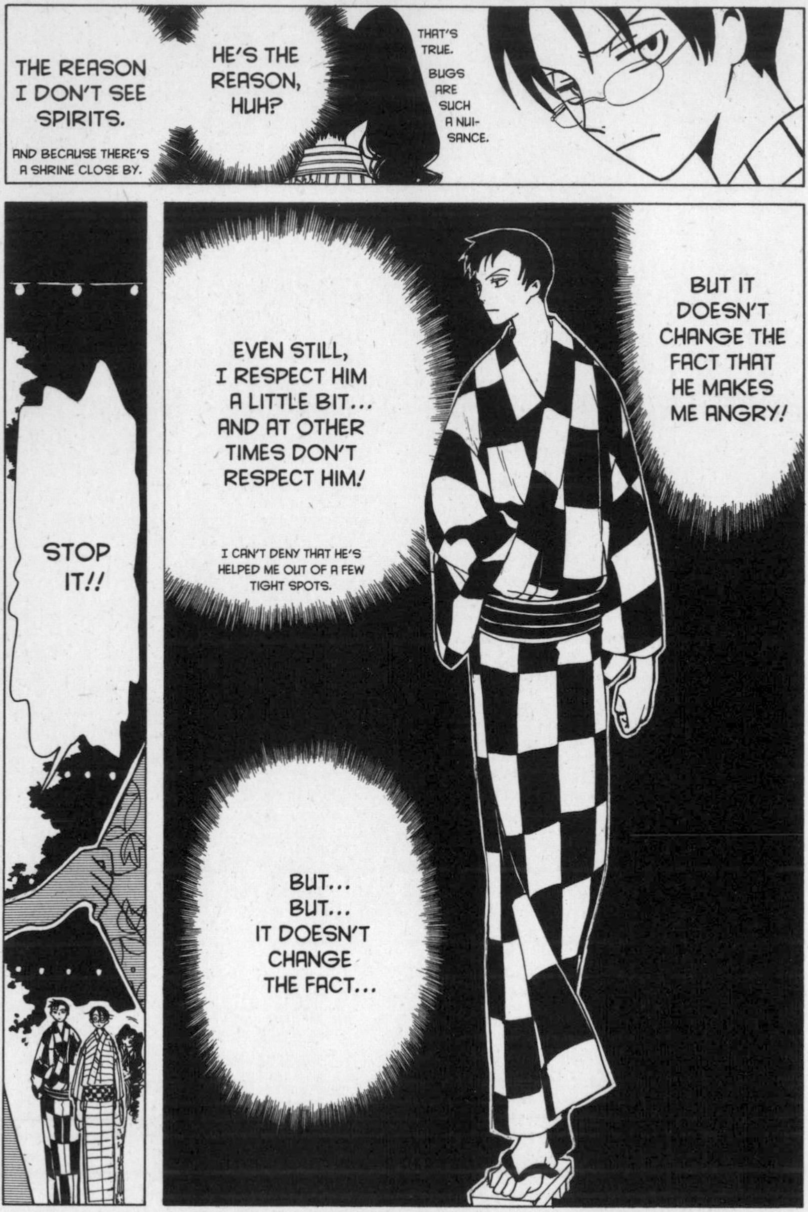
THAT'S TRUE.
BUGS ARE SUCH A NUI-SANCE.
HE'S THE REASON, HUH?
THE REASON I DON'T SEE SPIRITS.
AND BECAUSE THERE'S A SHRINE CLOSE BY.
BUT IT DOESN'T CHANGE THE FACT THAT HE MAKES ME ANGRY!
EVEN STILL, I RESPECT HIM A LITTLE BIT... AND AT OTHER TIMES DON'T RESPECT HIM!
I CAN'T DENY THAT HE'S HELPED ME OUT OF A FEW TIGHT SPOTS.
BUT... BUT... IT DOESN'T CHANGE THE FACT...
STOP IT!!

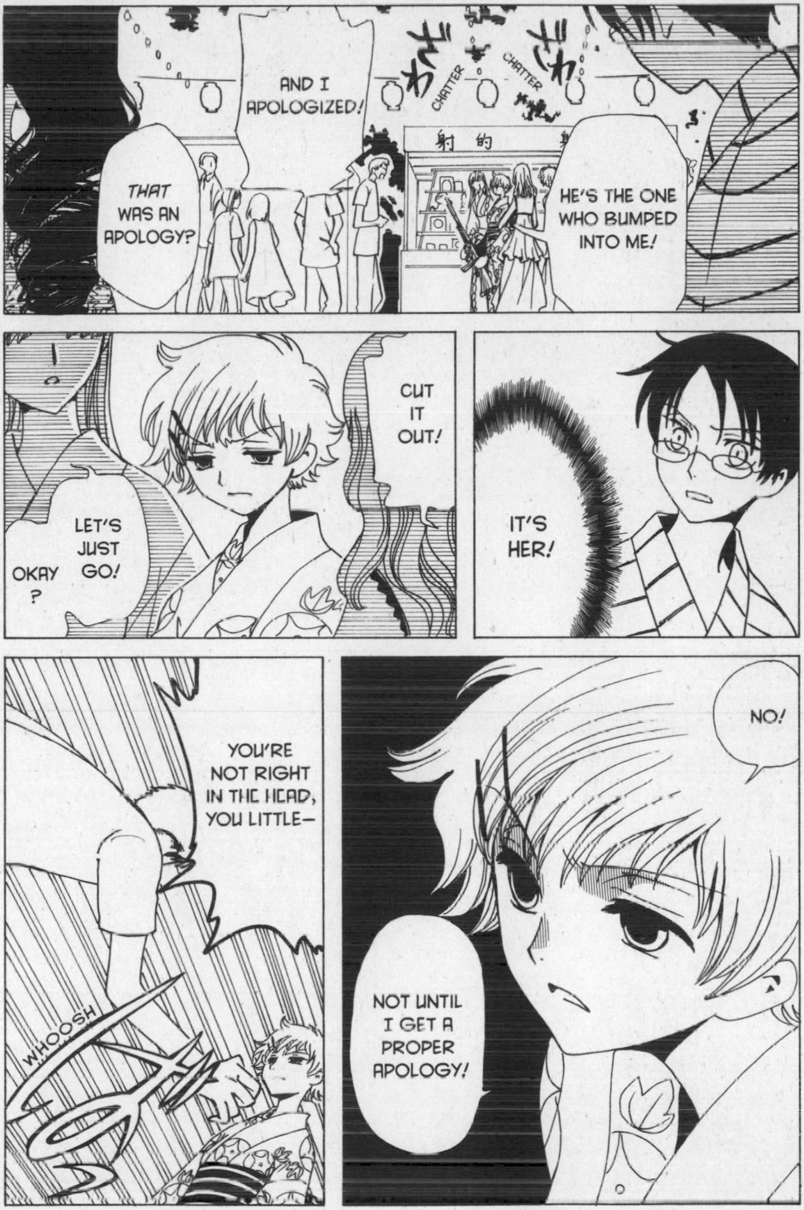
HE'S THE ONE WHO BUMPED INTO ME!
ざわ
CHATTER
ざわ
CHATTER
AND I APOLOGIZED!
射的
THAT WAS AN APOLOGY?
IT'S HER!
CUT IT OUT!
LET'S JUST GO!
OKAY?
NO!
NOT UNTIL I GET A PROPER APOLOGY!
YOU'RE NOT RIGHT IN THE HEAD, YOU LITTLE—
WHOOSH

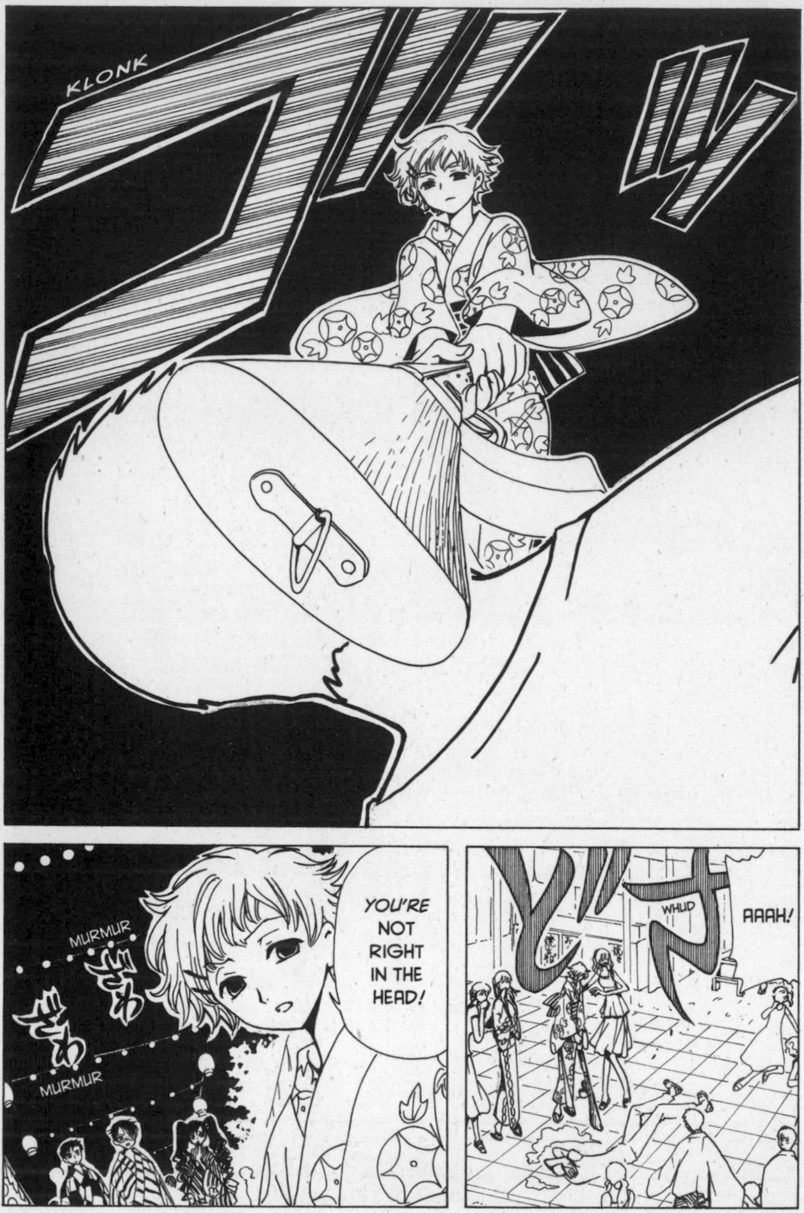
KLONK
WHUD
AAAH!
YOU'RE NOT RIGHT IN THE HEAD!
MURMUR
ざわ
ざわ
MURMUR

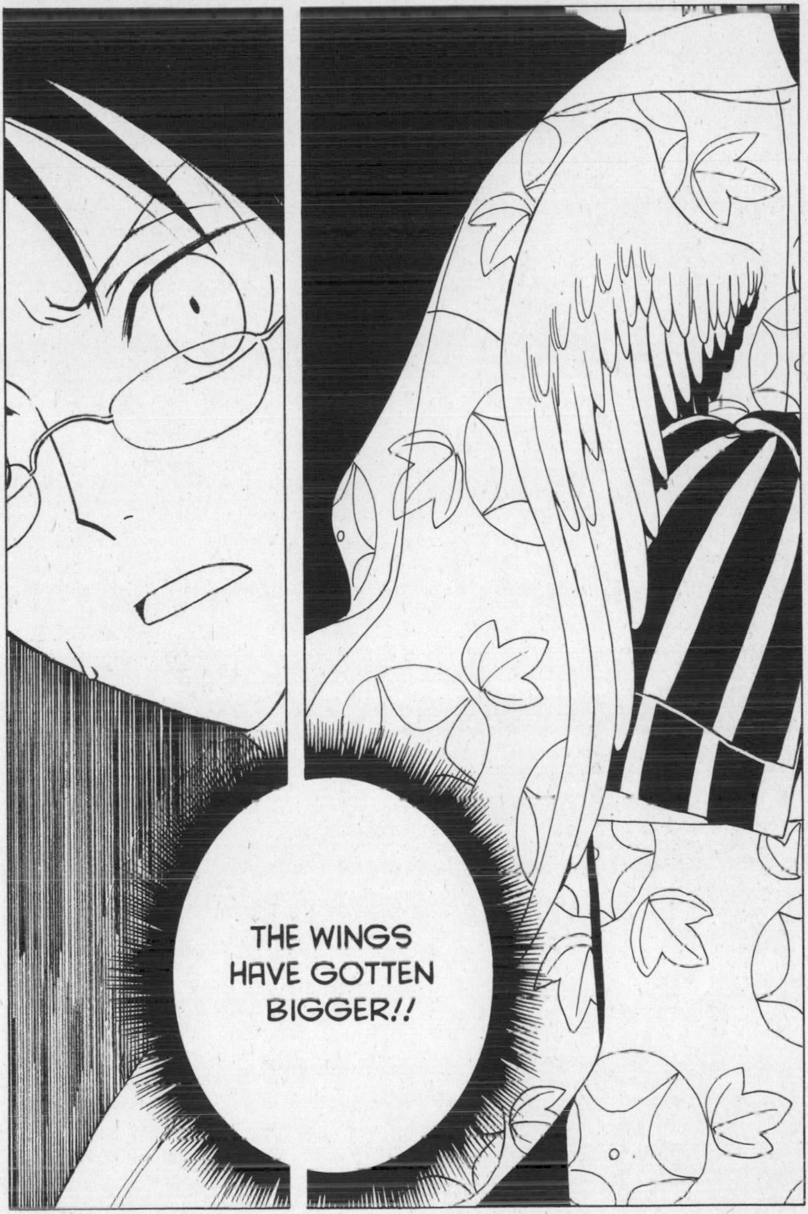
THE WINGS HAVE GOTTEN BIGGER!!

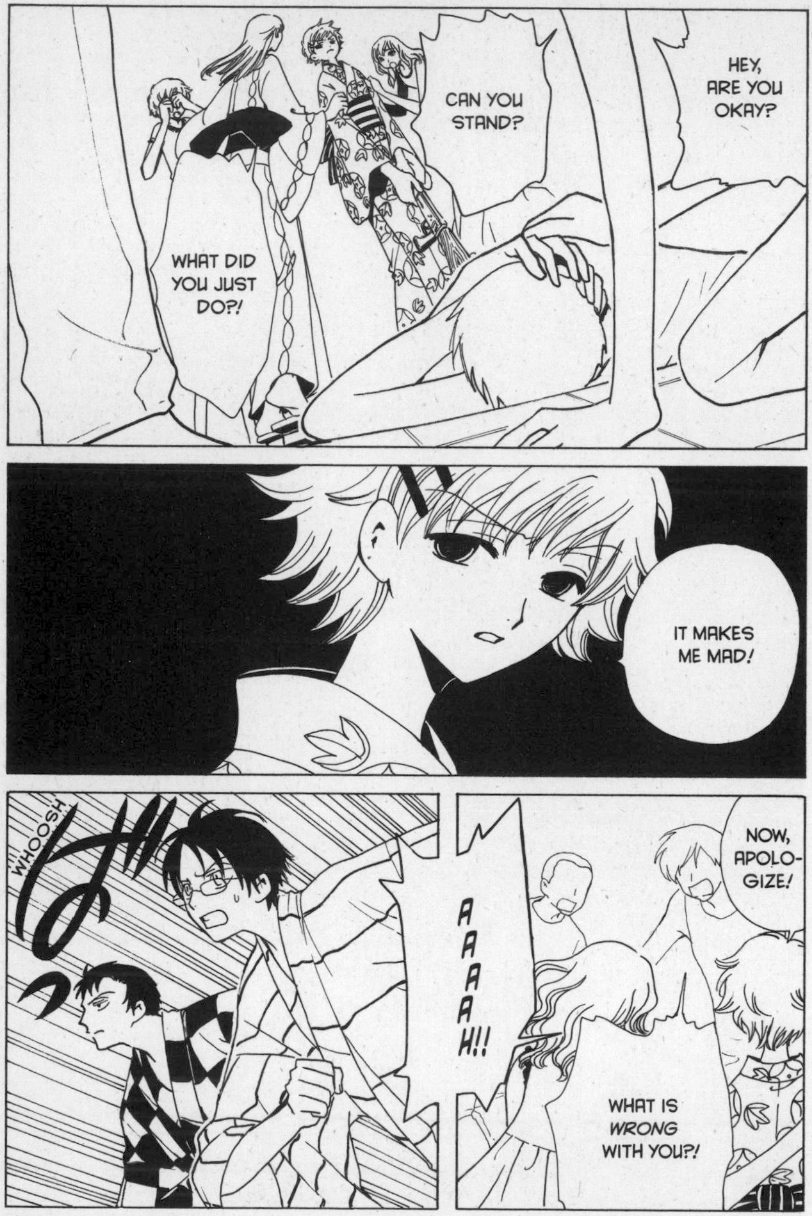
HEY, ARE YOU OKAY?
CAN YOU STAND?
WHAT DID YOU JUST DO?!
IT MAKES ME MAD!
NOW, APOLO-GIZE!
AAAAAH!!
WHAT IS *WRONG* WITH YOU?!
WHOOSH

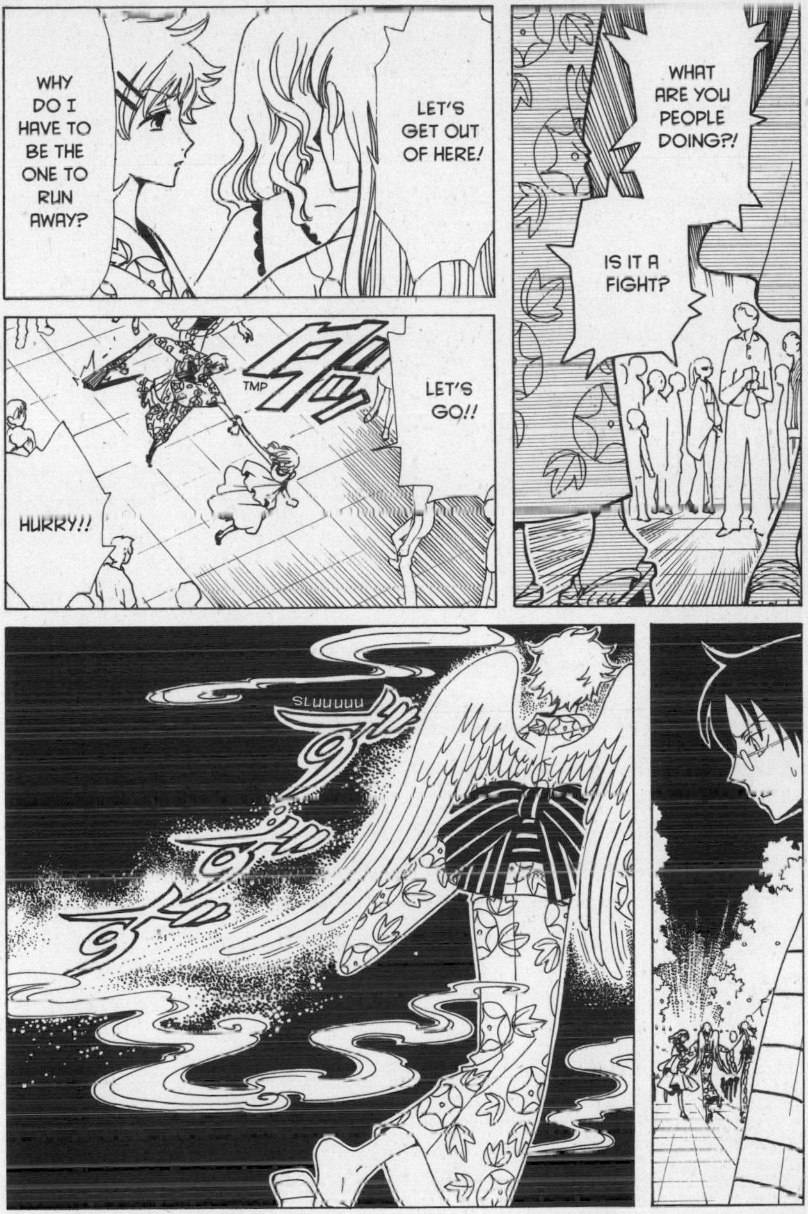
WHAT ARE YOU PEOPLE DOING?!
IS IT A FIGHT?
LET'S GET OUT OF HERE!
WHY DO I HAVE TO BE THE ONE TO RUN AWAY?
LET'S GO!!
TMP
HURRY!!
SLUUUUN

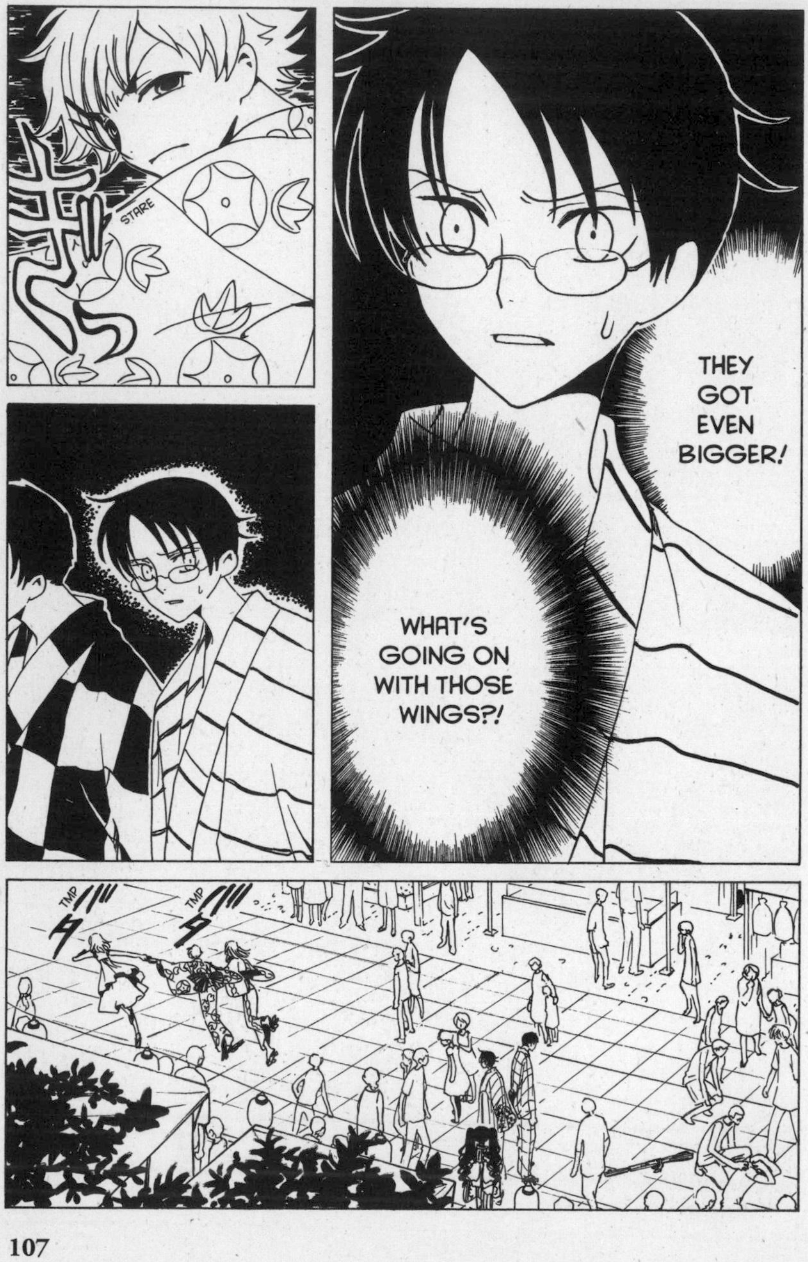
THEY GOT EVEN BIGGER!
WHAT'S GOING ON WITH THOSE WINGS?!
STARE
TMP
TMP

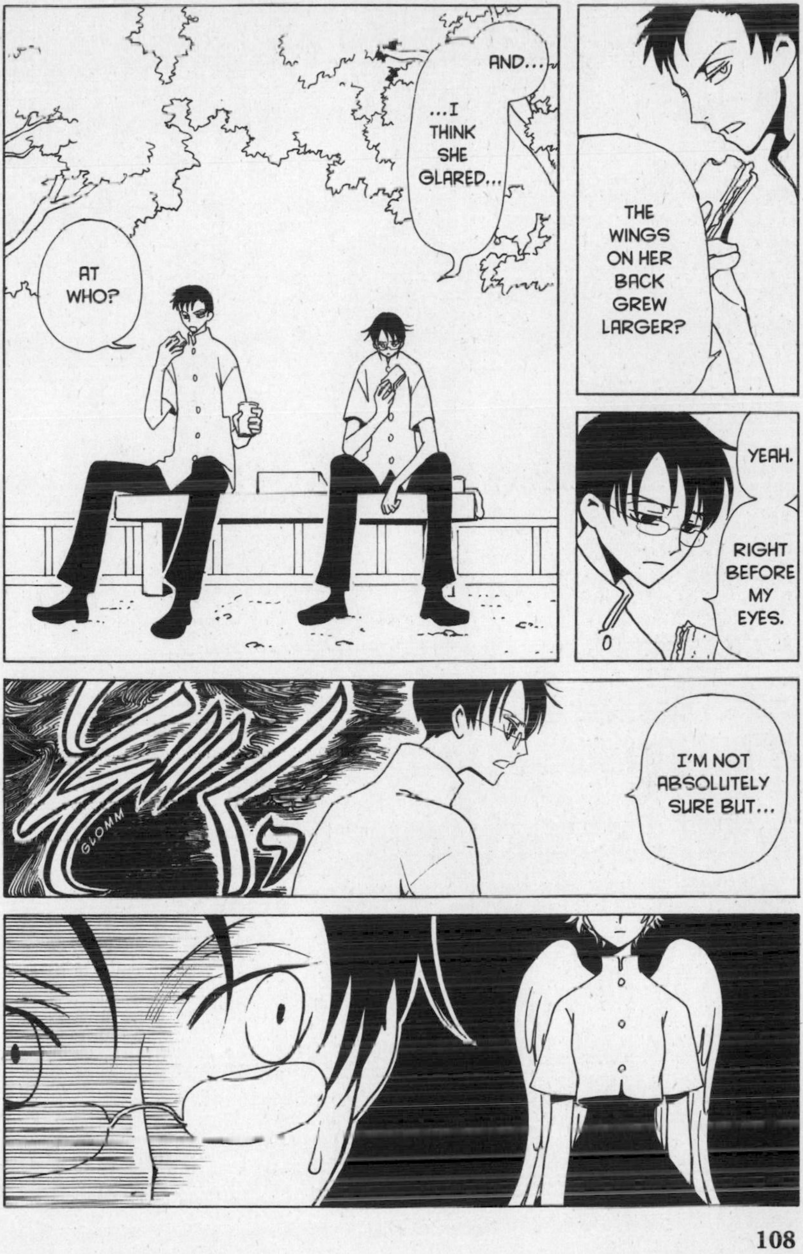
THE WINGS ON HER BACK GREW LARGER?
YEAH.
RIGHT BEFORE MY EYES.
AND...
...I THINK SHE GLARED...
AT WHO?
I'M NOT ABSOLUTELY SURE BUT...
GLOMM

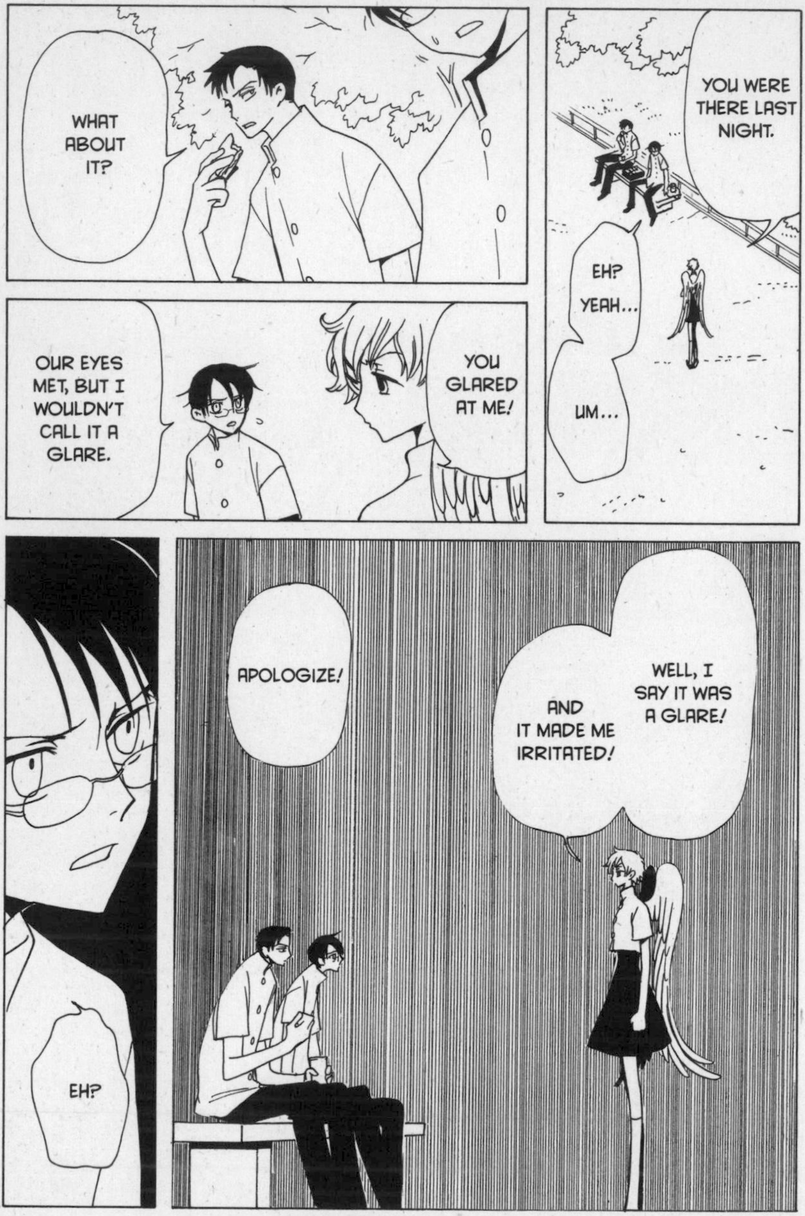
YOU WERE THERE LAST NIGHT.
EH? YEAH...
UM...
WHAT ABOUT IT?
YOU GLARED AT ME!
OUR EYES MET, BUT I WOULDN'T CALL IT A GLARE.
WELL, I SAY IT WAS A GLARE!
AND IT MADE ME IRRITATED!
APOLOGIZE!
EH?

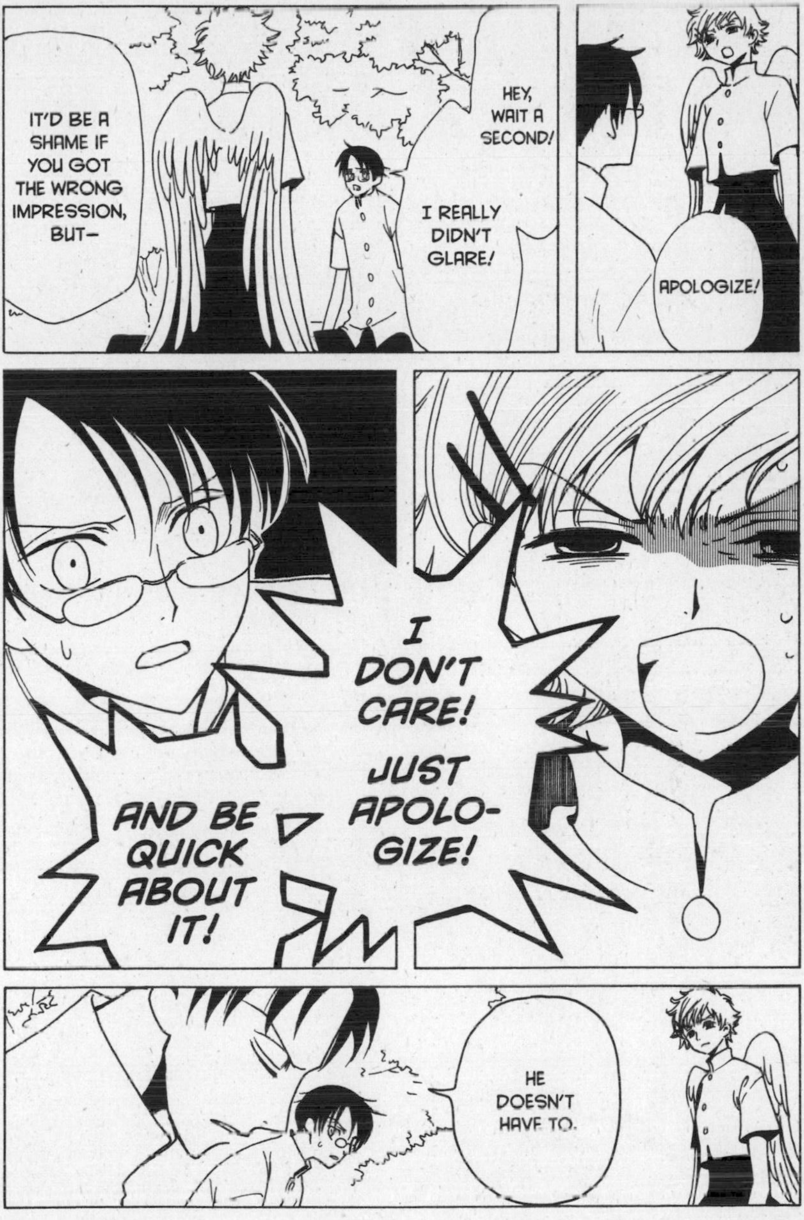
APOLOGIZE!
HEY, WAIT A SECOND!
I REALLY DIDN'T GLARE!
IT'D BE A SHAME IF YOU GOT THE WRONG IMPRESSION, BUT–
I DON'T CARE!
JUST APOLO-GIZE!
AND BE QUICK ABOUT IT!
HE DOESN'T HAVE TO.

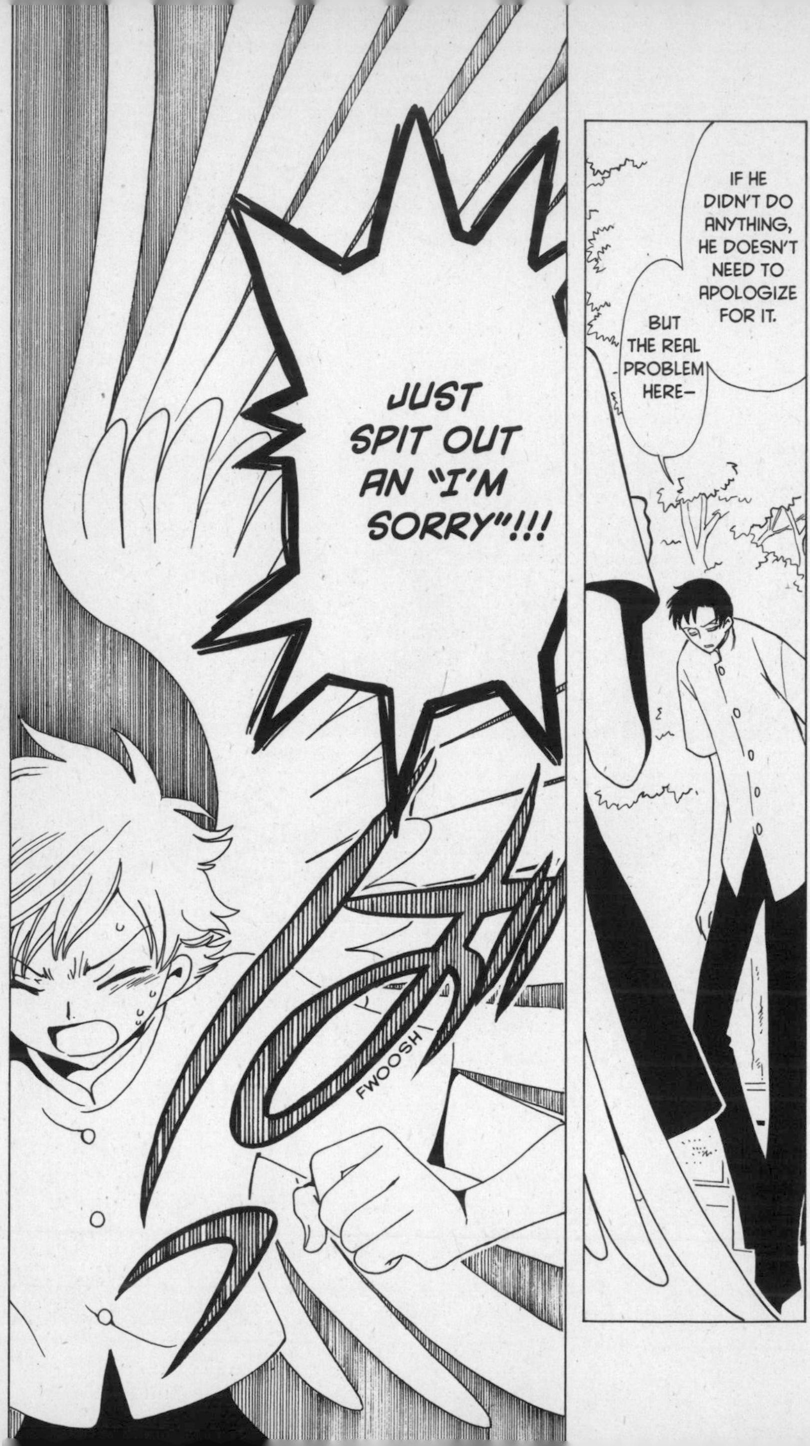
IF HE DIDN'T DO ANYTHING, HE DOESN'T NEED TO APOLOGIZE FOR IT.
BUT THE REAL PROBLEM HERE–
JUST SPIT OUT AN "I'M SORRY"!!!
FWOOSH

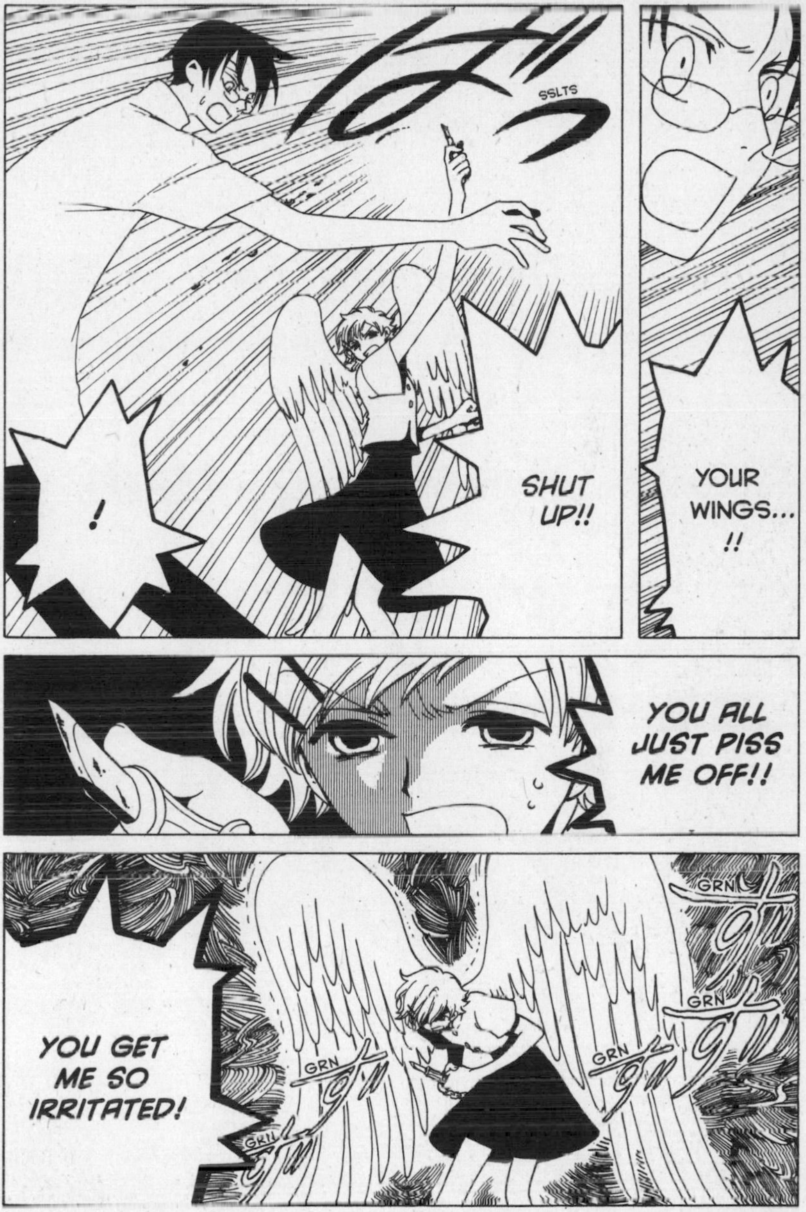
YOUR WINGS... !!
SSLTS
SHUT UP!!
!
YOU ALL JUST PISS ME OFF!!
GRN
GRN
GRN
YOU GET ME SO IRRITATED!
GRN

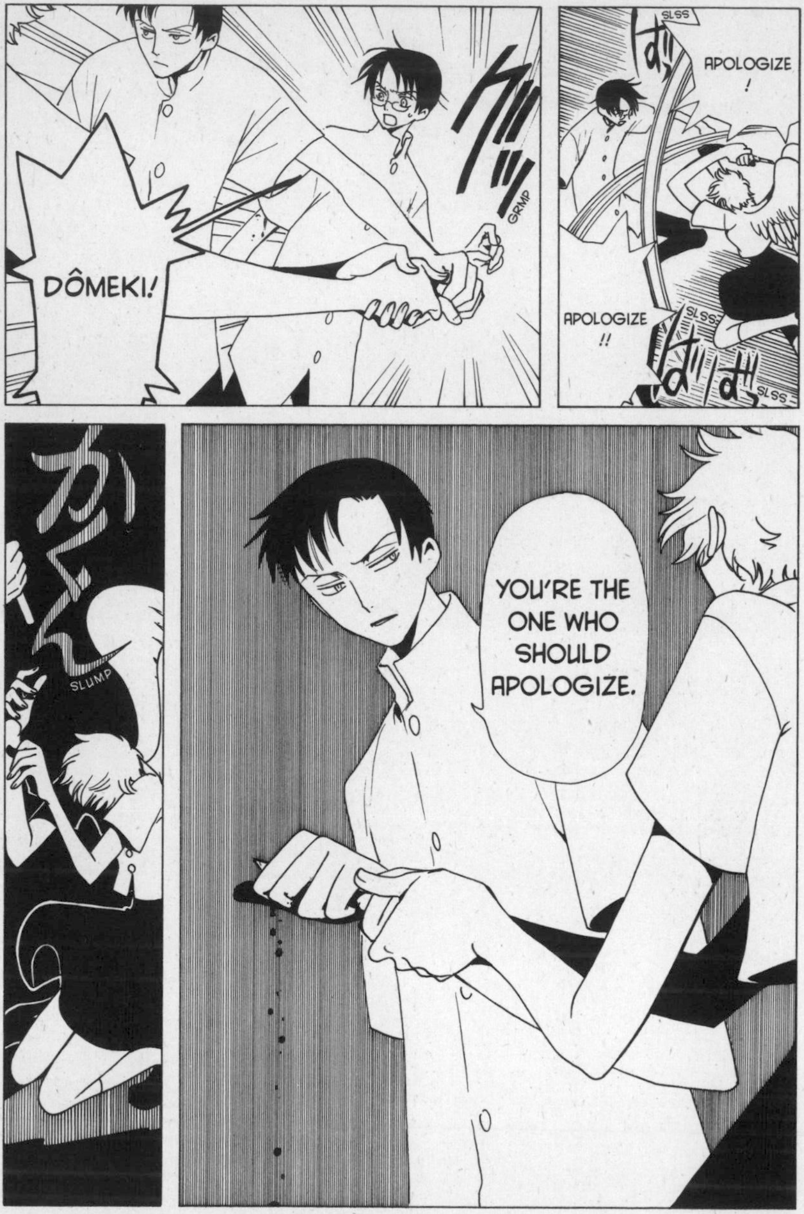
SLSS
APOLOGIZE !
APOLOGIZE !!
SLSS
SLSS
GRMP
DÔMEKI!
YOU'RE THE ONE WHO SHOULD APOLOGIZE.
SLUMP

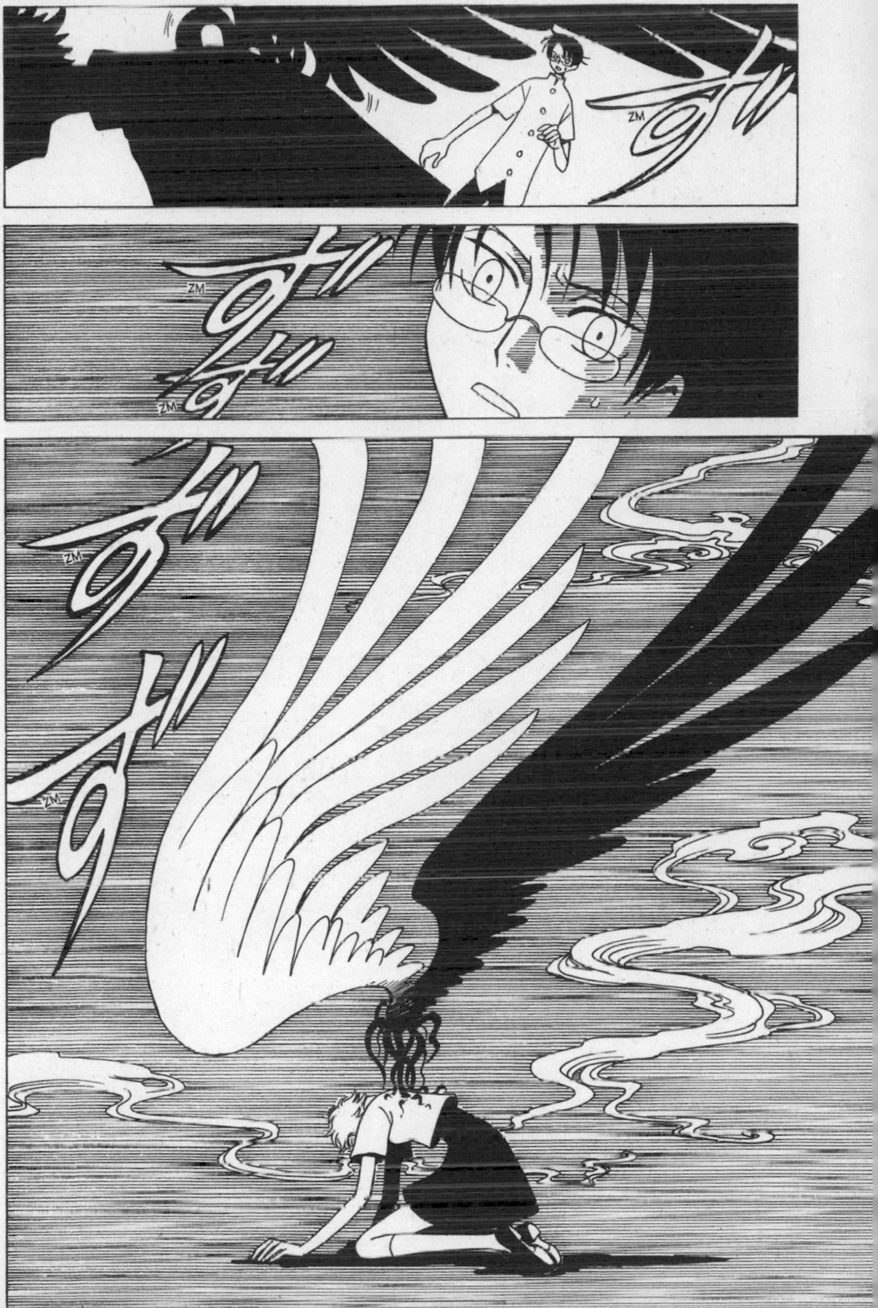
ZM
ZM
ZM
ZM
ZM

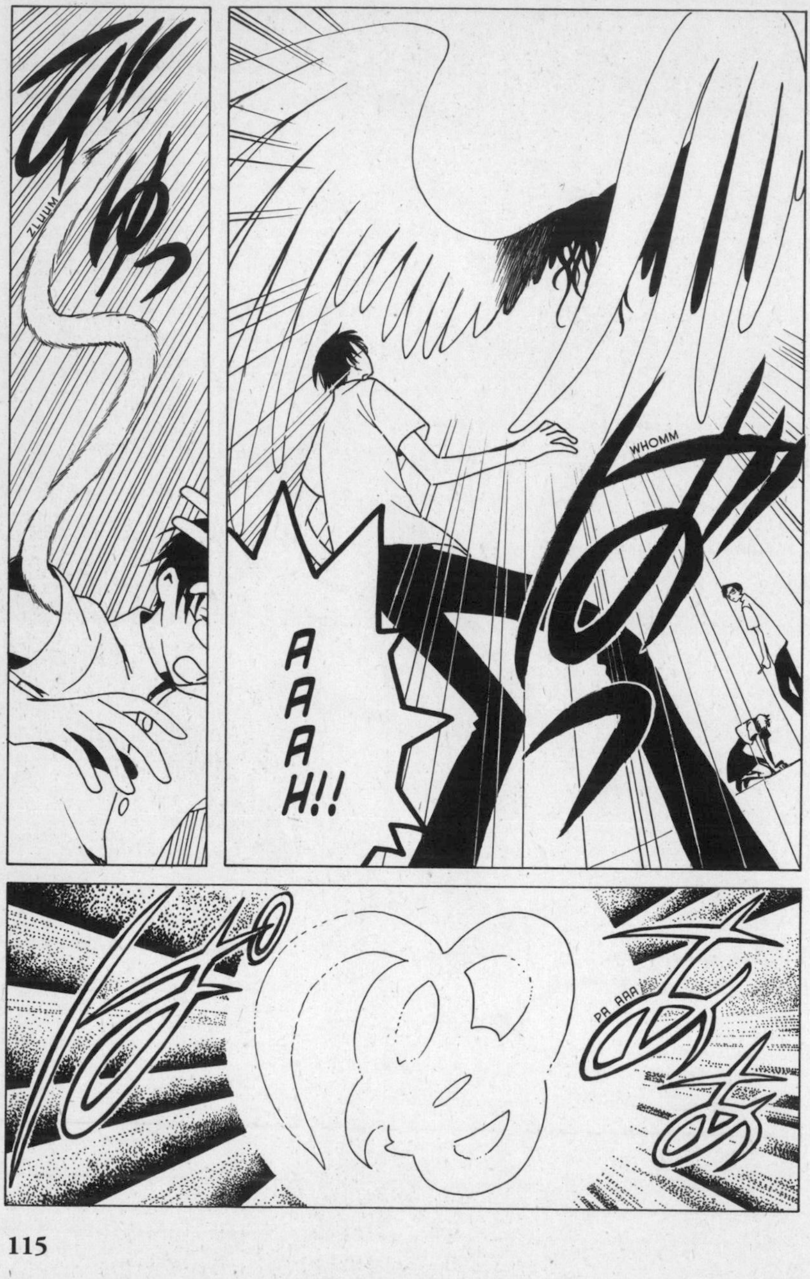
WHOMM
AAAAH!!
ZLUUM
PA AAA

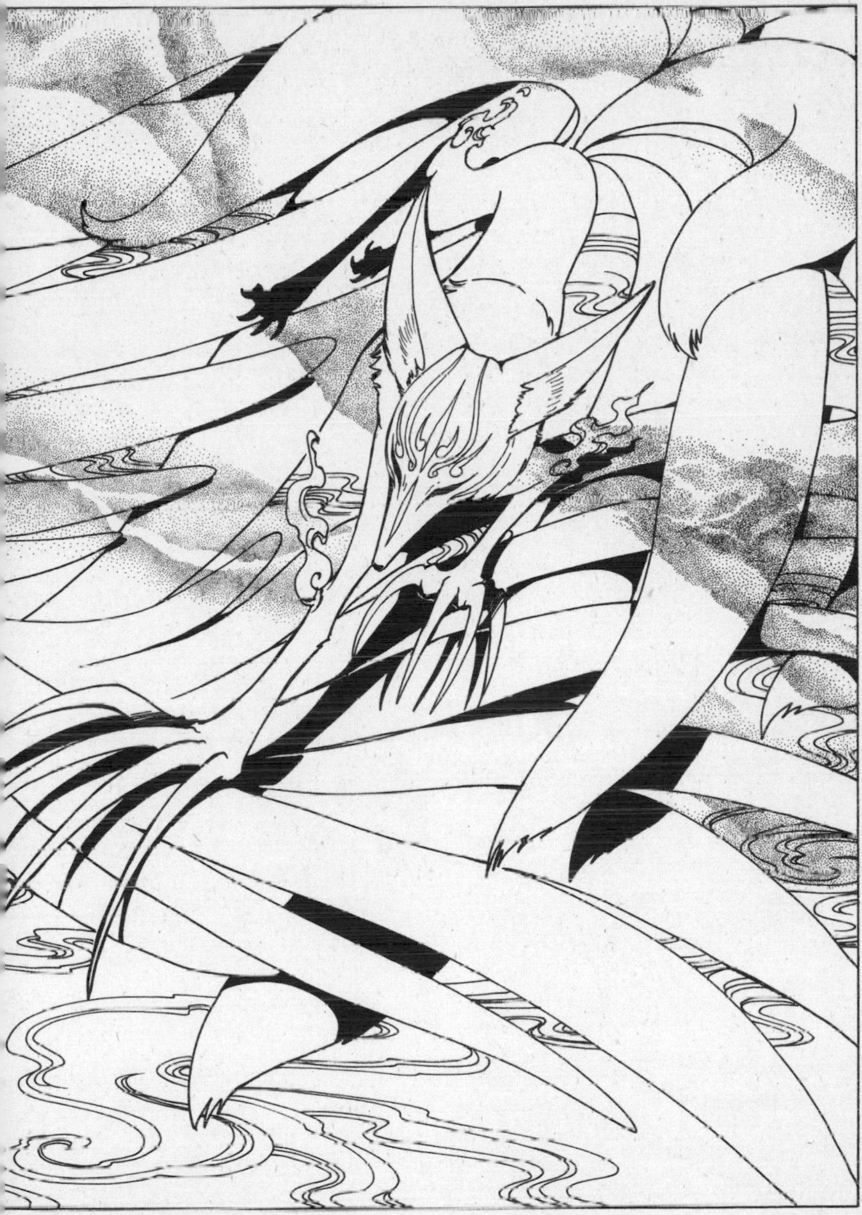

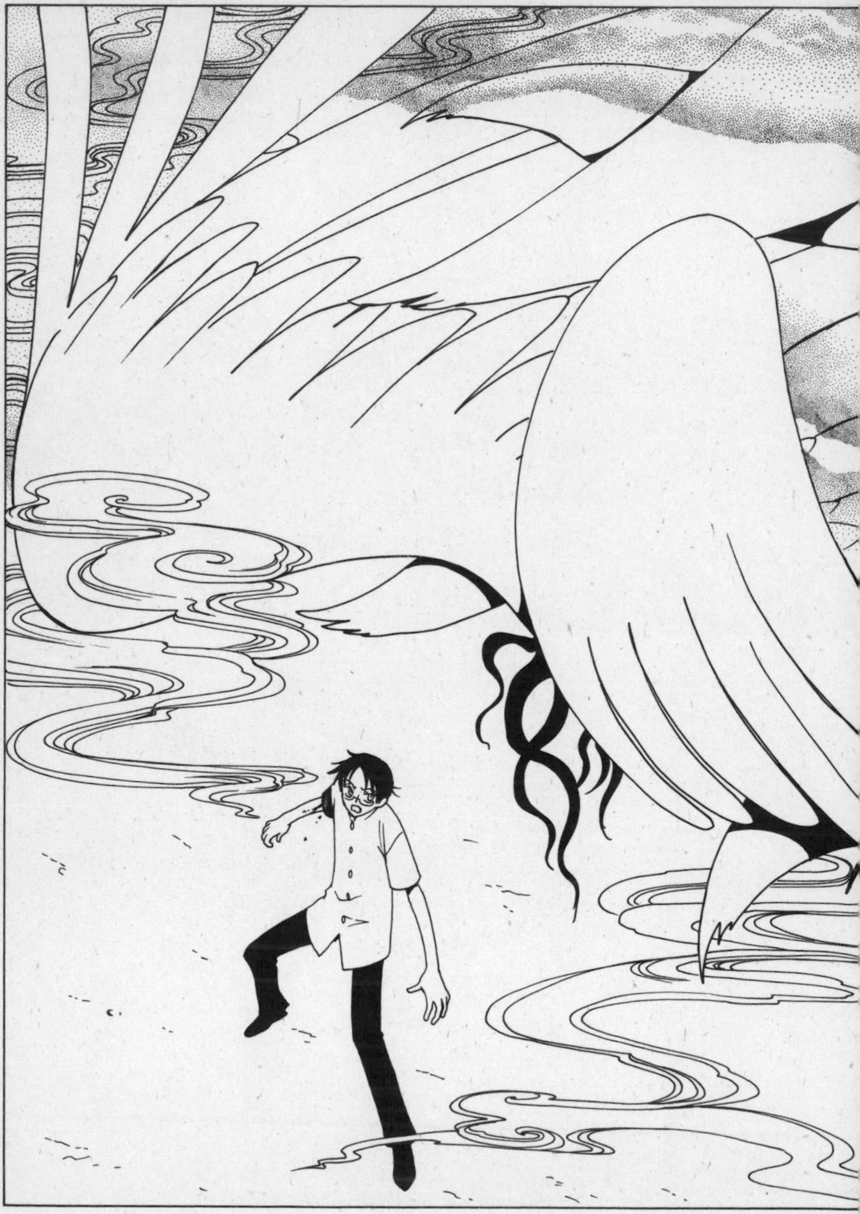

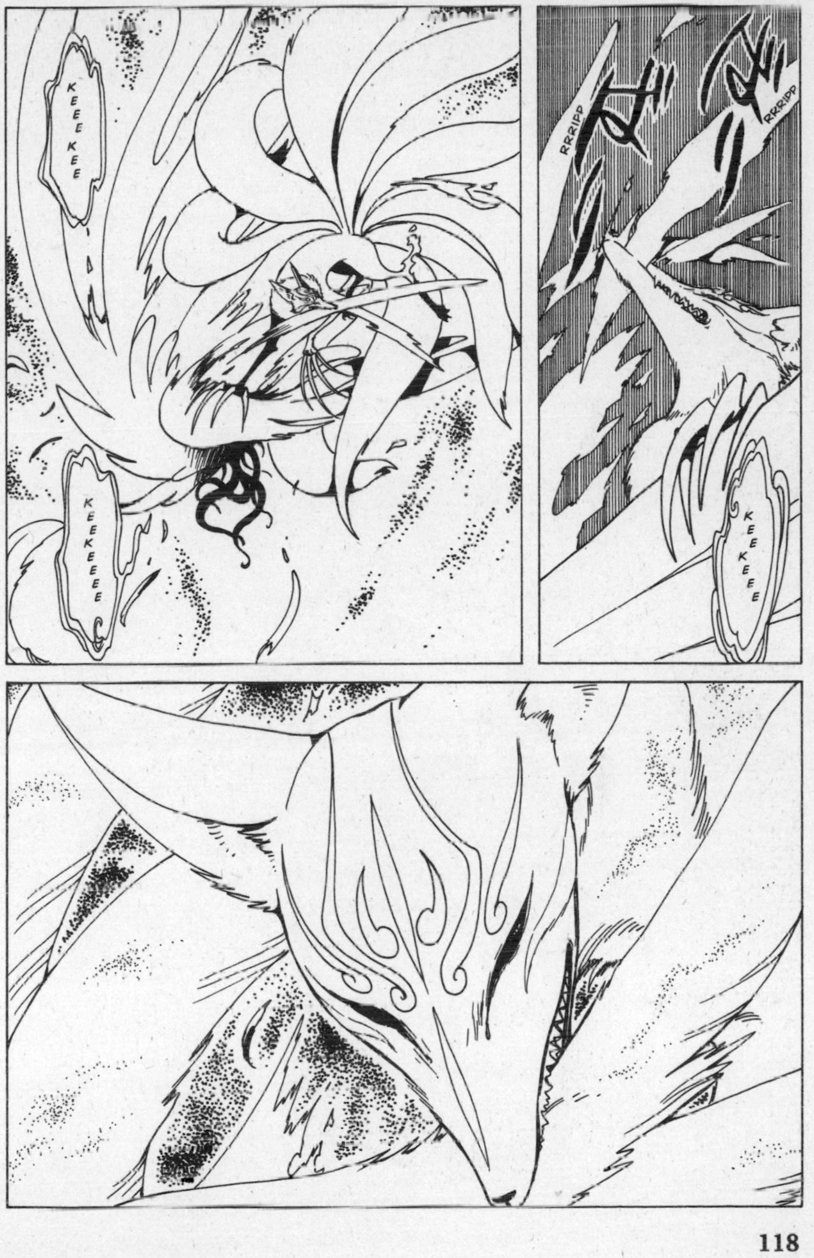
RRRIPP
RRRIPP
KEEKEEE
KEEE KEE
KEEKEEEE

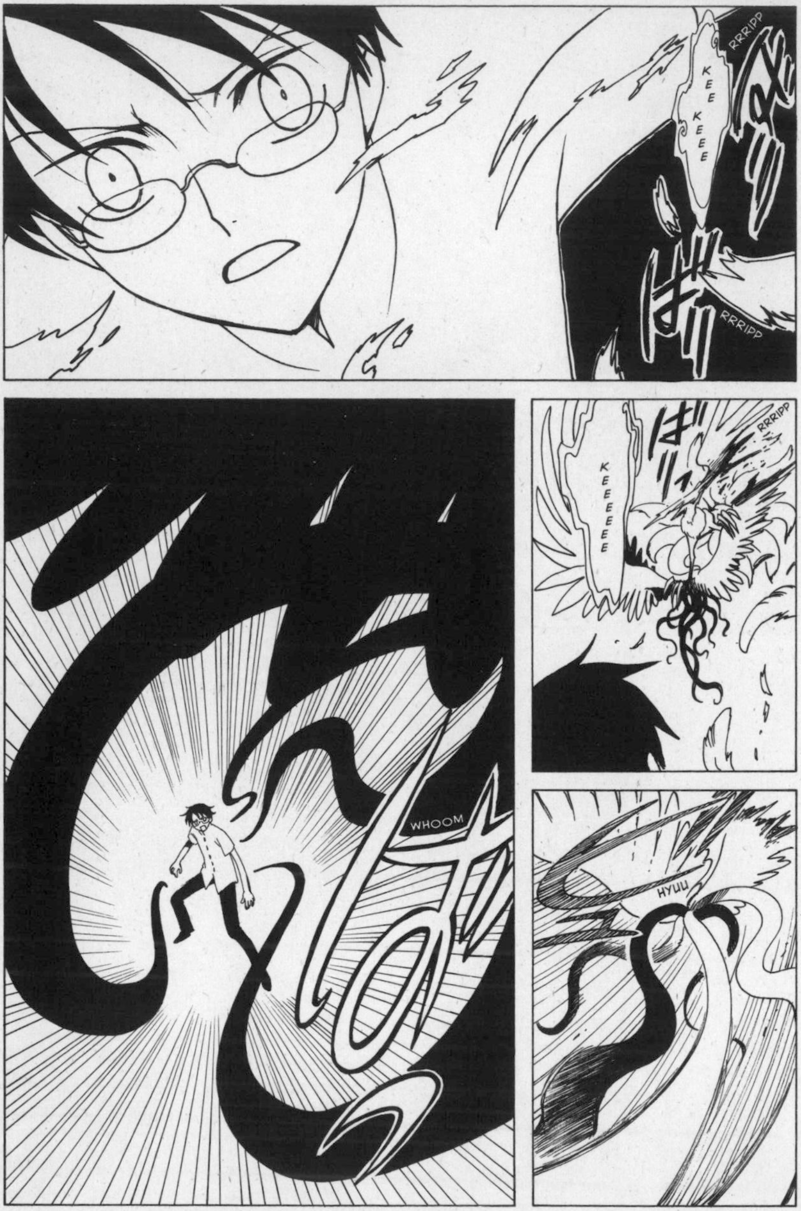
RRRIPP
KEE KEE KEEE
RRRIPP
RRRIPP
KEEEEEEE
HYUU
WHOOM

WHOOO
OOOO
FLOOM
ZOOM
!!
GHWOO

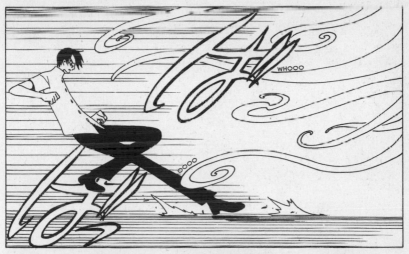

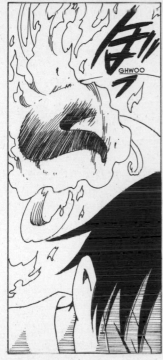

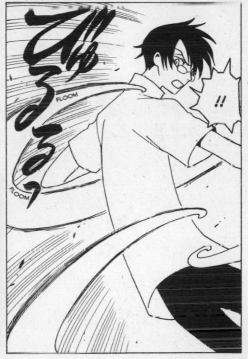

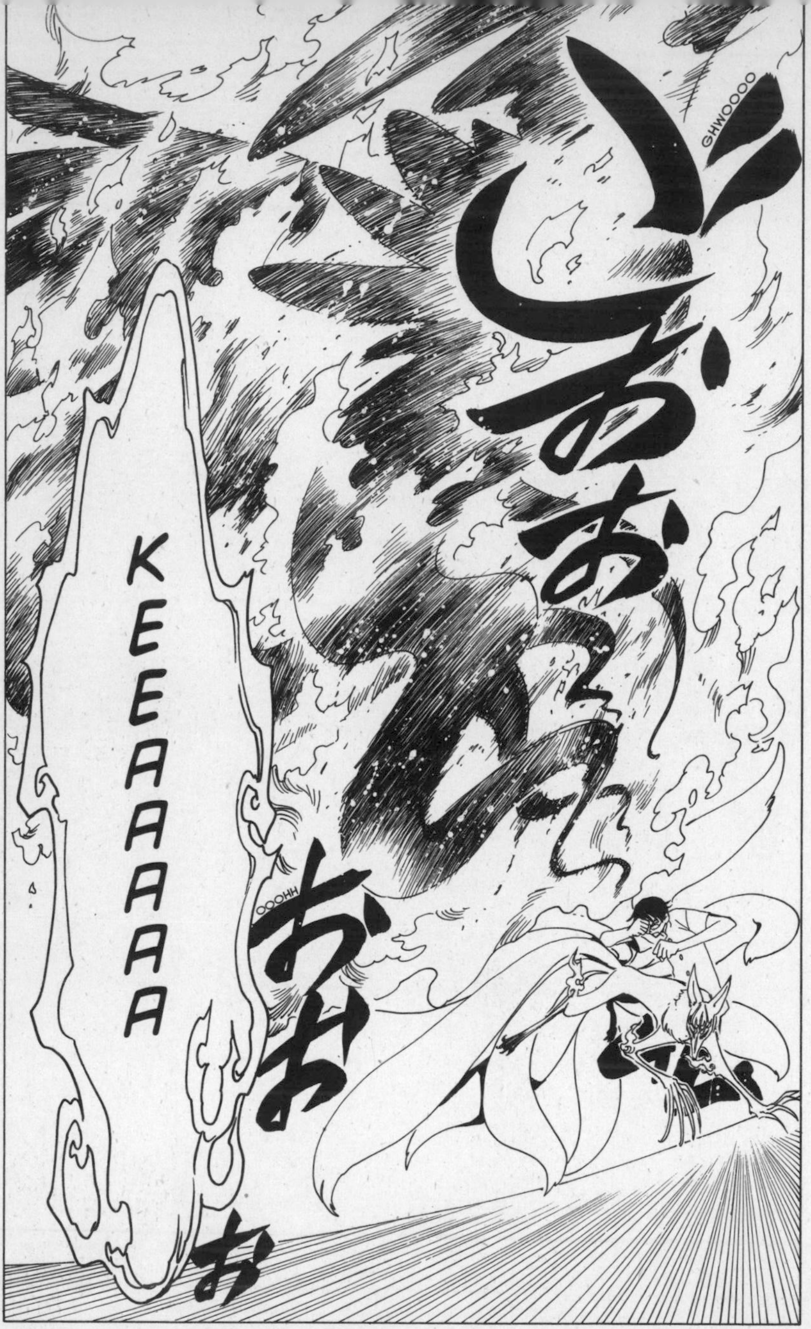
GHWOOOO
OOOHH
KEEAAAAAA

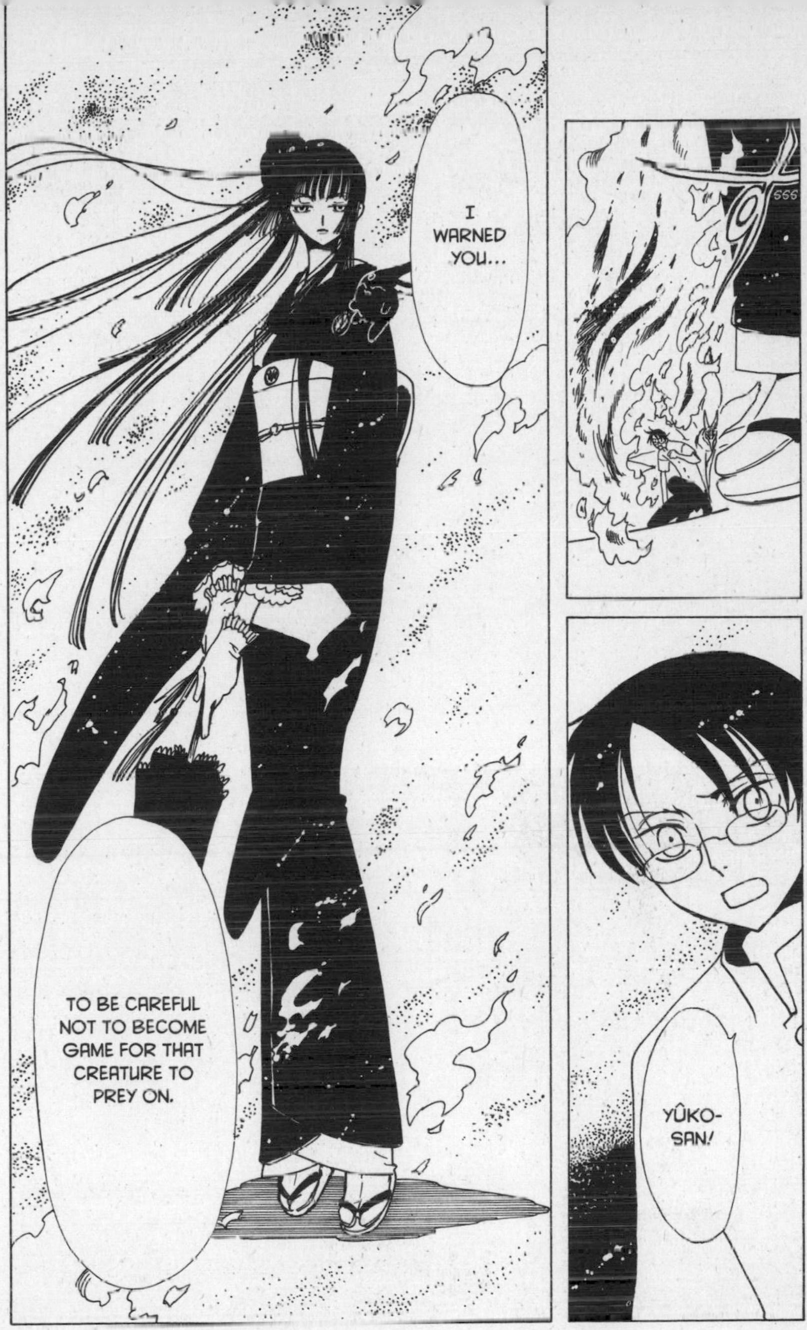
YÛKO-
SAN!
I WARNED YOU...
TO BE CAREFUL NOT TO BECOME GAME FOR THAT CREATURE TO PREY ON.

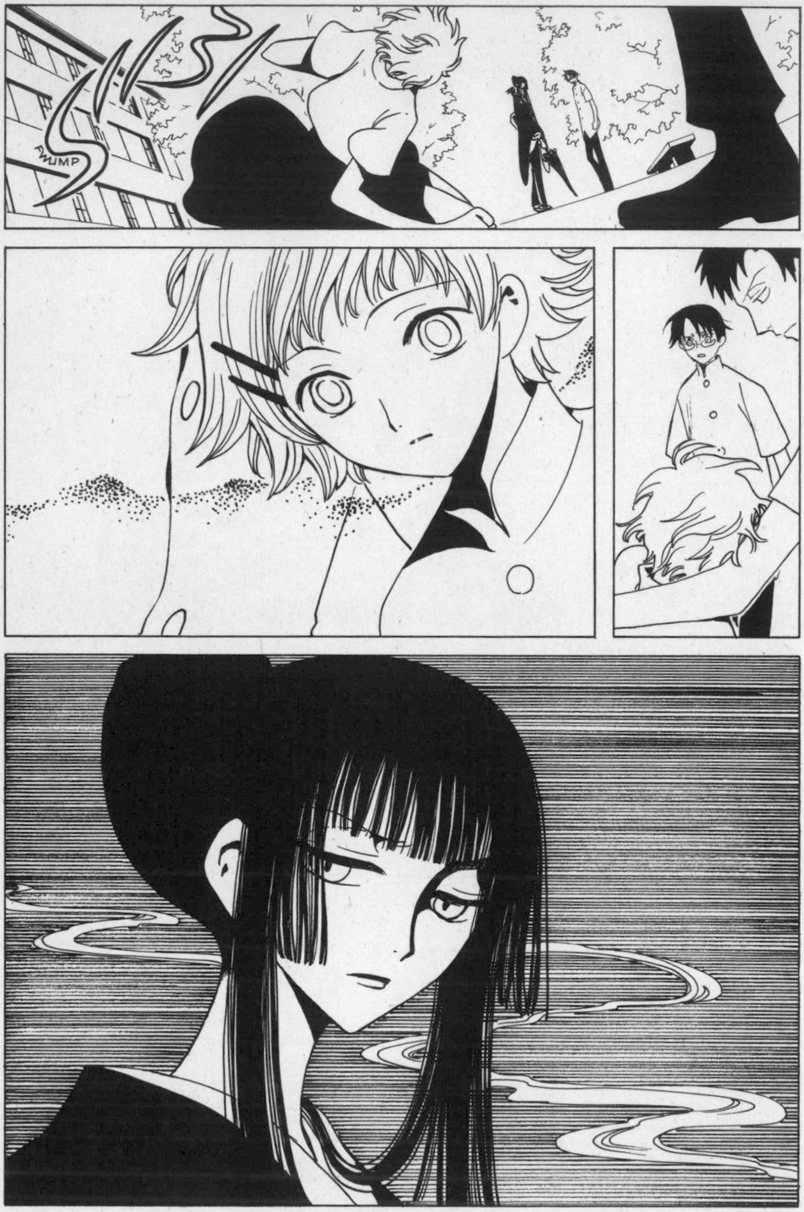
FWUMP

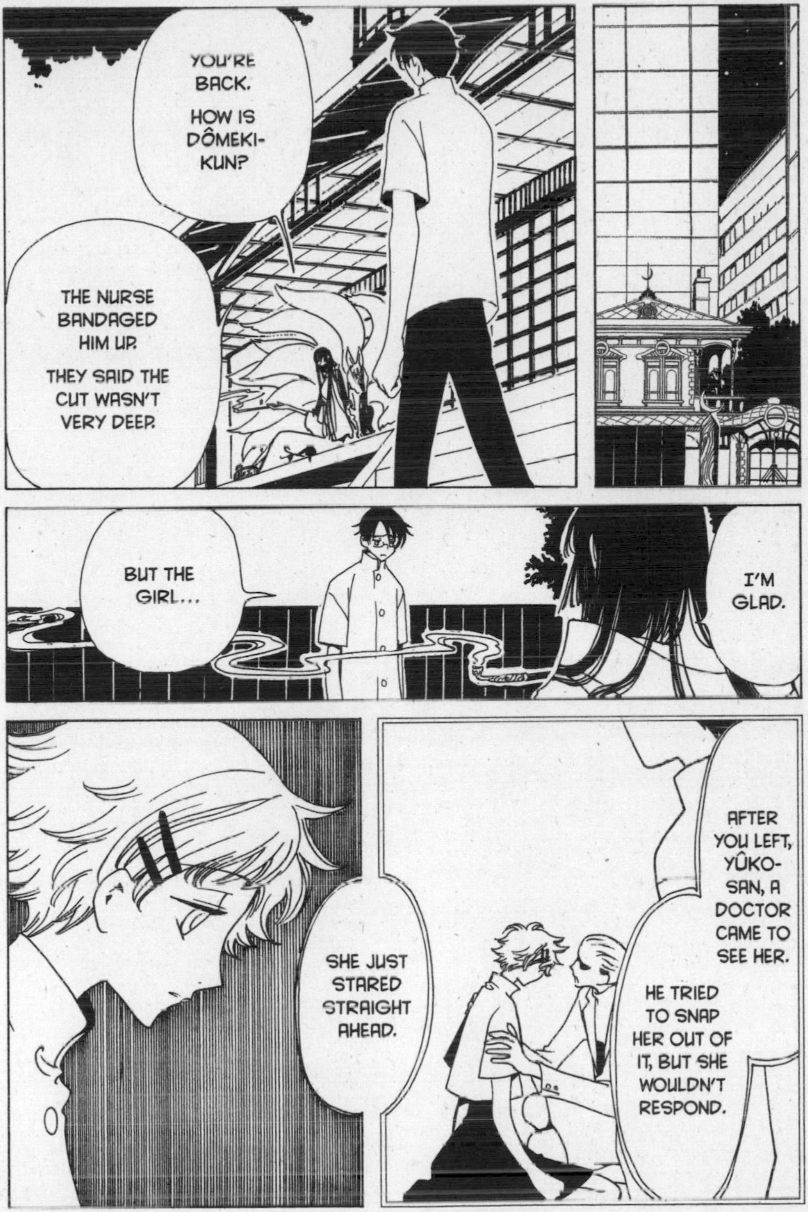
YOU'RE BACK.
HOW IS DÔMEKI-KUN?
THE NURSE BANDAGED HIM UP.
THEY SAID THE CUT WASN'T VERY DEEP.
I'M GLAD.
BUT THE GIRL...
AFTER YOU LEFT, YÛKO-SAN, A DOCTOR CAME TO SEE HER.
HE TRIED TO SNAP HER OUT OF IT, BUT SHE WOULDN'T RESPOND.
SHE JUST STARED STRAIGHT AHEAD.

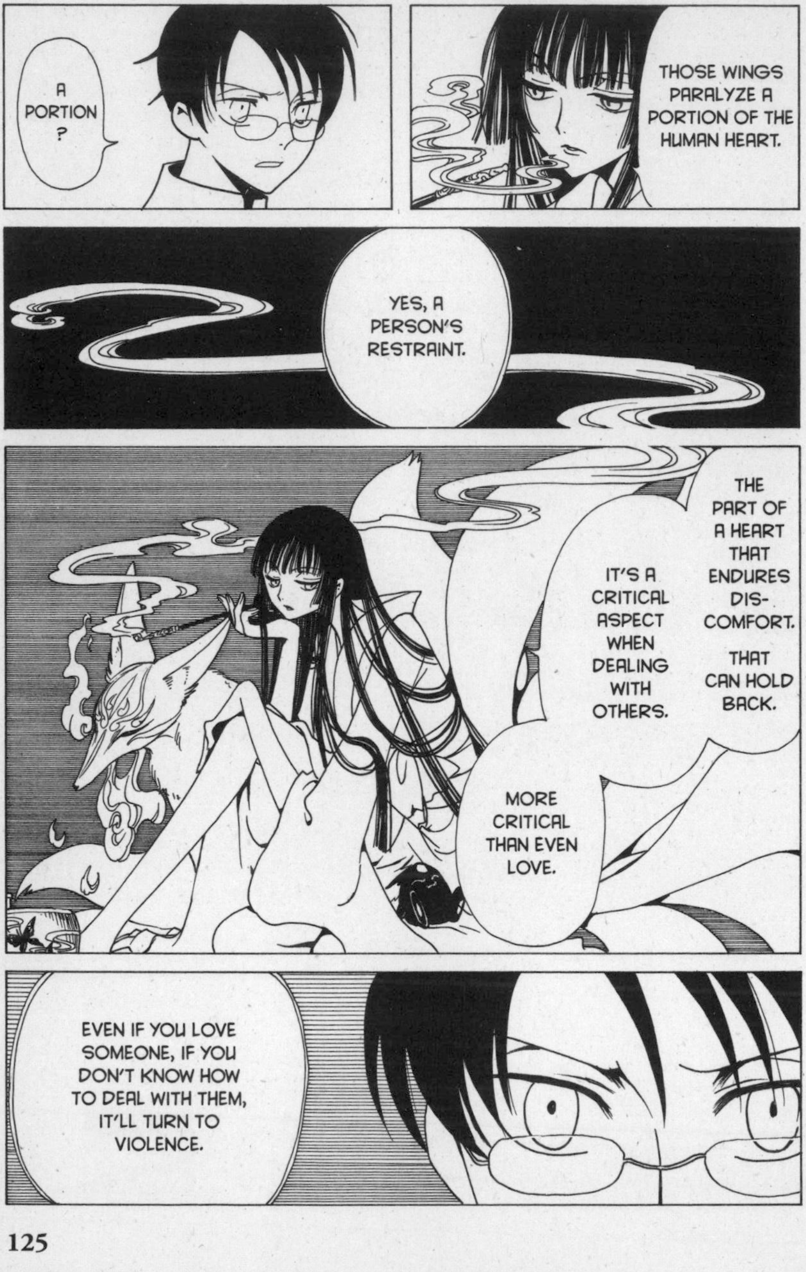
THOSE WINGS PARALYZE A PORTION OF THE HUMAN HEART.
A PORTION?
YES, A PERSON'S RESTRAINT.
THE PART OF A HEART THAT ENDURES DIS-COMFORT.
THAT CAN HOLD BACK.
IT'S A CRITICAL ASPECT WHEN DEALING WITH OTHERS.
MORE CRITICAL THAN EVEN LOVE.
EVEN IF YOU LOVE SOMEONE, IF YOU DON'T KNOW HOW TO DEAL WITH THEM, IT'LL TURN TO VIOLENCE.

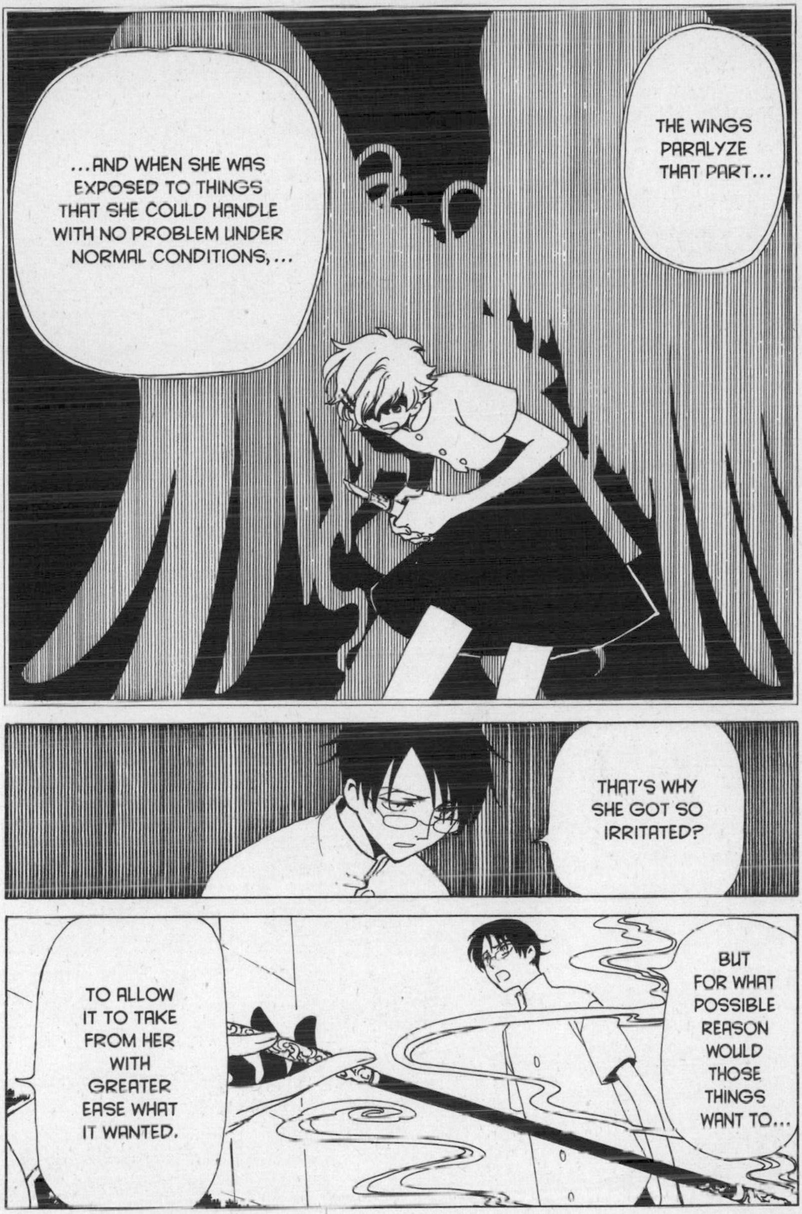
THE WINGS PARALYZE THAT PART...
...AND WHEN SHE WAS EXPOSED TO THINGS THAT SHE COULD HANDLE WITH NO PROBLEM UNDER NORMAL CONDITIONS,...
THAT'S WHY SHE GOT SO IRRITATED?
BUT FOR WHAT POSSIBLE REASON WOULD THOSE THINGS WANT TO...
TO ALLOW IT TO TAKE FROM HER WITH GREATER EASE WHAT IT WANTED.

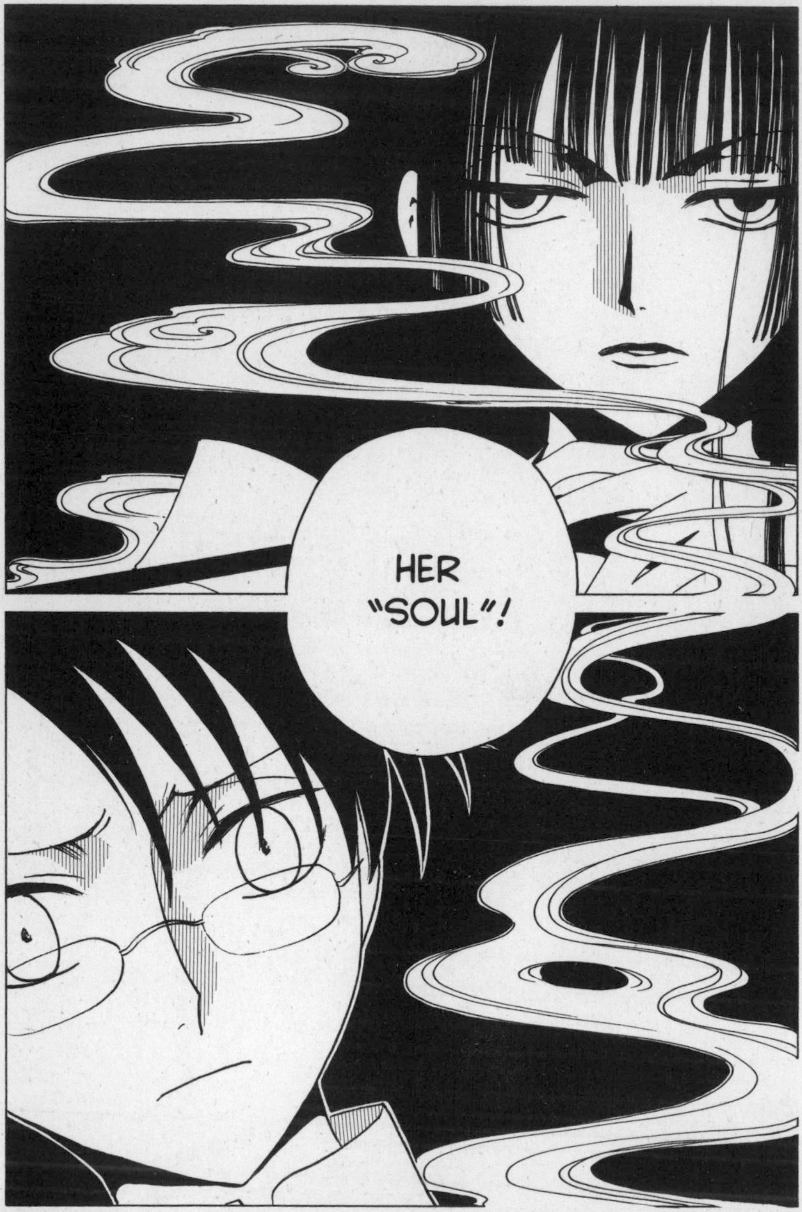
HER "SOUL"!

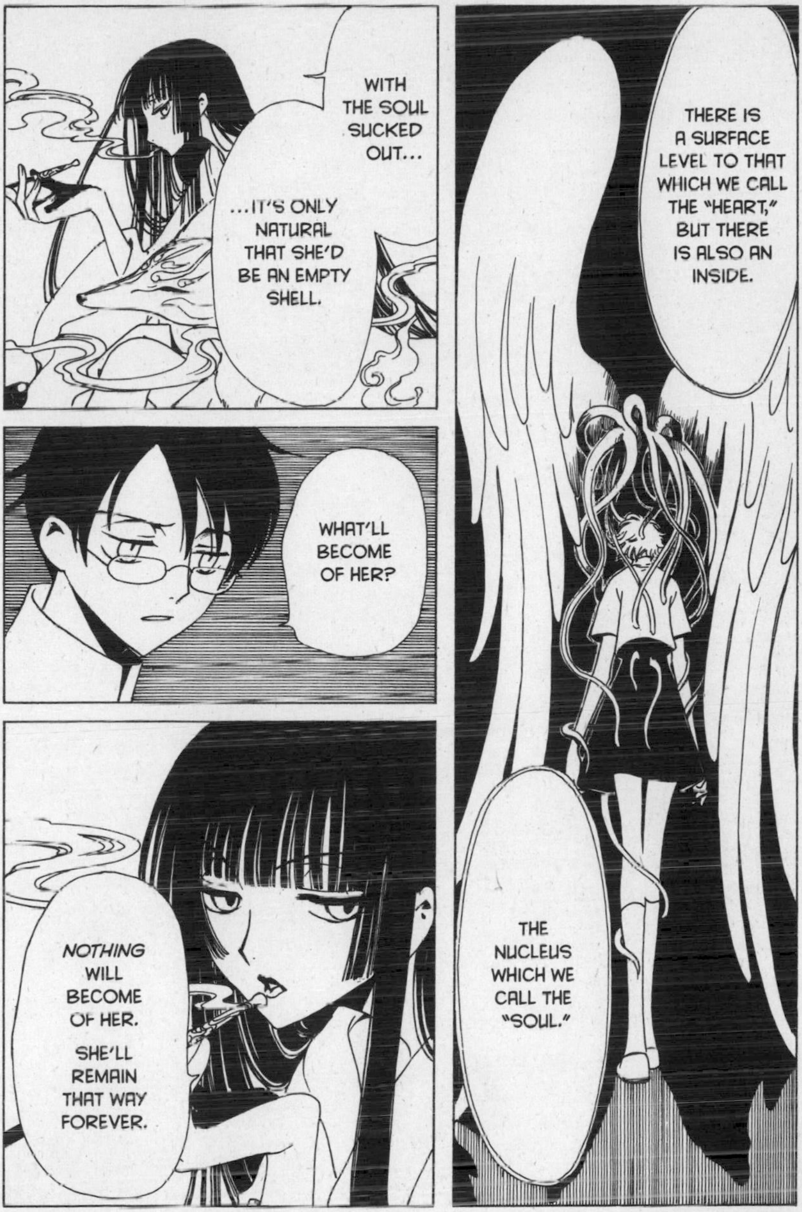
THERE IS A SURFACE LEVEL TO THAT WHICH WE CALL THE "HEART," BUT THERE IS ALSO AN INSIDE.
THE NUCLEUS WHICH WE CALL THE "SOUL."
WITH THE SOUL SUCKED OUT...
...IT'S ONLY NATURAL THAT SHE'D BE AN EMPTY SHELL.
WHAT'LL BECOME OF HER?
NOTHING WILL BECOME OF HER.
SHE'LL REMAIN THAT WAY FOREVER.

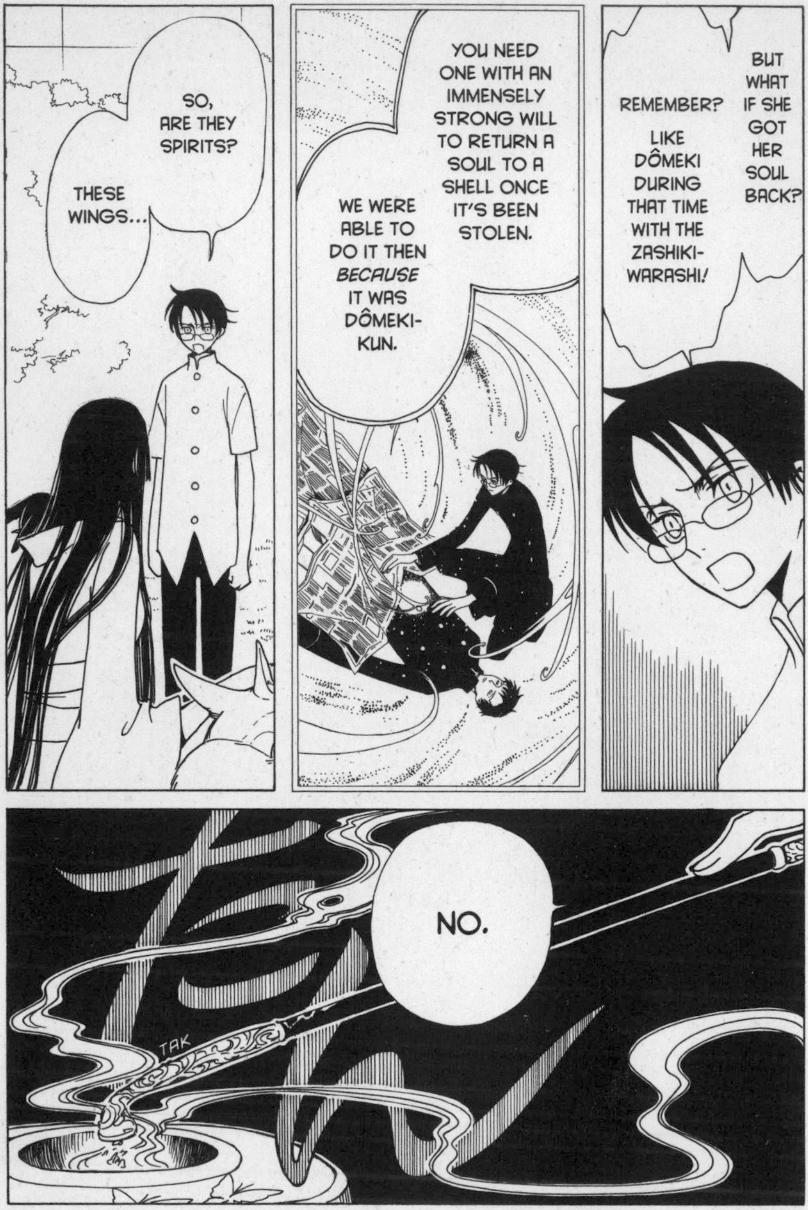
BUT WHAT IF SHE GOT HER SOUL BACK?
REMEMBER?
LIKE DÔMEKI DURING THAT TIME WITH THE ZASHIKI-WARASHI!
YOU NEED ONE WITH AN IMMENSELY STRONG WILL TO RETURN A SOUL TO A SHELL ONCE IT'S BEEN STOLEN.
WE WERE ABLE TO DO IT THEN *BECAUSE* IT WAS DÔMEKI-KUN.
SO, ARE THEY SPIRITS?
THESE WINGS...
NO.
TAK

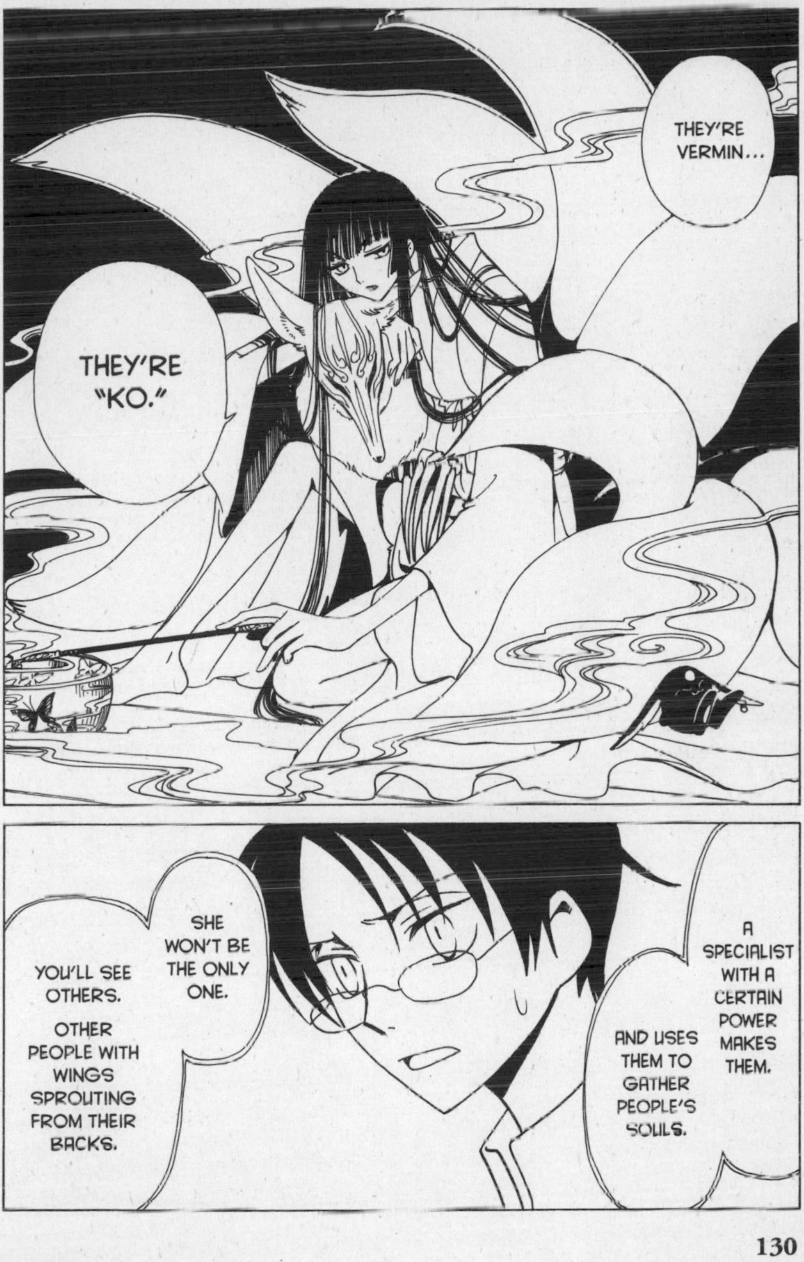
THEY'RE VERMIN...
THEY'RE "KO."
A SPECIALIST WITH A CERTAIN POWER MAKES THEM.
AND USES THEM TO GATHER PEOPLE'S SOULS.
SHE WON'T BE THE ONLY ONE.
YOU'LL SEE OTHERS.
OTHER PEOPLE WITH WINGS SPROUTING FROM THEIR BACKS.

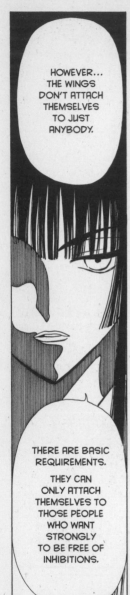

YOU SEE IT ALL THE TIME ON TELEVISION, DON'T YOU?
SOMEONE COMMITS A HORRIBLE CRIME, AND WHEN THEY INTERVIEW A PERSON WHO KNOWS THE CRIMINAL...
...THEY SAY, "THE MOST NORMAL PERSON YOU EVER SAW," OR, "THAT'D BE THE LAST PERSON I'D SUSPECT OF DOING IT!"
AND AFTER THE CRIME IS OVER, THE ONE WHO DID IT LOOKS SO SERENE.
EVERYONE HAS TO ASK THEMSELVES, "HOW DID IT HAPPEN?"
HOWEVER... THE WINGS DON'T ATTACH THEMSELVES TO JUST ANYBODY.
THERE ARE BASIC REQUIREMENTS.
THEY CAN ONLY ATTACH THEMSELVES TO THOSE PEOPLE WHO WANT STRONGLY TO BE FREE OF INHIBITIONS.

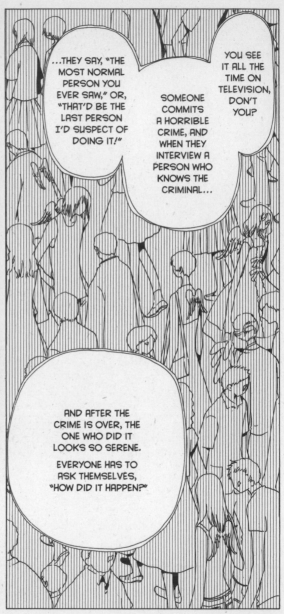

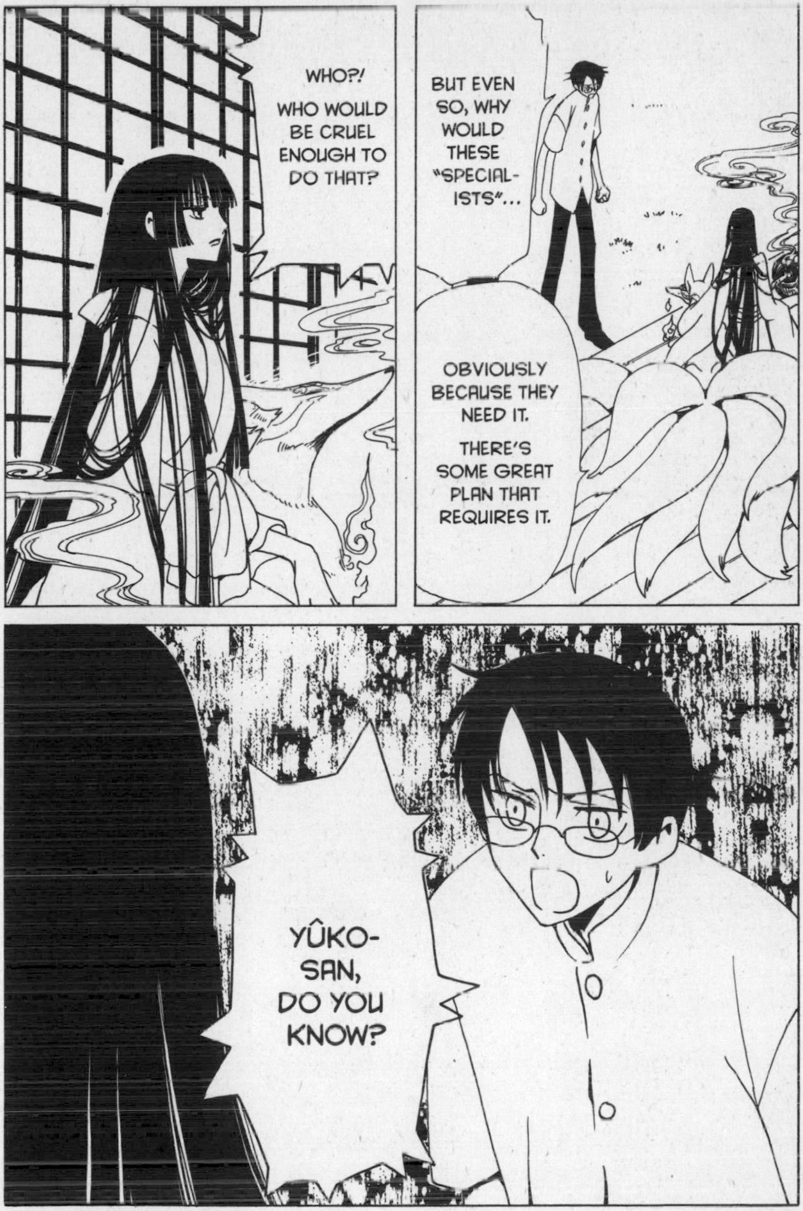
BUT EVEN SO, WHY WOULD THESE "SPECIAL-ISTS"...
OBVIOUSLY BECAUSE THEY NEED IT.
THERE'S SOME GREAT PLAN THAT REQUIRES IT.
WHO?!
WHO WOULD BE CRUEL ENOUGH TO DO THAT?
YÛKO-SAN, DO YOU KNOW?

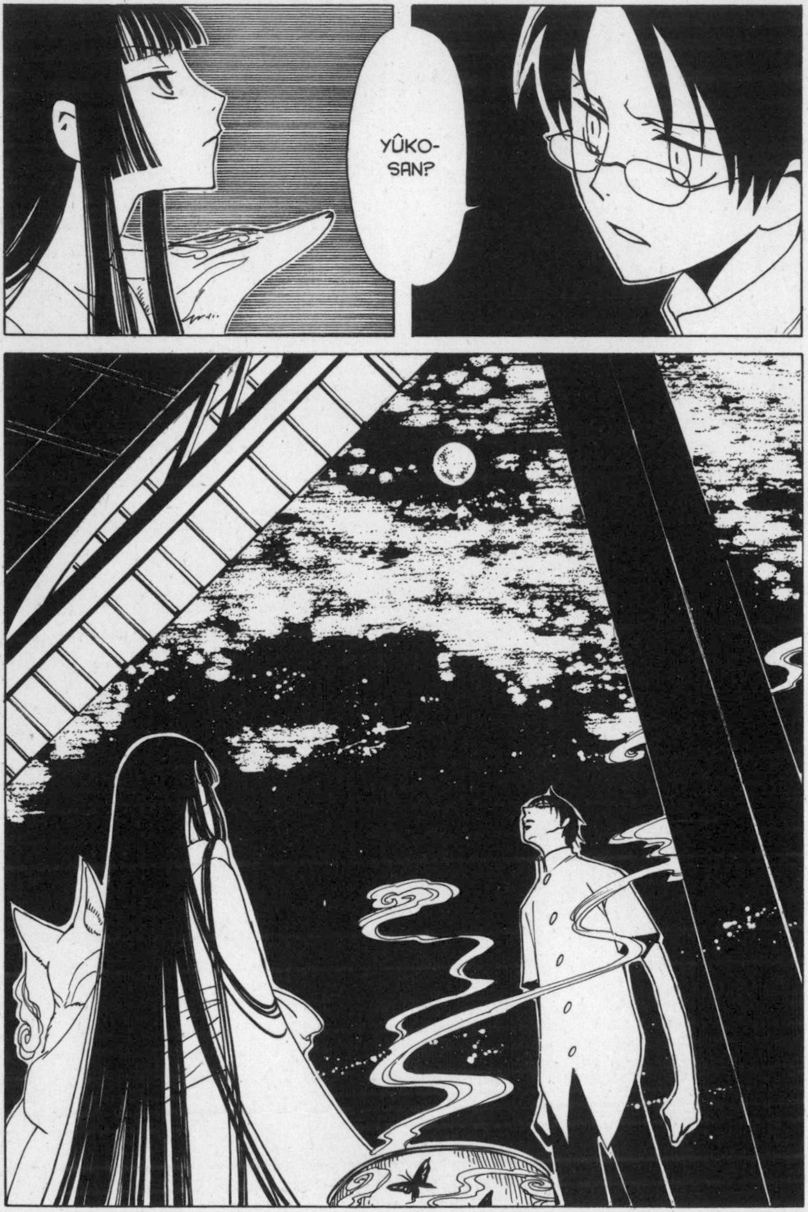
YÛKO-SAN?

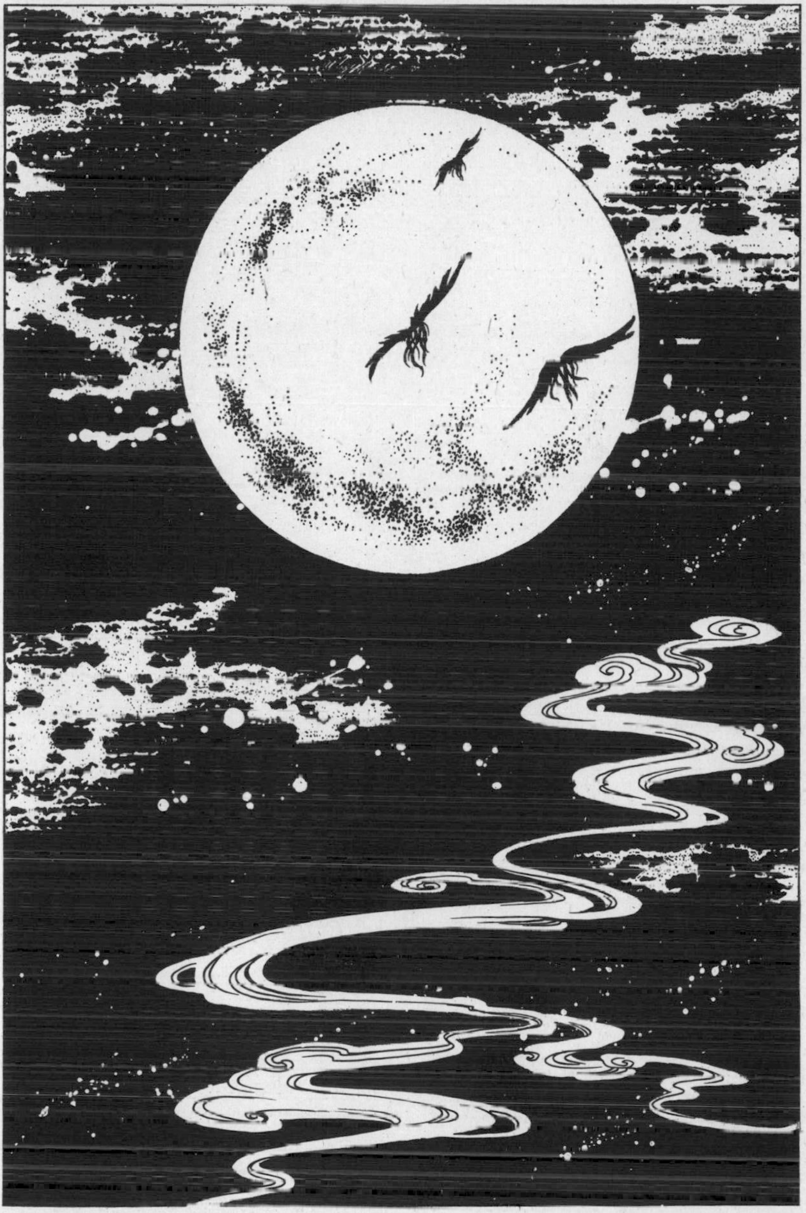

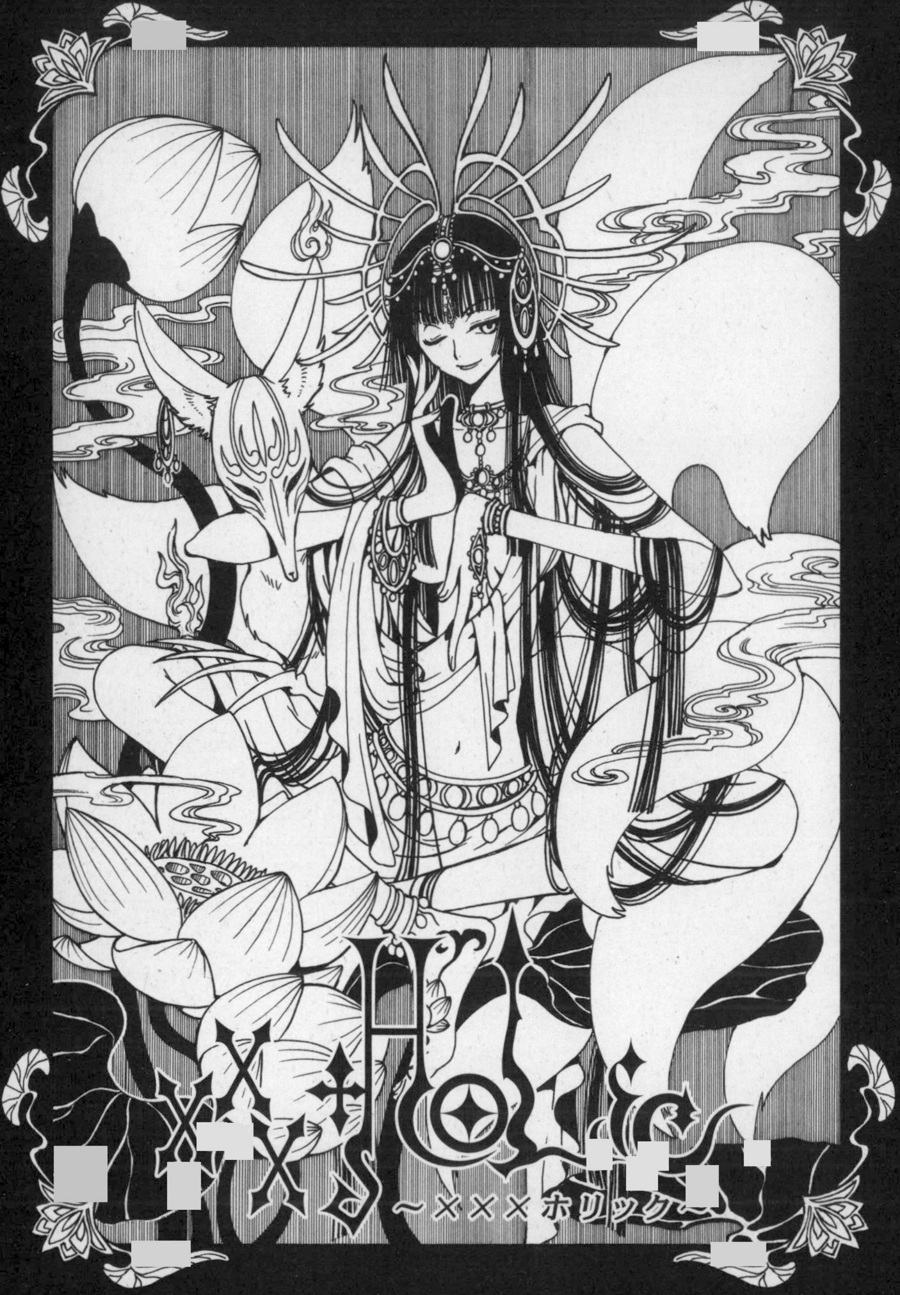
xxxHOLiC
〜×××ホリック〜

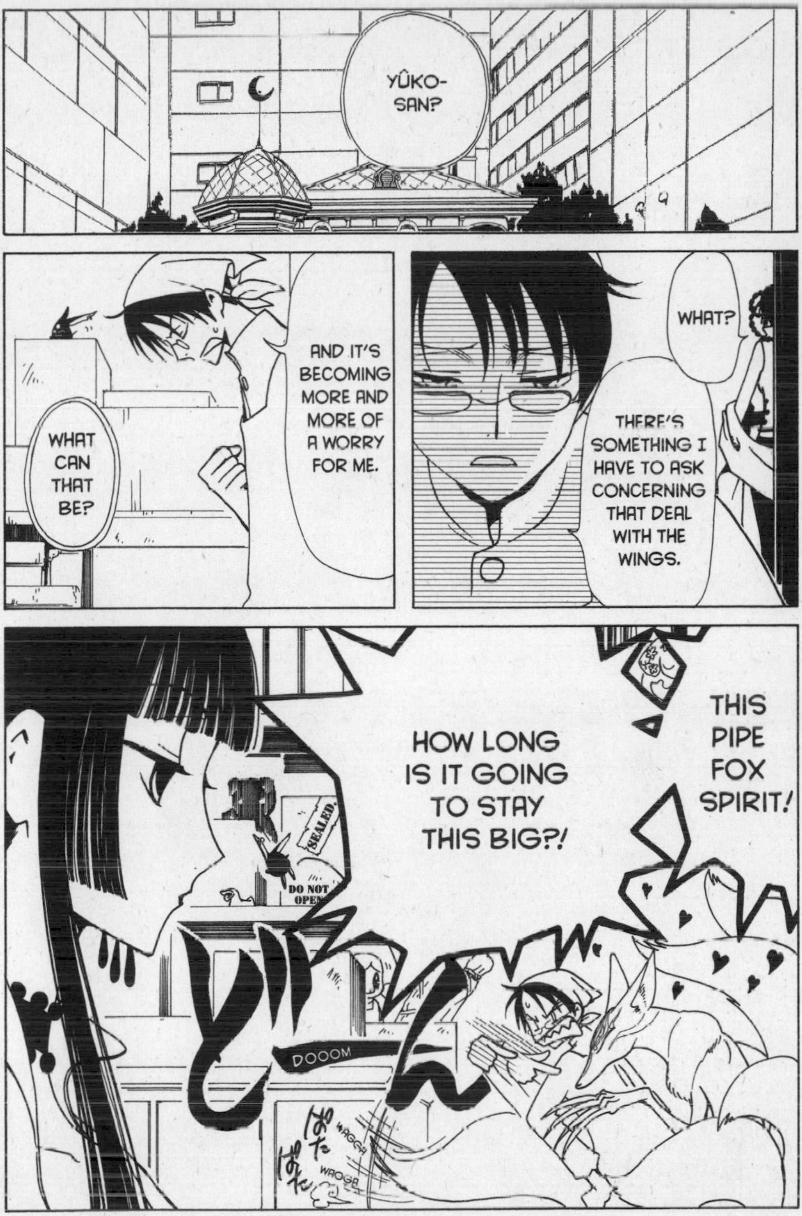
YÛKO-SAN?
WHAT?
THERE'S SOMETHING I HAVE TO ASK CONCERNING THAT DEAL WITH THE WINGS.
AND IT'S BECOMING MORE AND MORE OF A WORRY FOR ME.
WHAT CAN THAT BE?
THIS PIPE FOX SPIRIT!
HOW LONG IS IT GOING TO STAY THIS BIG?!
SEALED.
DOOOM
WAGGA
WAGGA

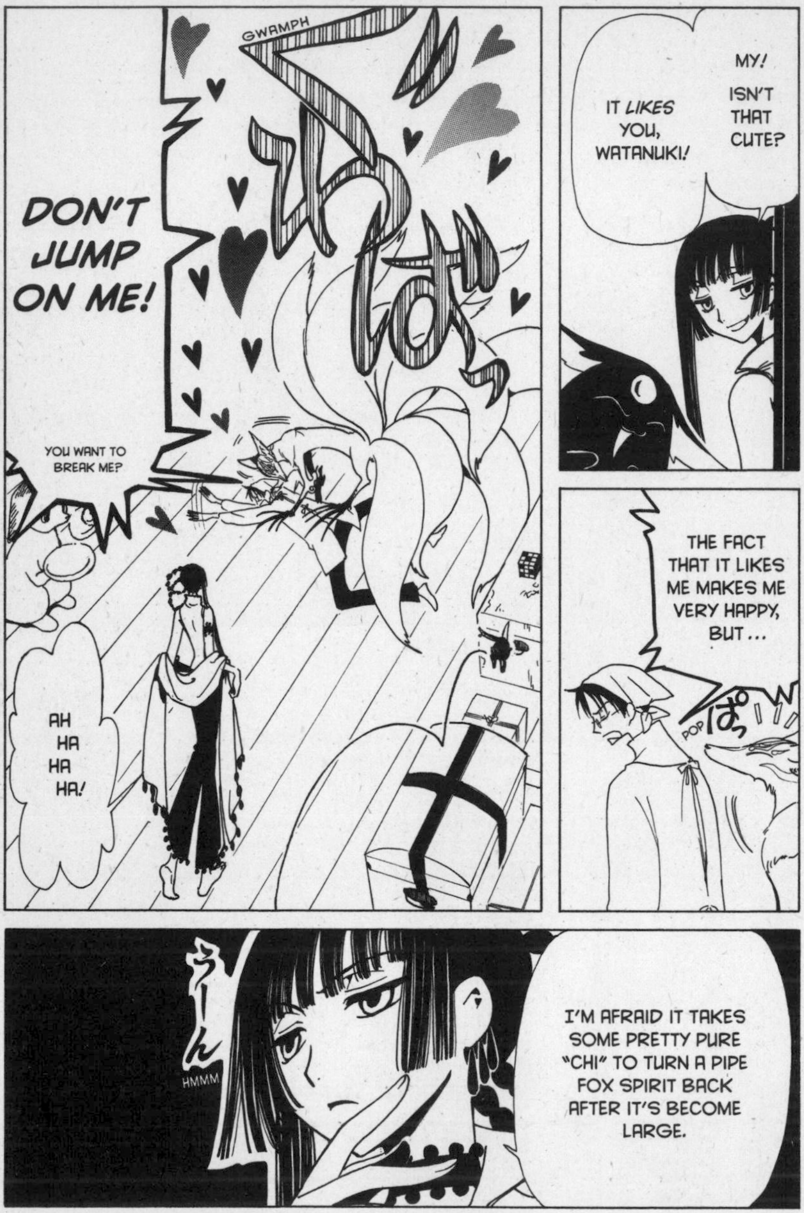
MY! ISN'T THAT CUTE?
IT *LIKES* YOU, WATANUKI!
THE FACT THAT IT LIKES ME MAKES ME VERY HAPPY, BUT...
POP
GWAMPH
DON'T JUMP ON ME!
YOU WANT TO BREAK ME?
AH HA HA HA!
I'M AFRAID IT TAKES SOME PRETTY PURE "CHI" TO TURN A PIPE FOX SPIRIT BACK AFTER IT'S BECOME LARGE.
HMMM

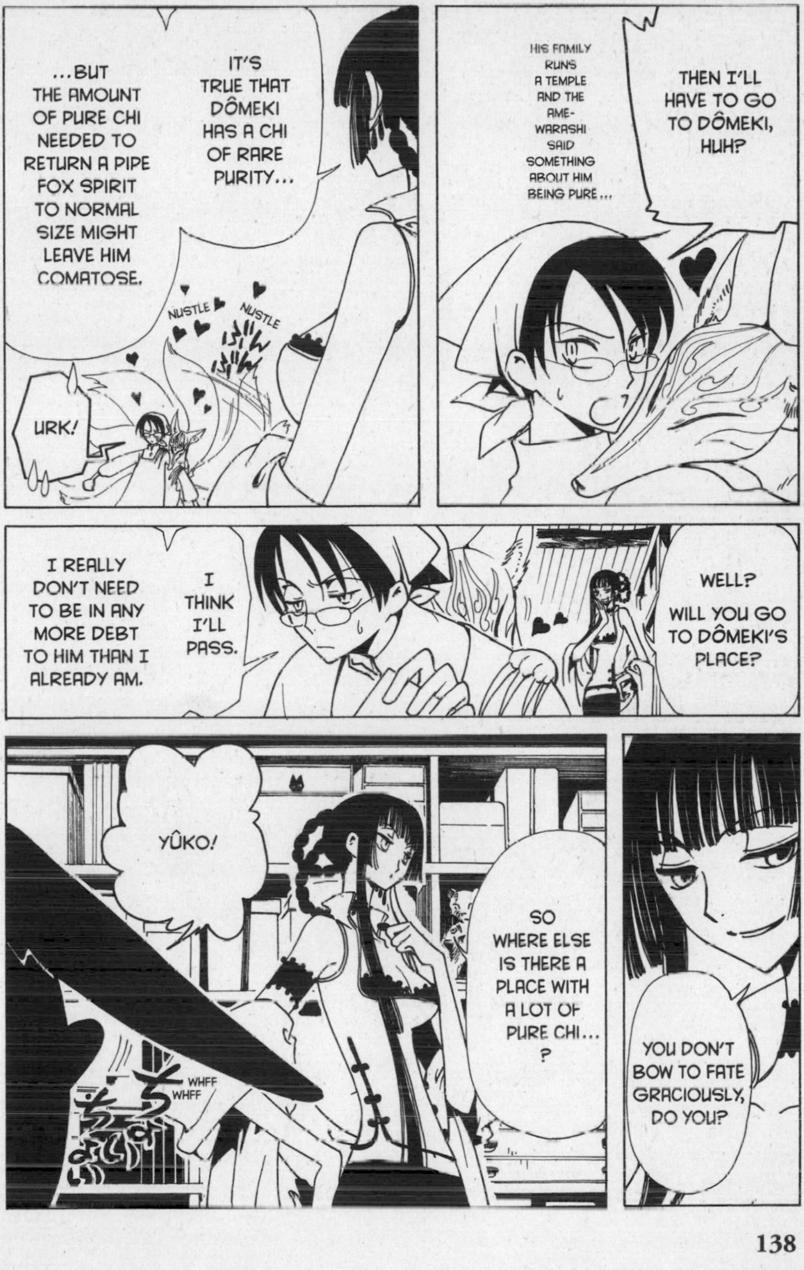
THEN I'LL HAVE TO GO TO DÔMEKI, HUH?
HIS FAMILY RUNS A TEMPLE AND THE AME-WARASHI SAID SOMETHING ABOUT HIM BEING PURE...
IT'S TRUE THAT DÔMEKI HAS A CHI OF RARE PURITY...
...BUT THE AMOUNT OF PURE CHI NEEDED TO RETURN A PIPE FOX SPIRIT TO NORMAL SIZE MIGHT LEAVE HIM COMATOSE.
NUSTLE
NUSTLE
URK!
WELL? WILL YOU GO TO DÔMEKI'S PLACE?
I THINK I'LL PASS.
I REALLY DON'T NEED TO BE IN ANY MORE DEBT TO HIM THAN I ALREADY AM.
YOU DON'T BOW TO FATE GRACIOUSLY, DO YOU?
SO WHERE ELSE IS THERE A PLACE WITH A LOT OF PURE CHI...?
YÛKO!
WHFF WHFF

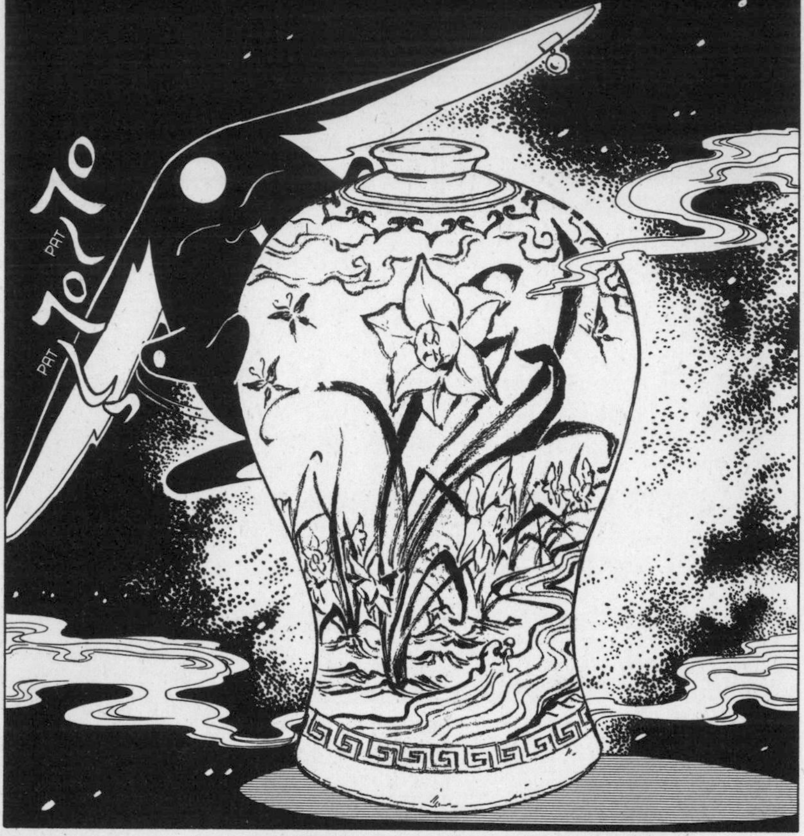
PAT
PAT

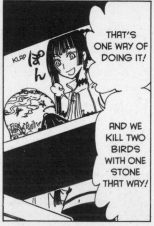

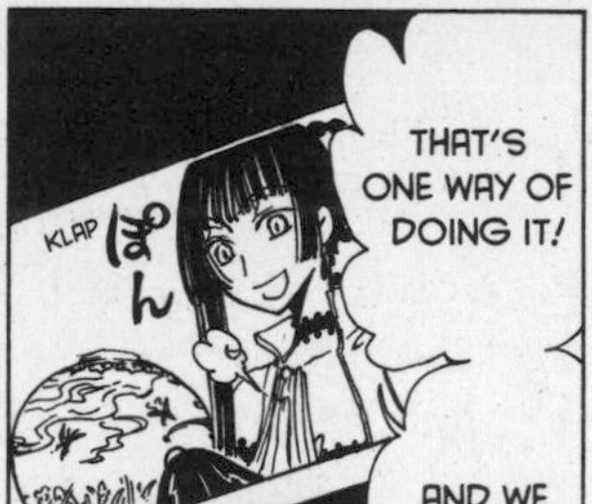
THAT'S ONE WAY OF DOING IT!
KLAP
ぽん
AND WE KILL TWO BIRDS WITH ONE STONE THAT WAY!

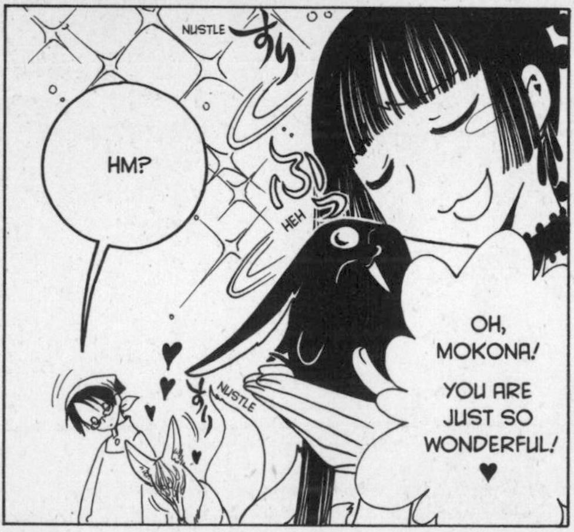
NUSTLE
すり
HEH
HM?
OH, MOKONA!
YOU ARE JUST SO WONDERFUL! ♥
NUSTLE

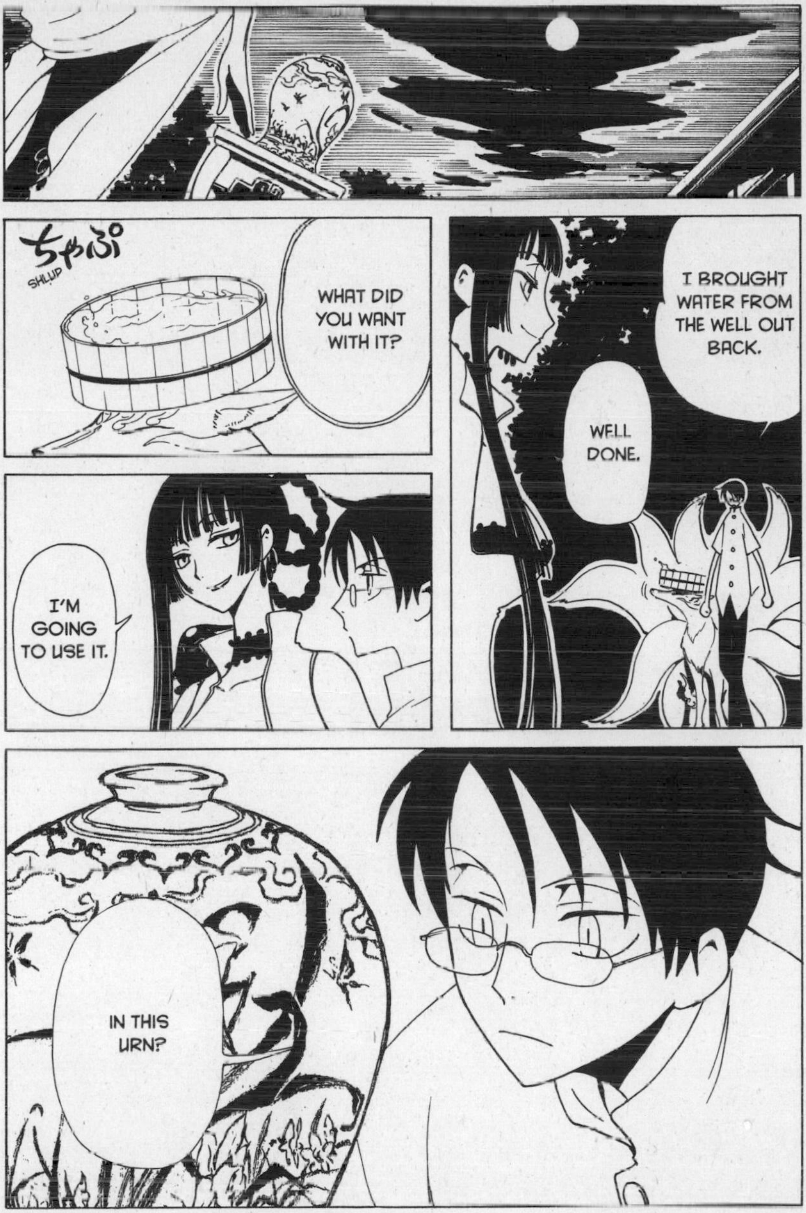
I BROUGHT WATER FROM THE WELL OUT BACK.
WELL DONE.
ちゃぷ
SHLUP
WHAT DID YOU WANT WITH IT?
I'M GOING TO USE IT.
IN THIS URN?

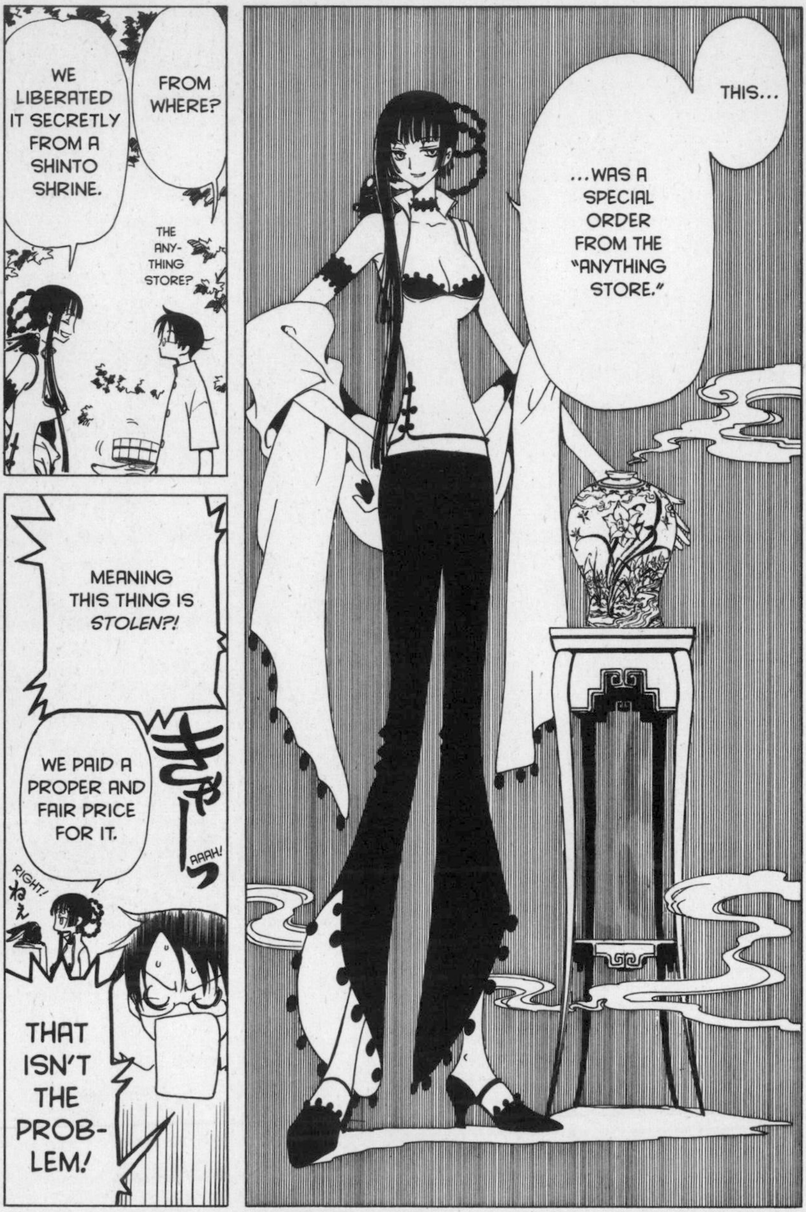
THIS...
...WAS A SPECIAL ORDER FROM THE "ANYTHING STORE."
FROM WHERE?
WE LIBERATED IT SECRETLY FROM A SHINTO SHRINE.
THE ANY-THING STORE?
MEANING THIS THING IS STOLEN?!
きゃーっ
AAAH!
WE PAID A PROPER AND FAIR PRICE FOR IT.
ねぇ
RIGHT!
THAT ISN'T THE PROB-LEM!

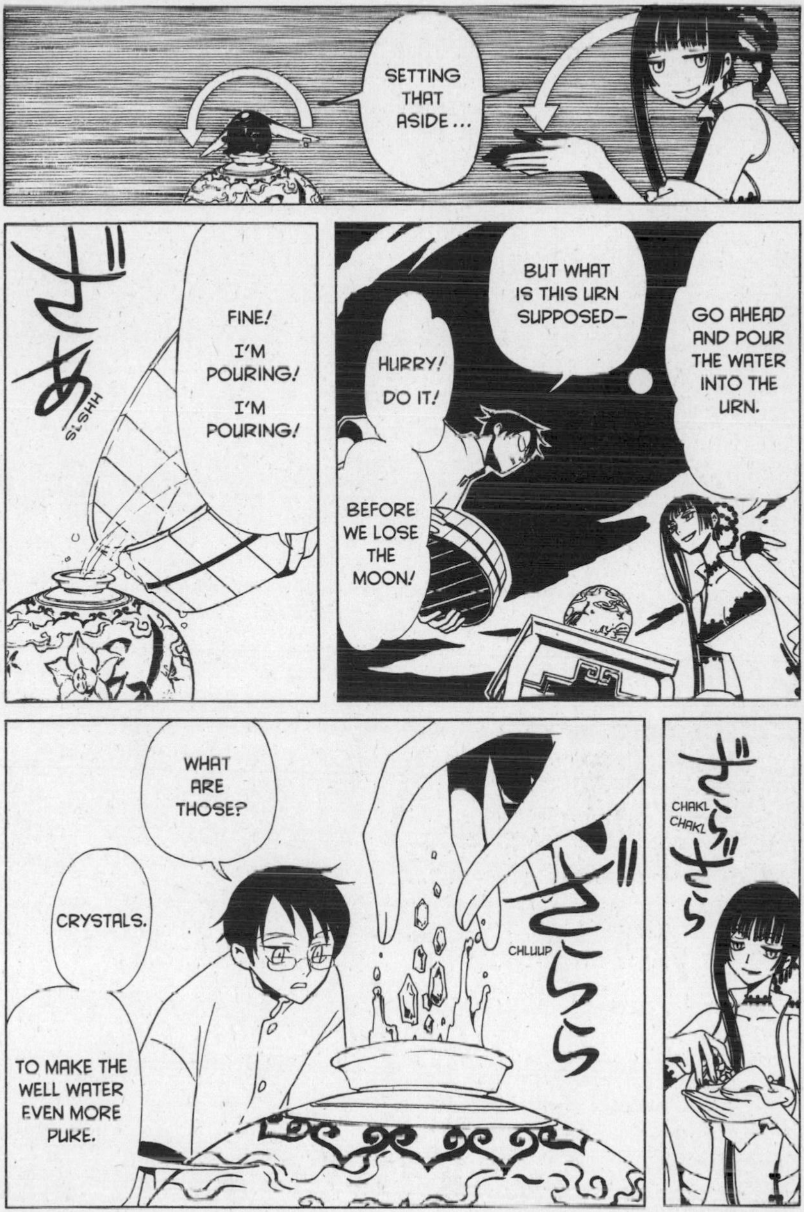

SETTING THAT ASIDE...
GO AHEAD AND POUR THE WATER INTO THE URN.
BUT WHAT IS THIS URN SUPPOSED—
HURRY! DO IT!
BEFORE WE LOSE THE MOON!
FINE! I'M POURING! I'M POURING!
ざあ
SLSHH
ざらざら
CHAKL CHAKL
WHAT ARE THOSE?
ざら
CHLUUP
CRYSTALS.
TO MAKE THE WELL WATER EVEN MORE PUKE.

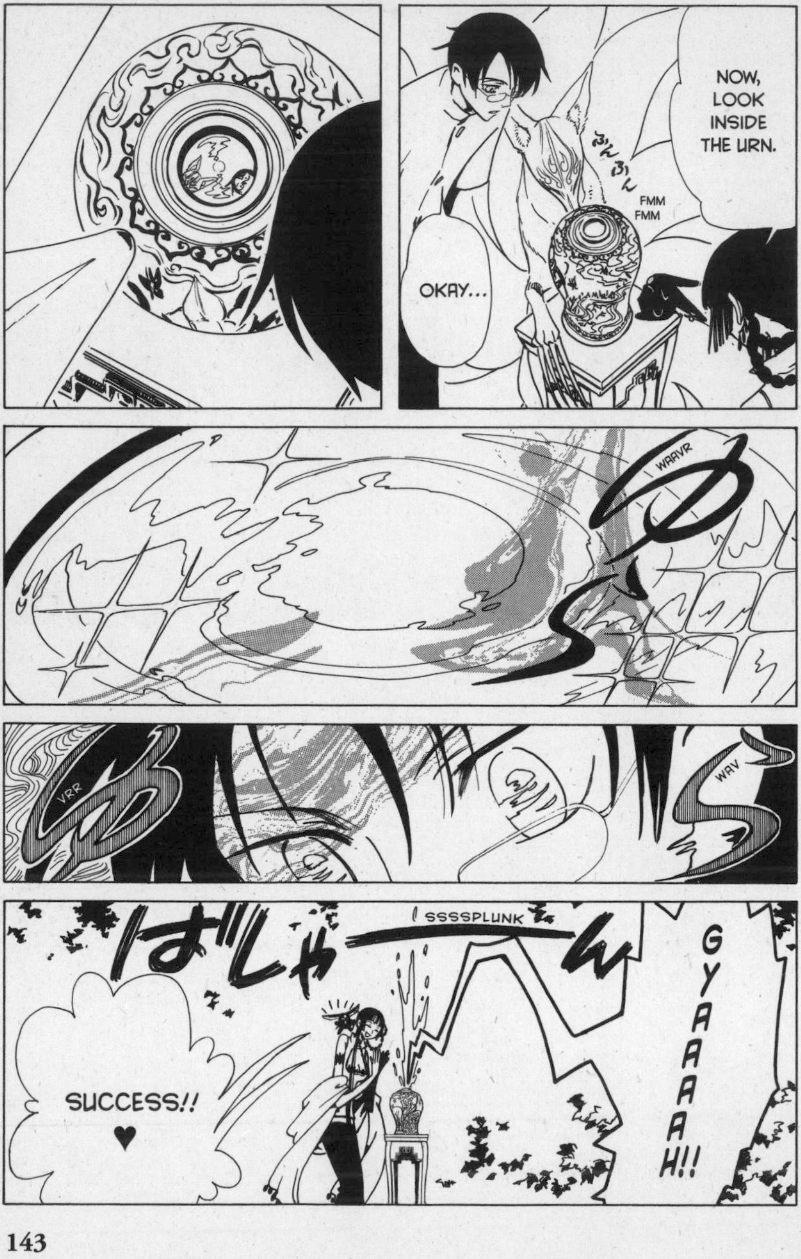
NOW, LOOK INSIDE THE URN.
ふんふん
FMM FMM
OKAY...
ゆ
WAAVR
WAV
VRR
GYAAAAAH!!
ばしゃーん
SSSSPLUNK
SUCCESS!! ♥

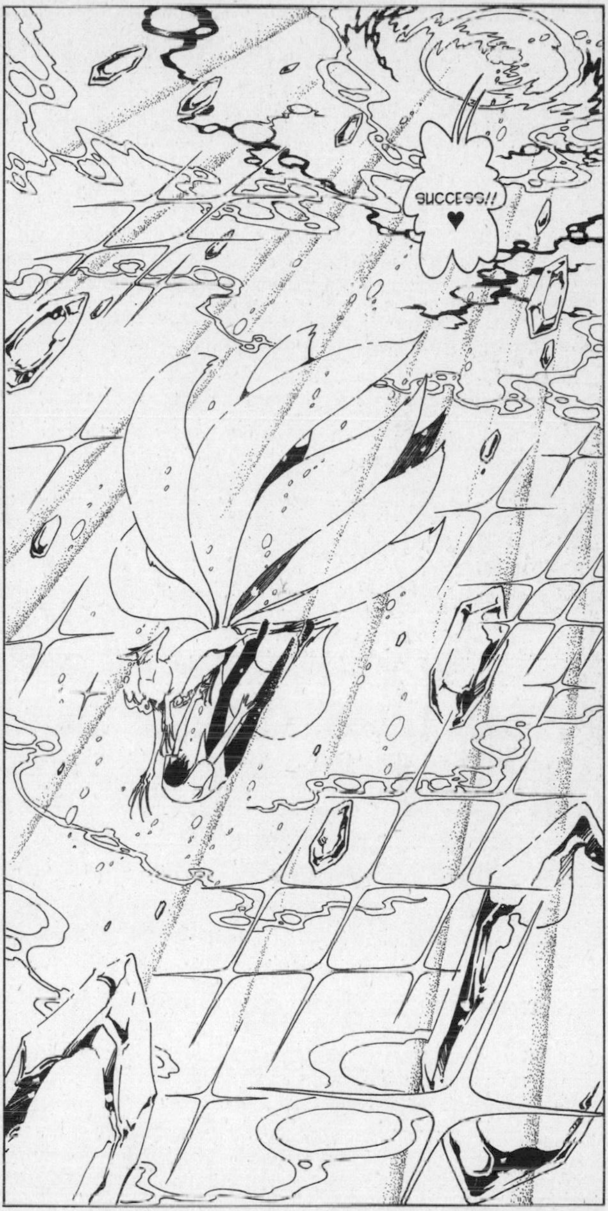
SUCCESS!!
♥
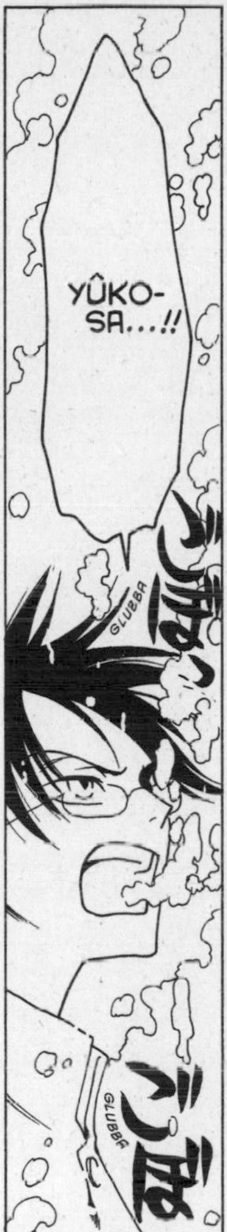
YÛKO-SA...!!
GLUBBA
GLUBBA
GLUBBA

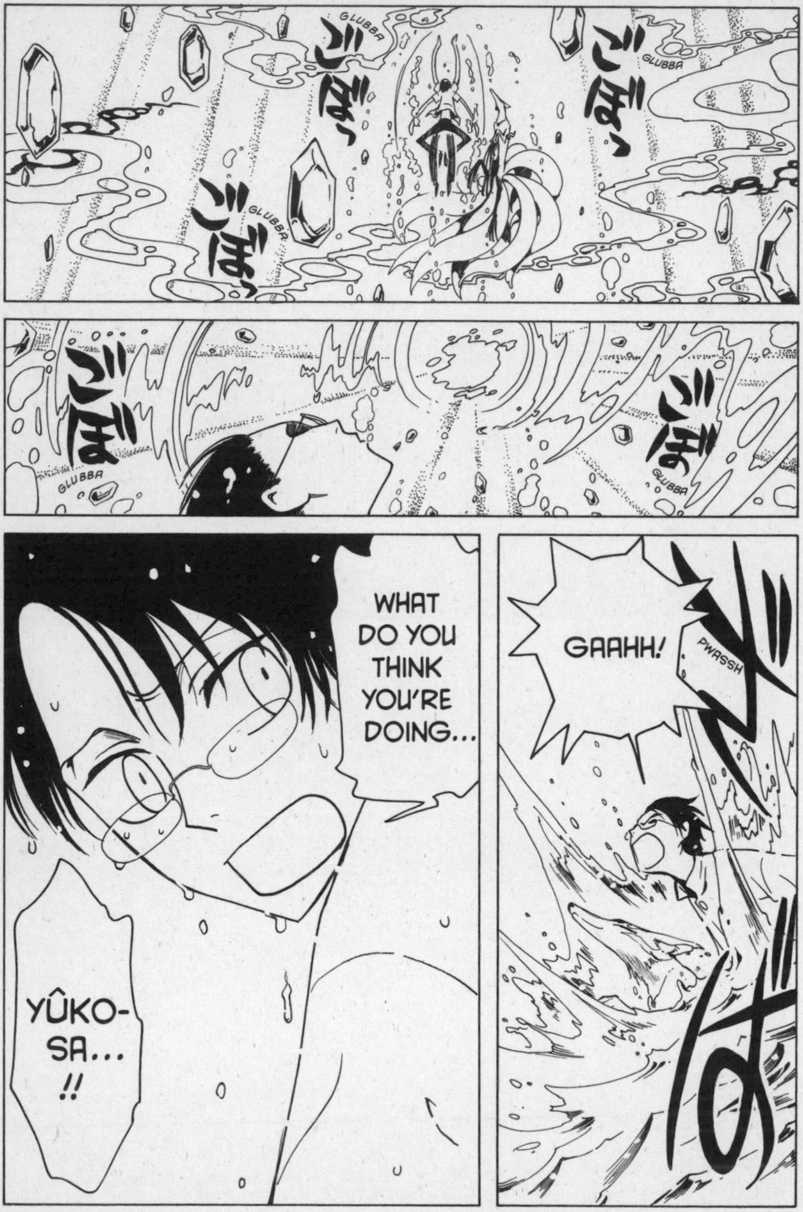
ごぼっ
GLUBBA
ごぼっ
GLUBBA
ごぼっ
GLUBBA
ごぼ
GLUBBA
ごぼ
GLUBBA
GAAHH!
PWASSH
WHAT DO YOU THINK YOU'RE DOING...
YÛKO-SA...!!

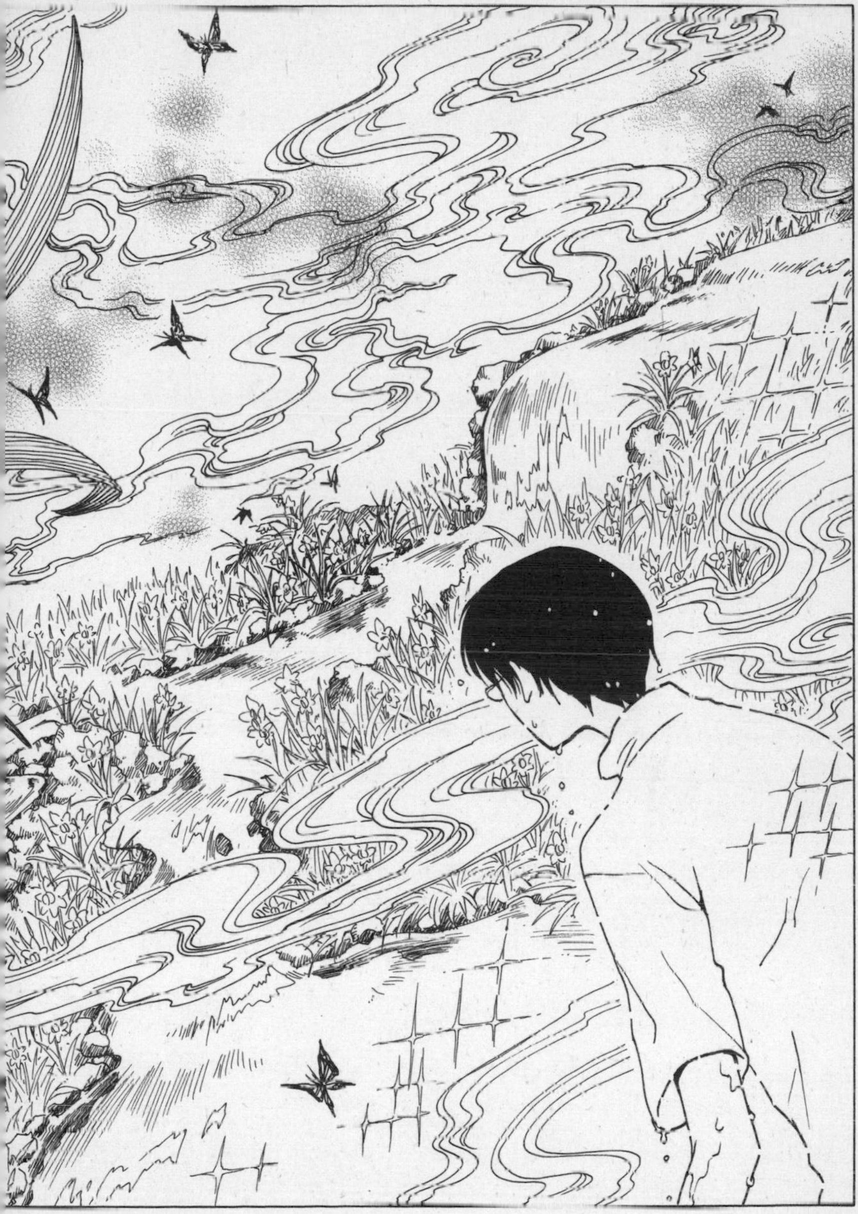

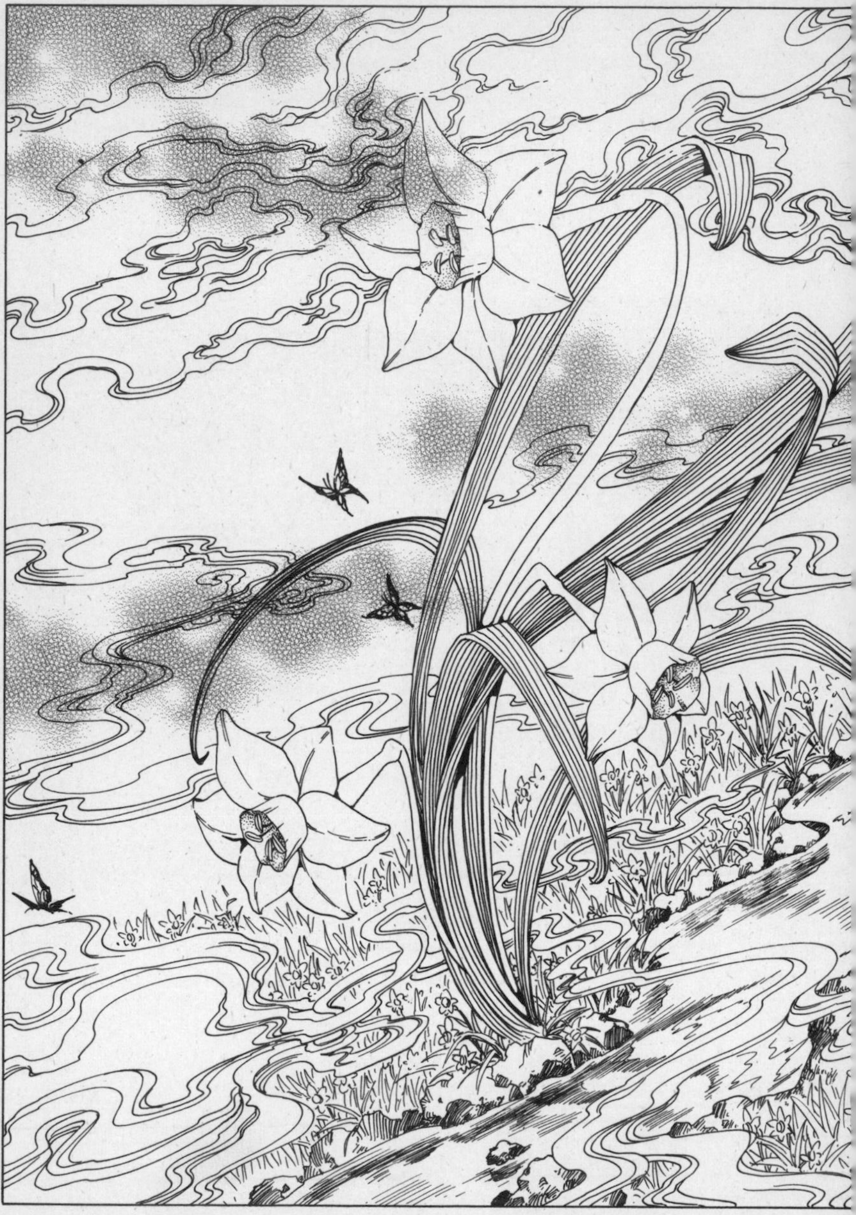

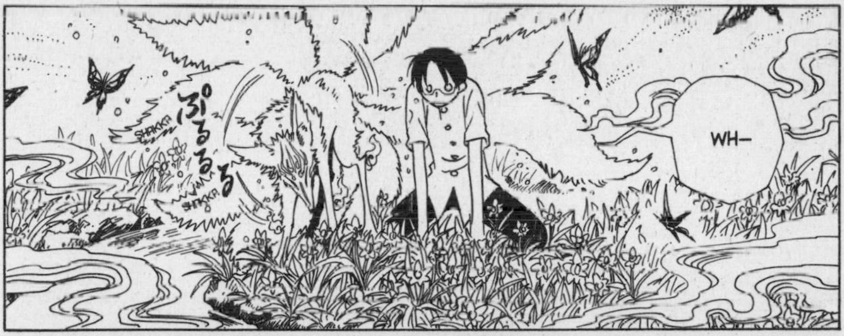
WH–
ぷるるる
SHAKKA
SHAKKA

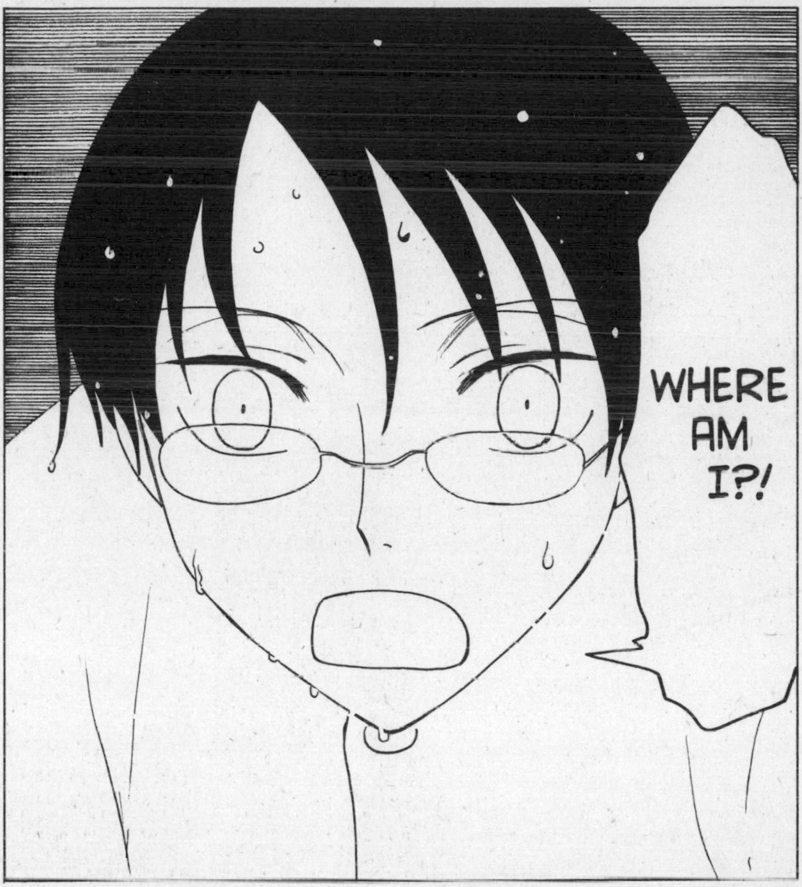
WHERE AM I?!

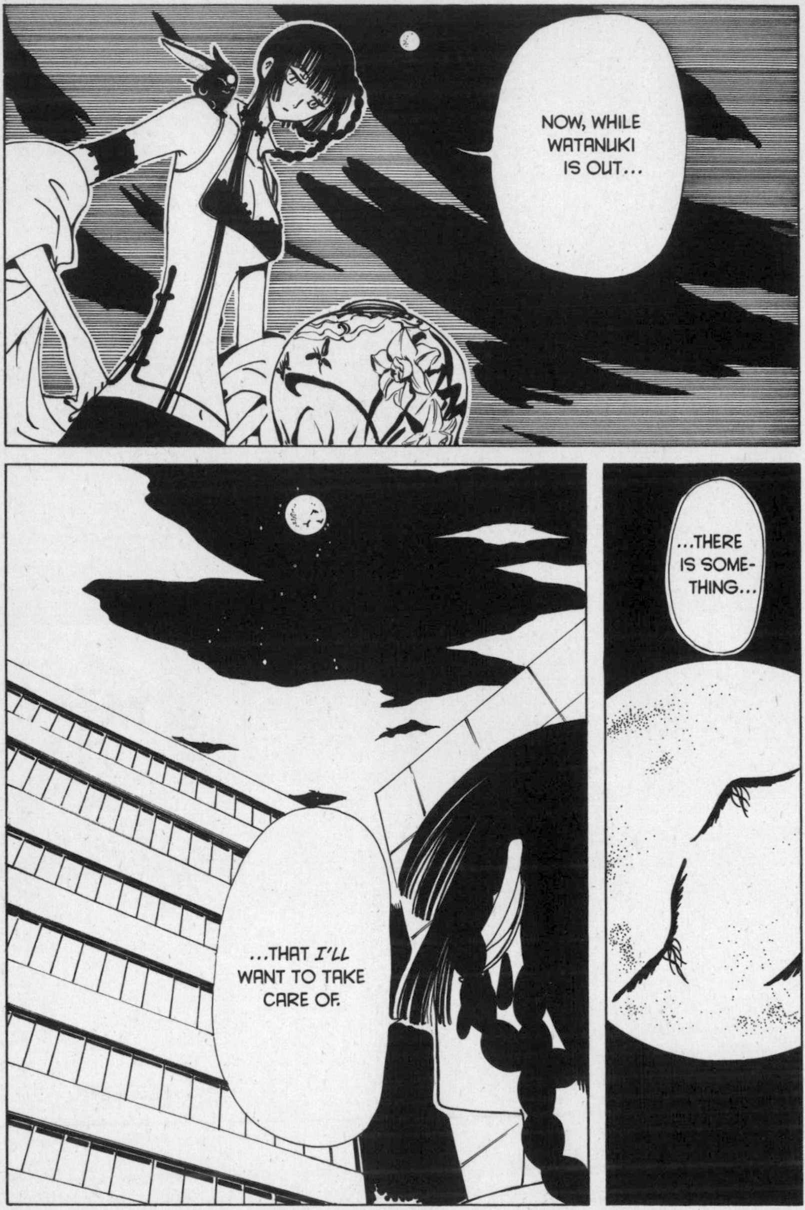
NOW, WHILE WATANUKI IS OUT...
...THERE IS SOME-THING...
...THAT I'LL WANT TO TAKE CARE OF.

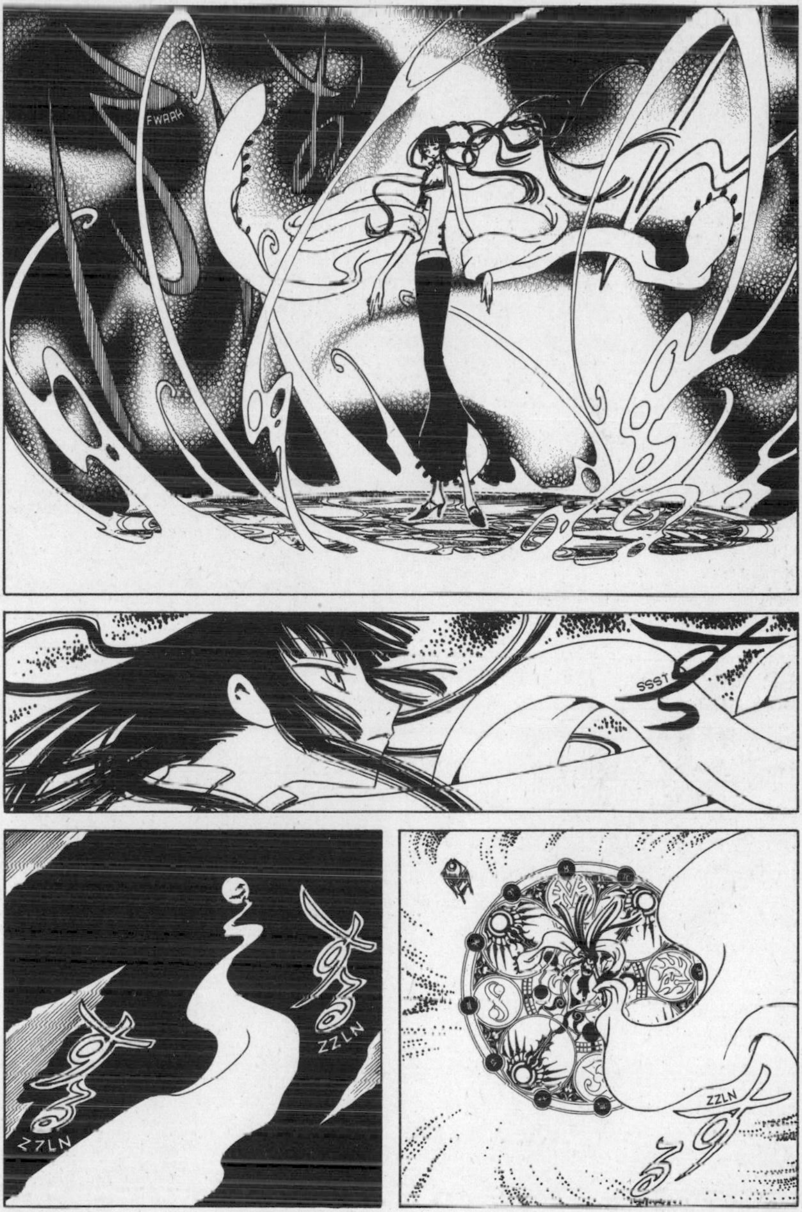
FWAAH
SSST
ZZLN
ZZLN
ZZLN

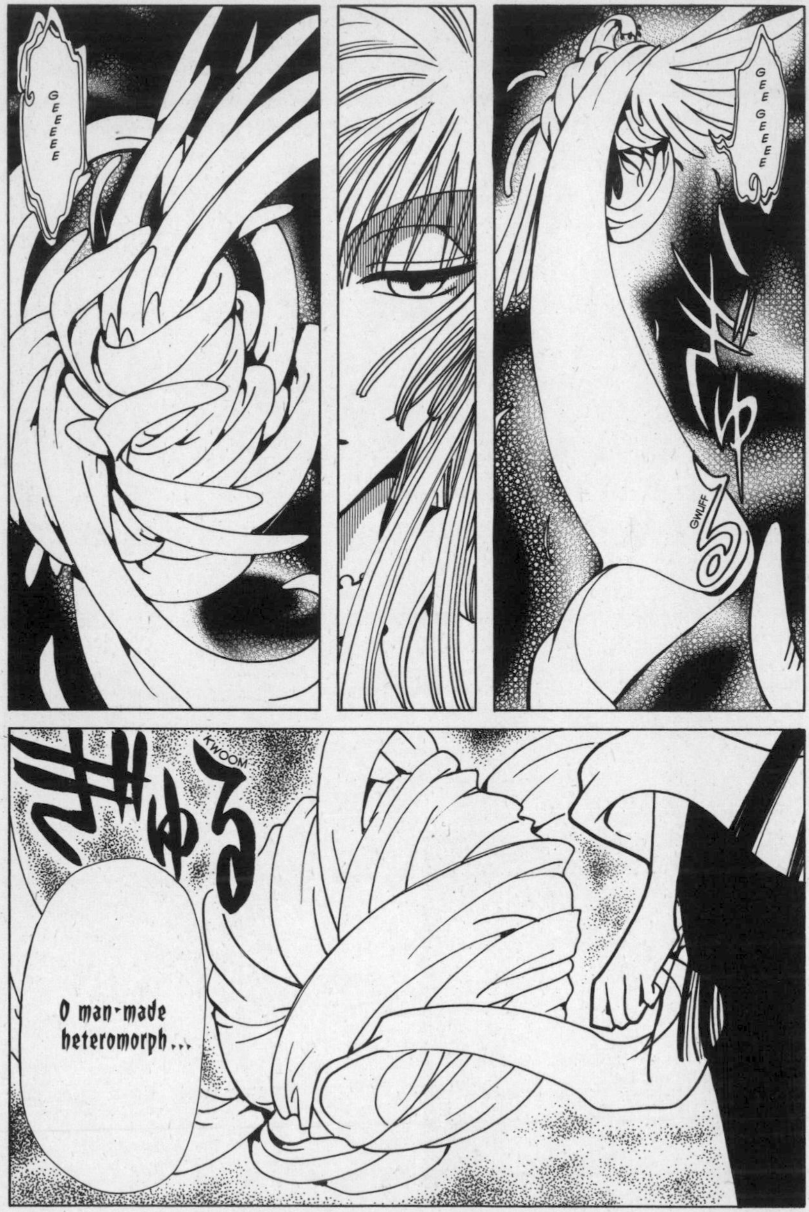
GEE GEEEE
きゅ
GWUFF
GEEEEE
きゅる
KWOOM
O man-made heteromorph...

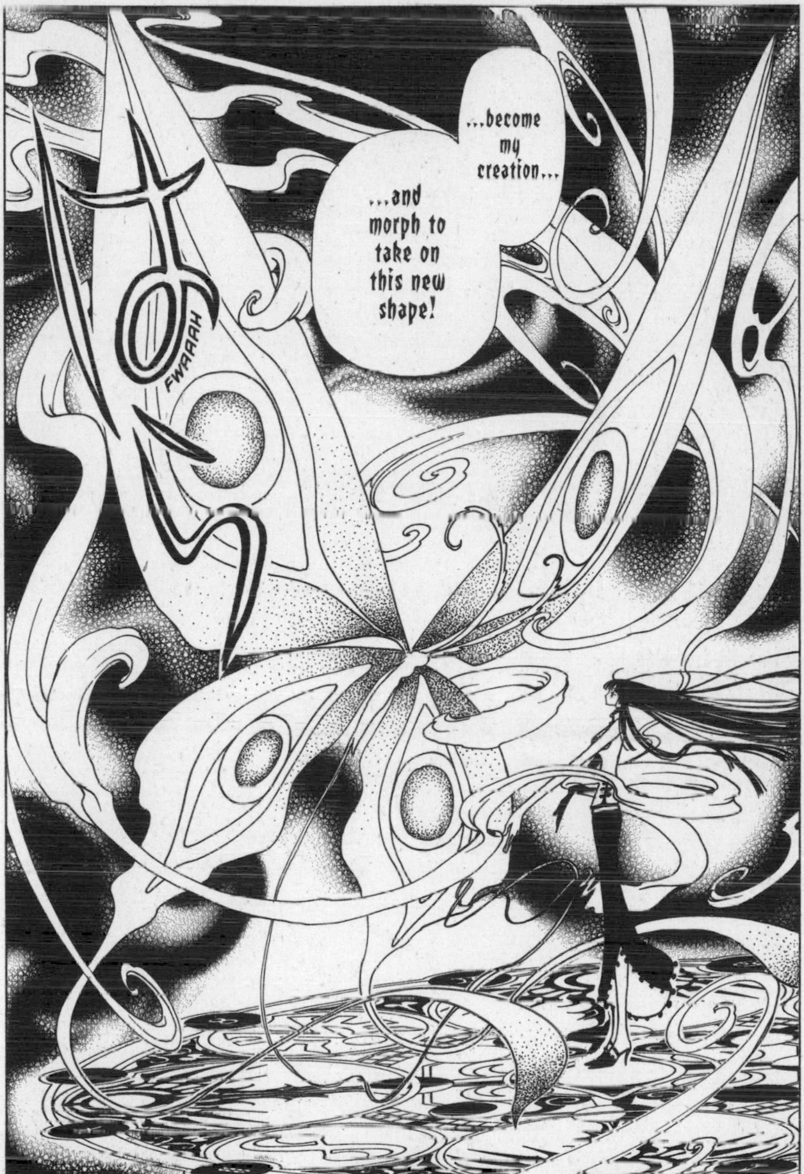
...become my creation...
...and morph to take on this new shape!
FWAAAH

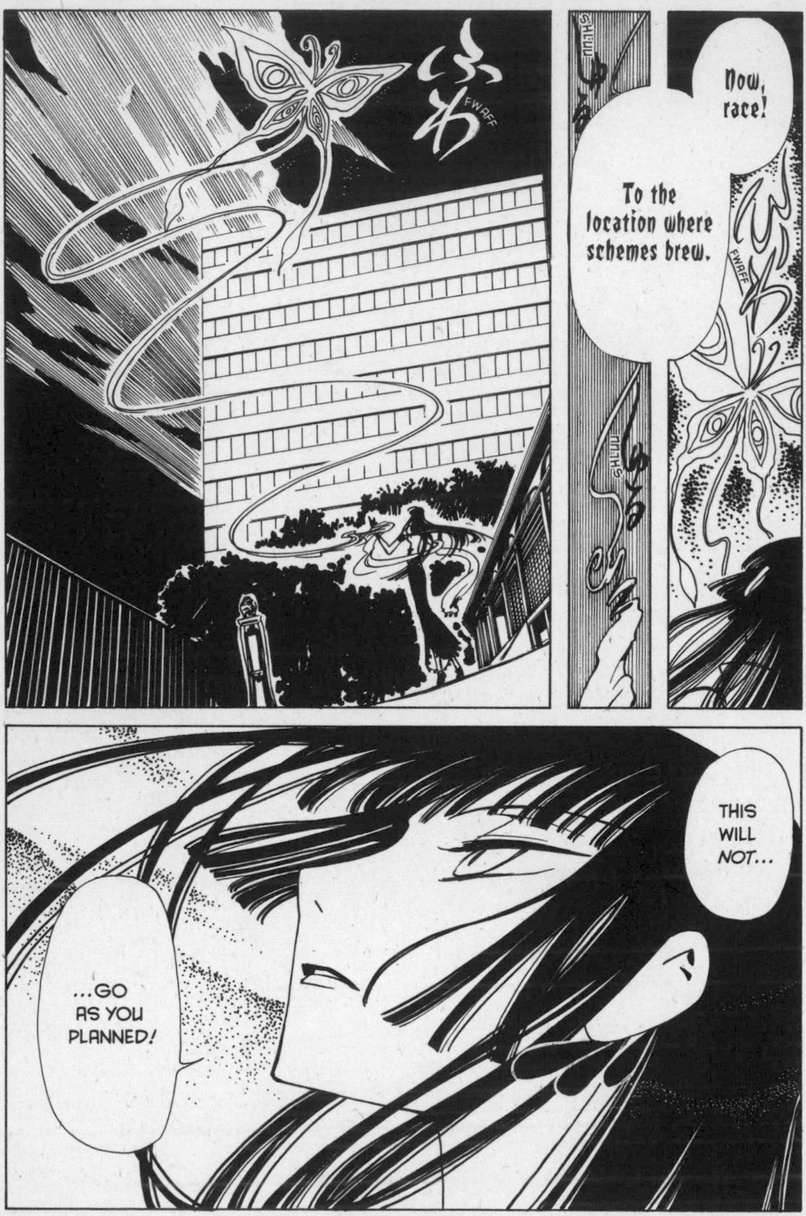
Now, race!
To the location where schemes brew.
ふわ
FWAFF
ゆる
SHEUU
ゆる
SHEUU
ふわ
FWAFF
THIS WILL *NOT*...
...GO AS YOU PLANNED!

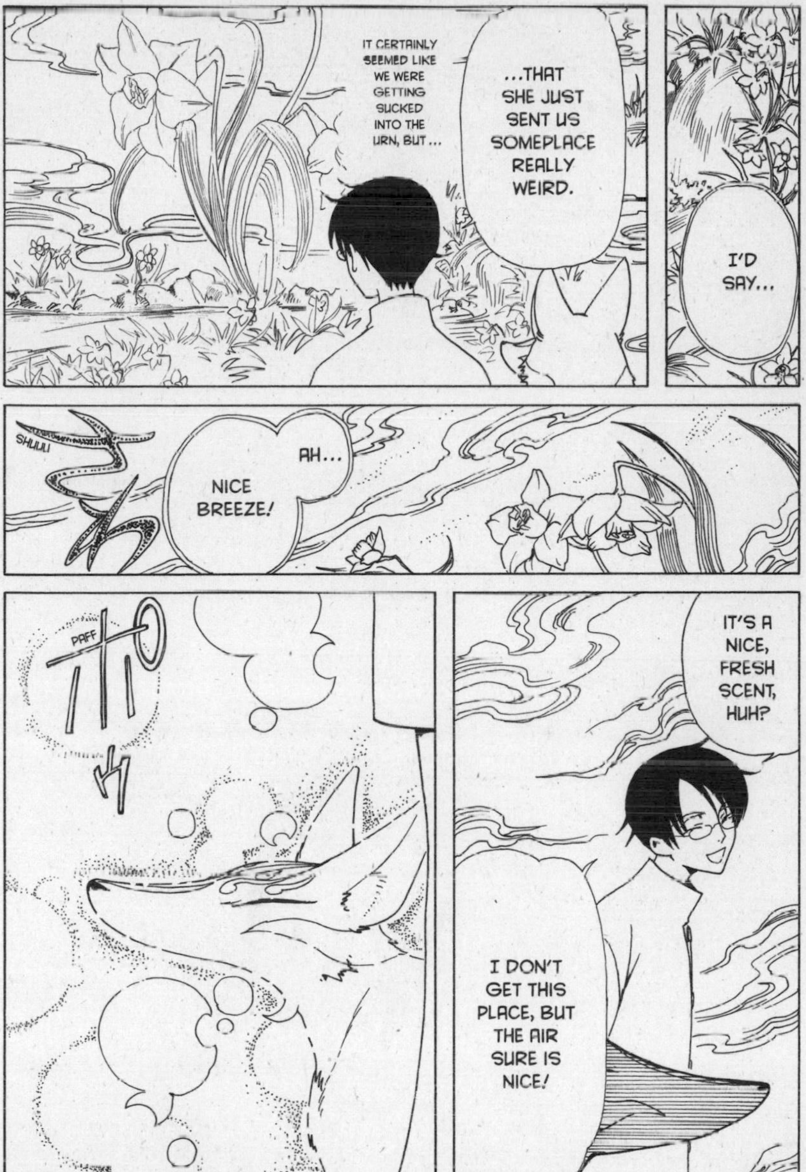
I'D SAY...
IT CERTAINLY SEEMED LIKE WE WERE GETTING SUCKED INTO THE URN, BUT...
...THAT SHE JUST SENT US SOMEPLACE REALLY WEIRD.
AH... NICE BREEZE!
SHUUU
IT'S A NICE, FRESH SCENT, HUH?
I DON'T GET THIS PLACE, BUT THE AIR SURE IS NICE!
PAFF

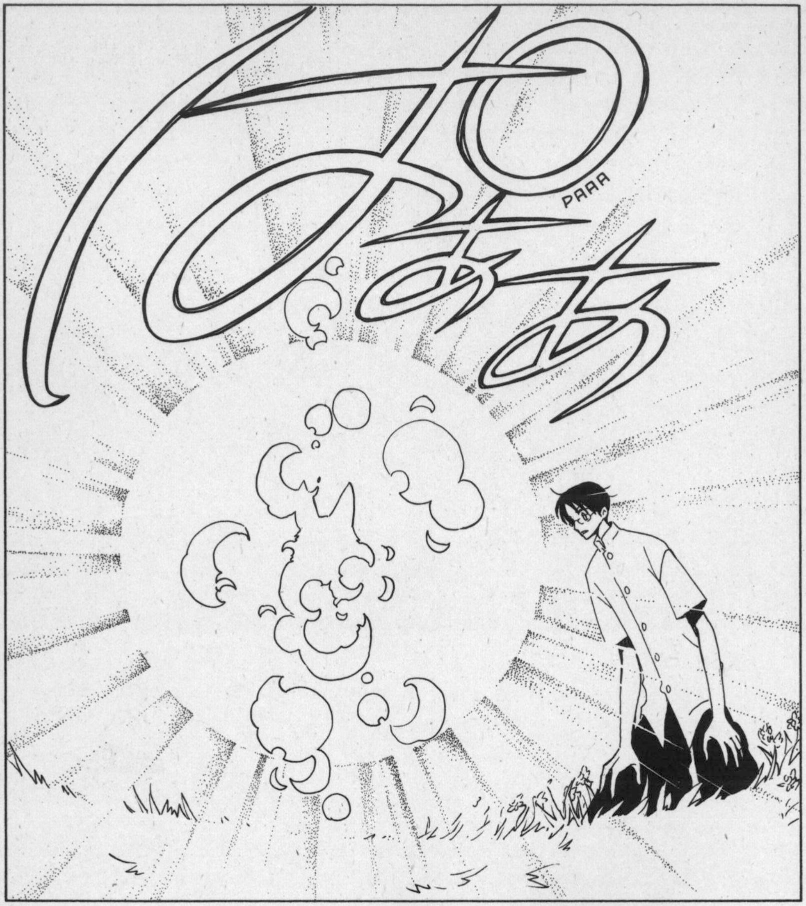
PAAA

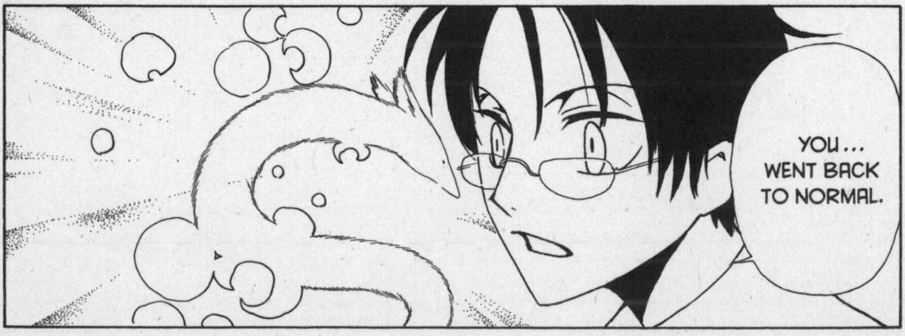
YOU... WENT BACK TO NORMAL.

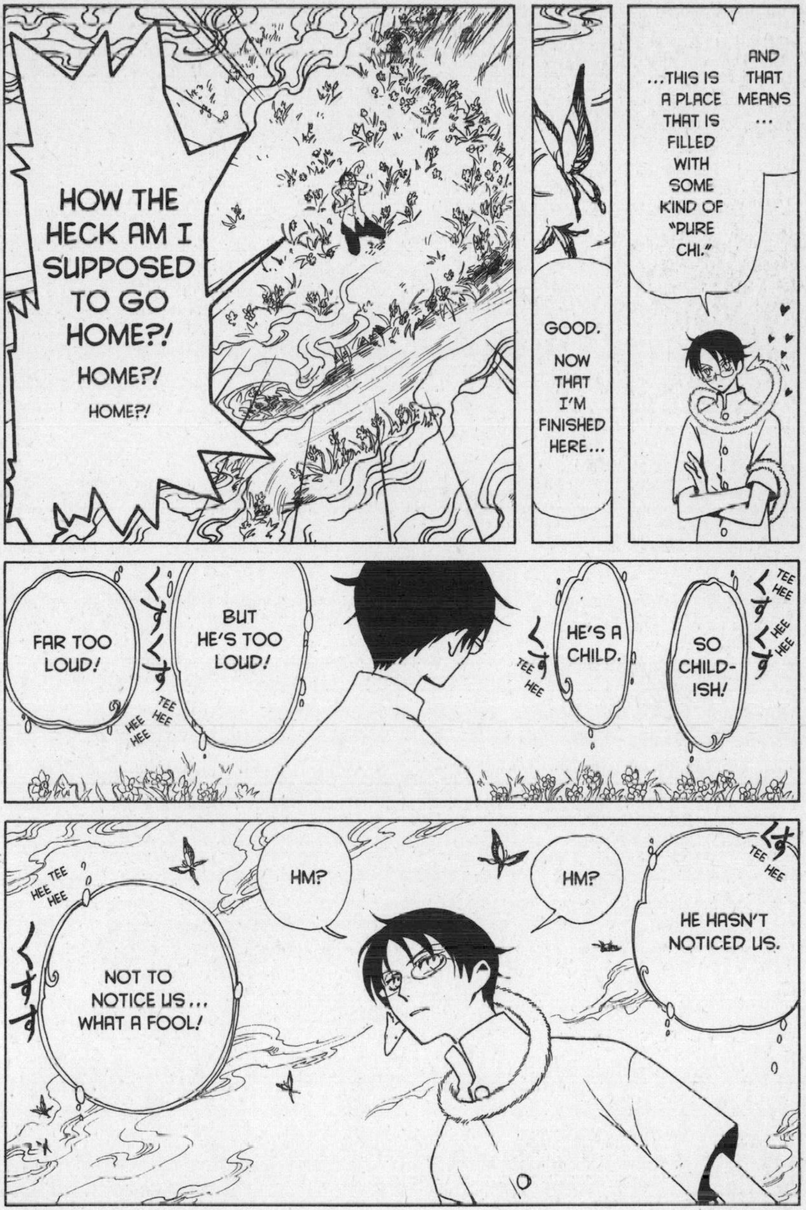
AND THAT MEANS...
...THIS IS A PLACE THAT IS FILLED WITH SOME KIND OF "PURE CHI."
GOOD. NOW THAT I'M FINISHED HERE...
HOW THE HECK AM I SUPPOSED TO GO HOME?!
HOME?!
HOME?!
くすくす
TEE HEE
HEE HEE
SO CHILD-ISH!
HE'S A CHILD.
くす
TEE HEE
BUT HE'S TOO LOUD!
くすくす
TEE HEE
HEE HEE
FAR TOO LOUD!
くす
TEE HEE
HE HASN'T NOTICED US.
HM?
HM?
TEE HEE HEE
くすす
NOT TO NOTICE US... WHAT A FOOL!

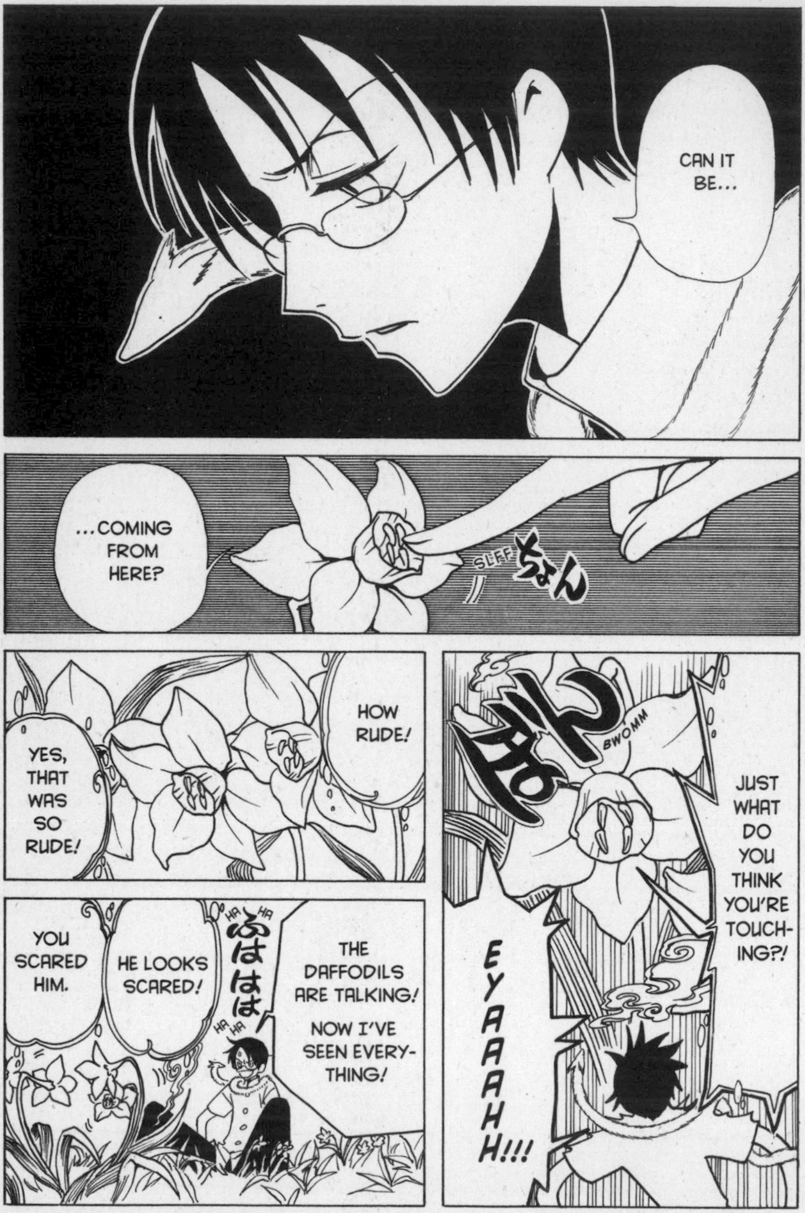
CAN IT BE...
...COMING FROM HERE?
SLIFF
ちょん
JUST WHAT DO YOU THINK YOU'RE TOUCHING?!
BWOMM
EYAAAAHH!!!
HOW RUDE!
YES, THAT WAS SO RUDE!
THE DAFFODILS ARE TALKING!
NOW I'VE SEEN EVERYTHING!
HA HA
ふははは
HA HA
HE LOOKS SCARED!
YOU SCARED HIM.

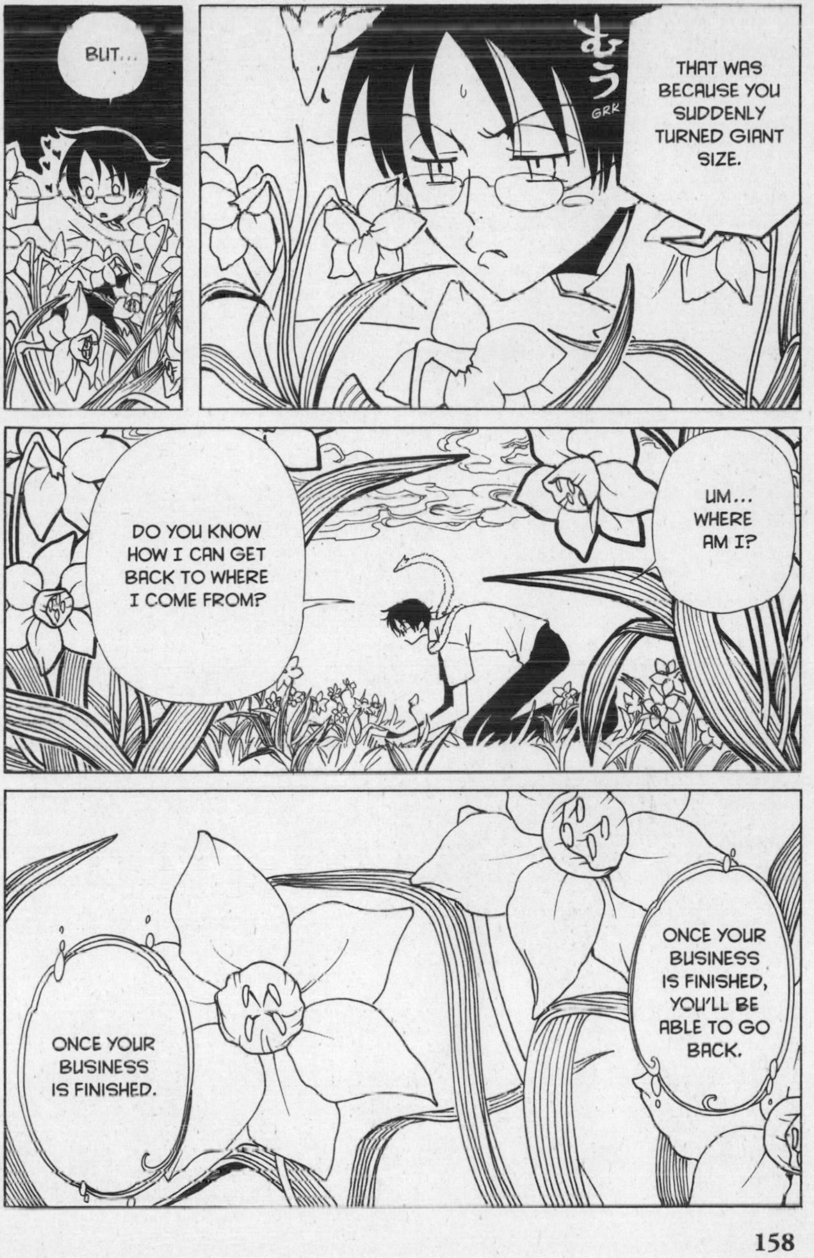
THAT WAS BECAUSE YOU SUDDENLY TURNED GIANT SIZE.
むう
GRK
BUT...
UM... WHERE AM I?
DO YOU KNOW HOW I CAN GET BACK TO WHERE I COME FROM?
ONCE YOUR BUSINESS IS FINISHED, YOU'LL BE ABLE TO GO BACK.
ONCE YOUR BUSINESS IS FINISHED.

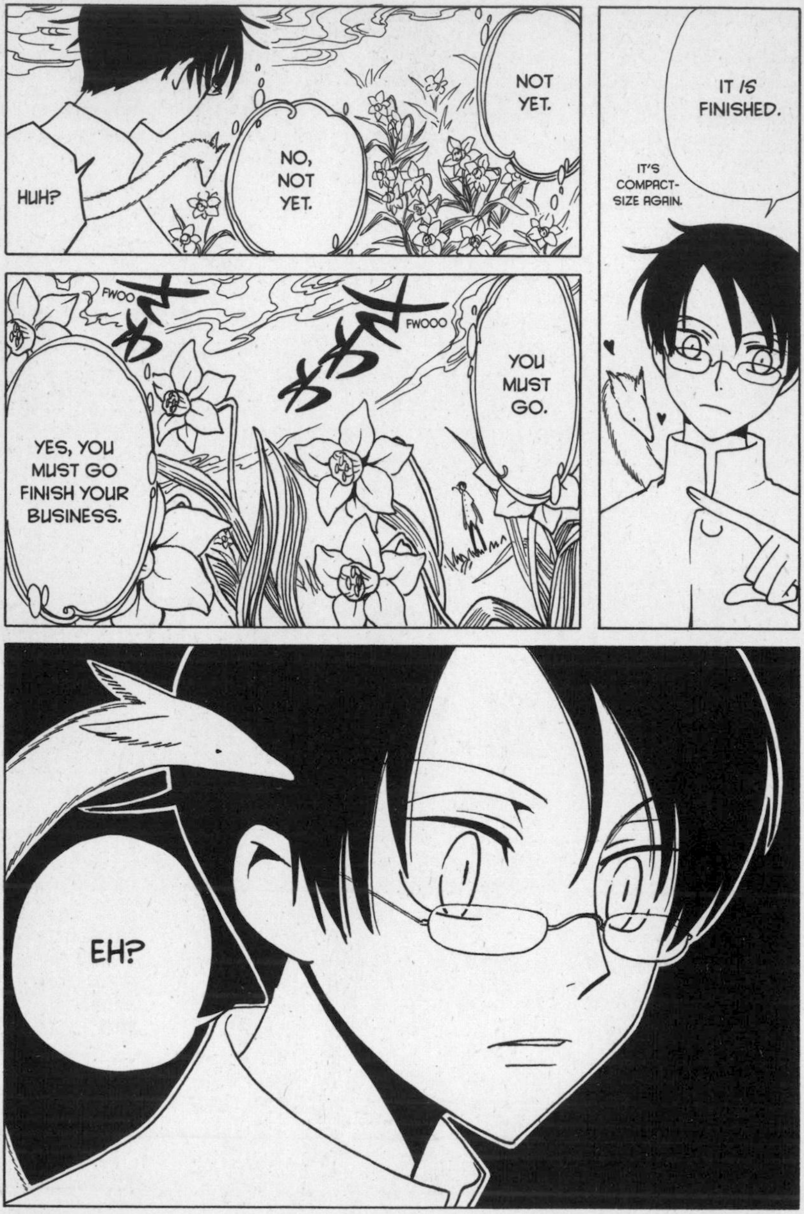
IT IS FINISHED.
IT'S COMPACT-SIZE AGAIN.
NOT YET.
NO, NOT YET.
HUH?
FWOOO
YOU MUST GO.
FWOO
YES, YOU MUST GO FINISH YOUR BUSINESS.
EH?

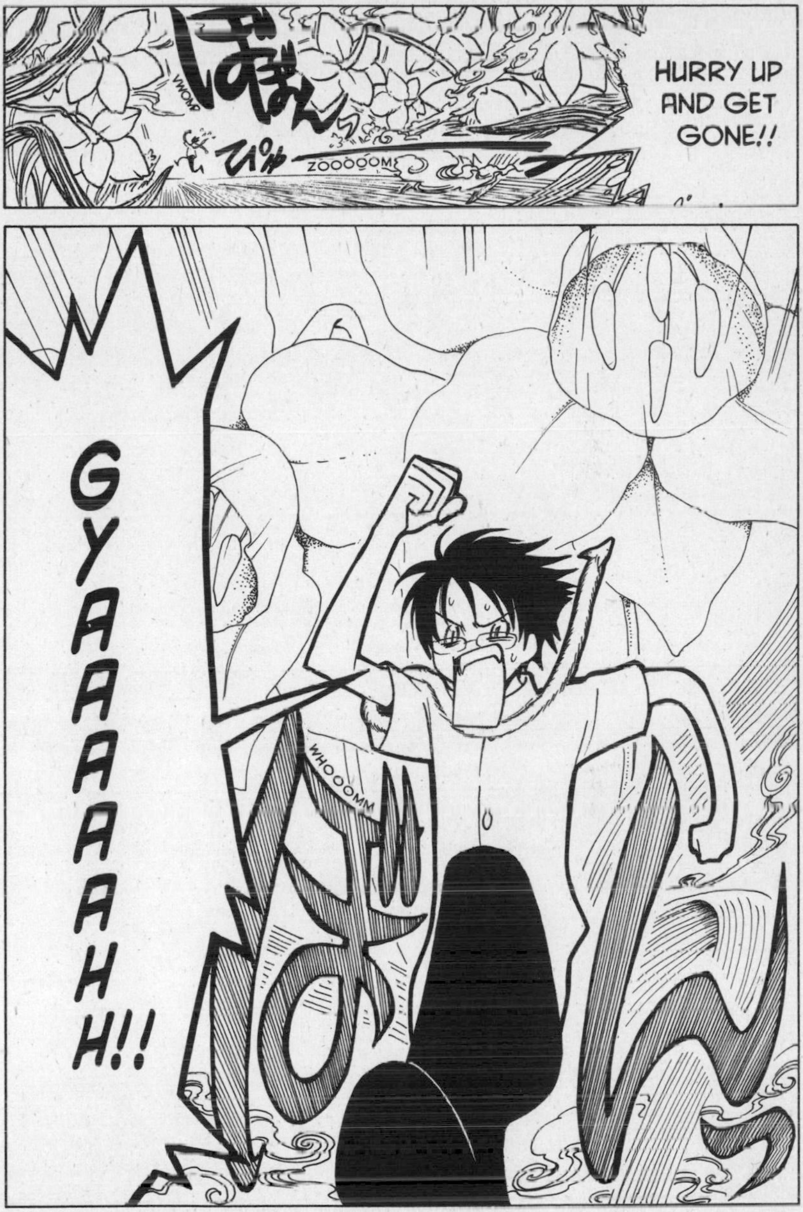
HURRY UP AND GET GONE!!
ZOOOOOM
VWOMP
GYAAAAAAAH!!
WHOOOMM

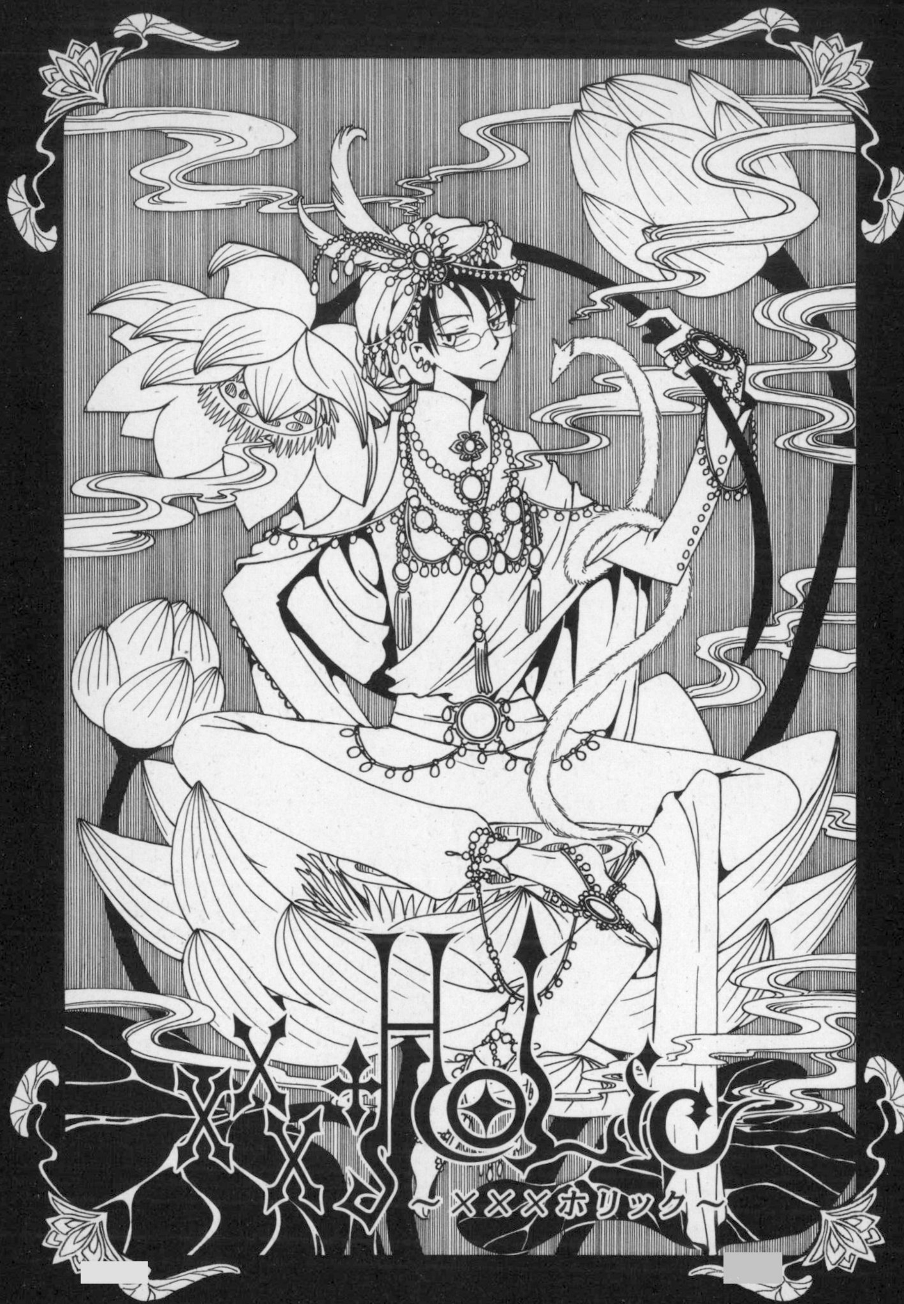
xxxHOLiC
〜×××ホリック〜

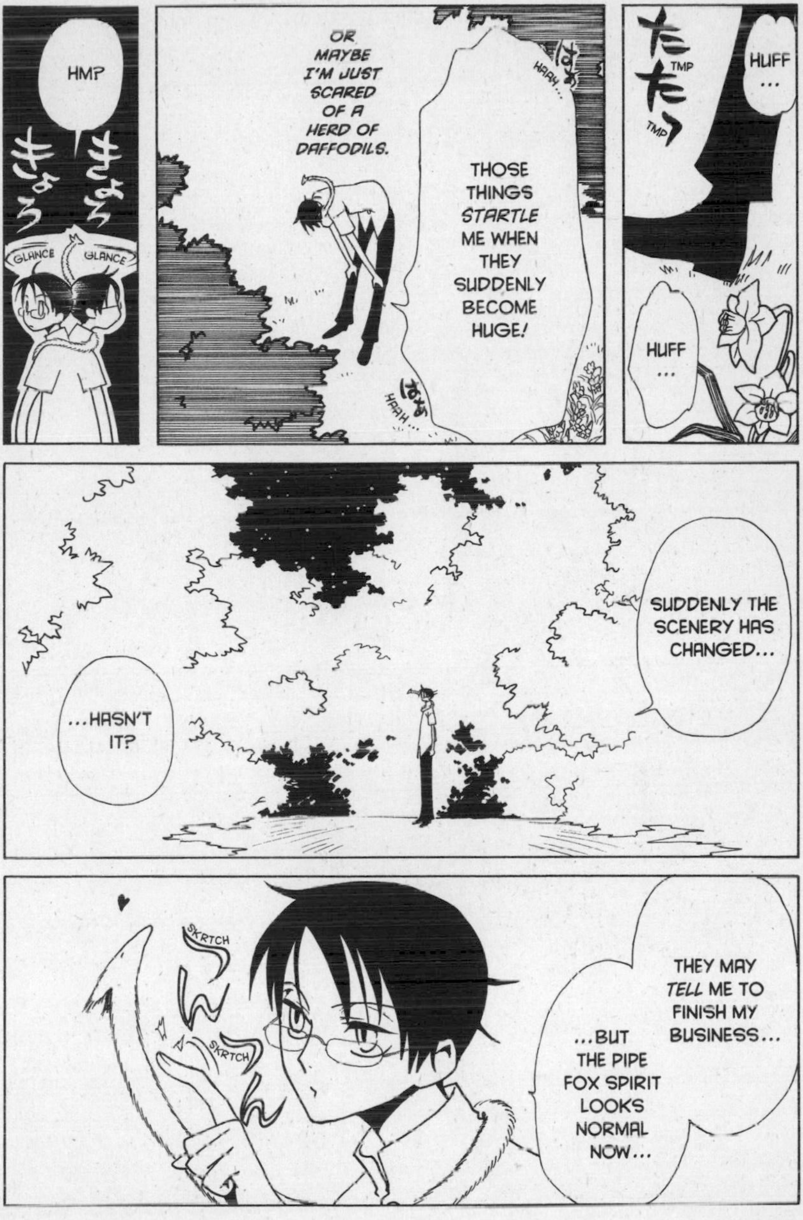
TMP TMP
HUFF...
HUFF...
OR MAYBE I'M JUST SCARED OF A HERD OF DAFFODILS.
HAAH...
THOSE THINGS STARTLE ME WHEN THEY SUDDENLY BECOME HUGE!
HAAH...
HM?
GLANCE GLANCE
SUDDENLY THE SCENERY HAS CHANGED...
...HASN'T IT?
THEY MAY TELL ME TO FINISH MY BUSINESS...
...BUT THE PIPE FOX SPIRIT LOOKS NORMAL NOW...
SKRTCH
SKRTCH

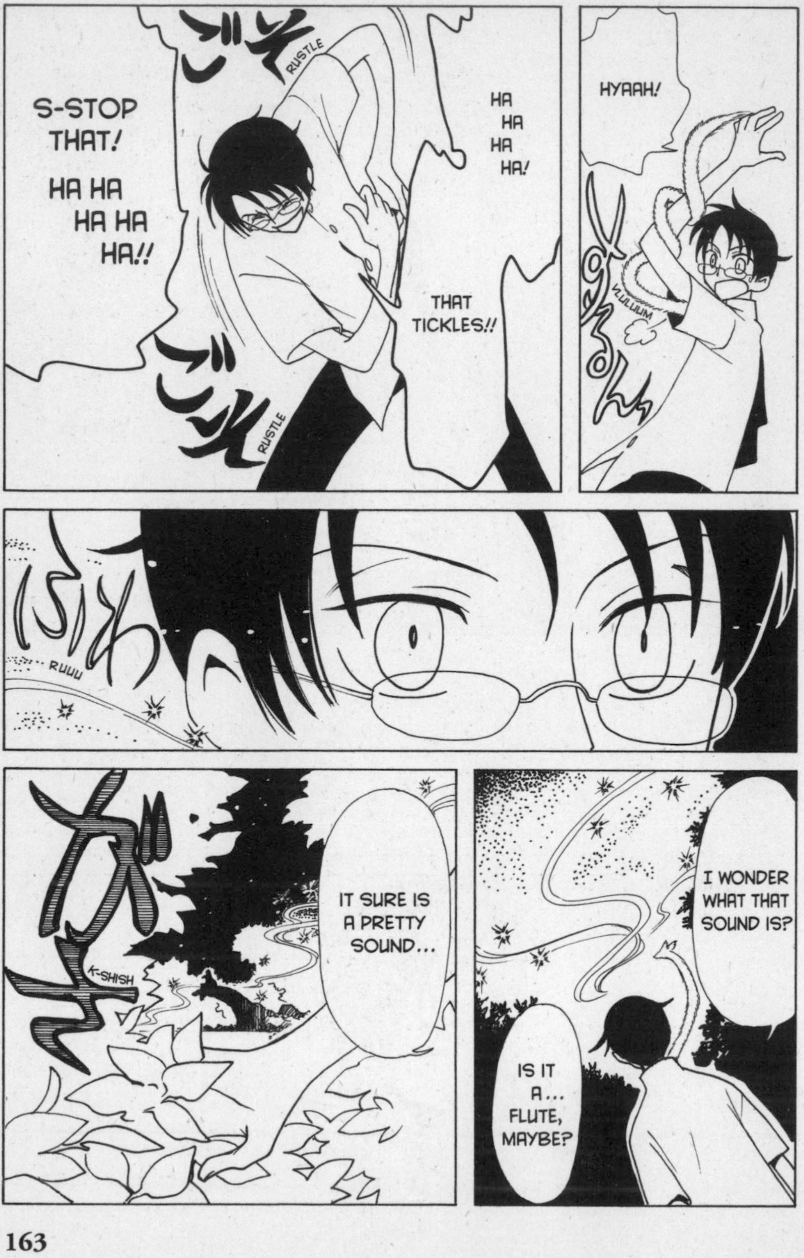
HYAAH!
VLULUUM
RUSTLE
HA HA HA HA!
S-STOP THAT!
HA HA HA HA HA!!
THAT TICKLES!!
RUSTLE
RUUU
I WONDER WHAT THAT SOUND IS?
IS IT A... FLUTE, MAYBE?
IT SURE IS A PRETTY SOUND...
K-SHISH

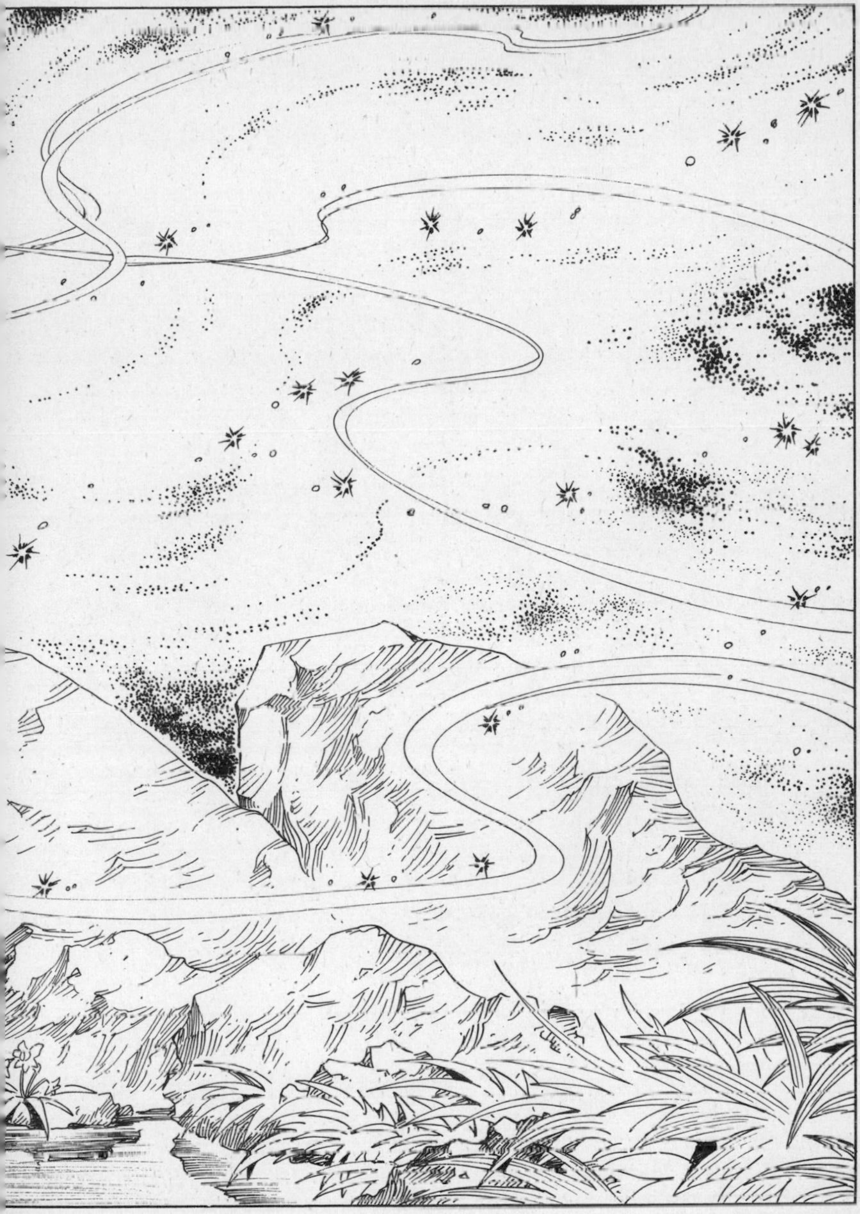

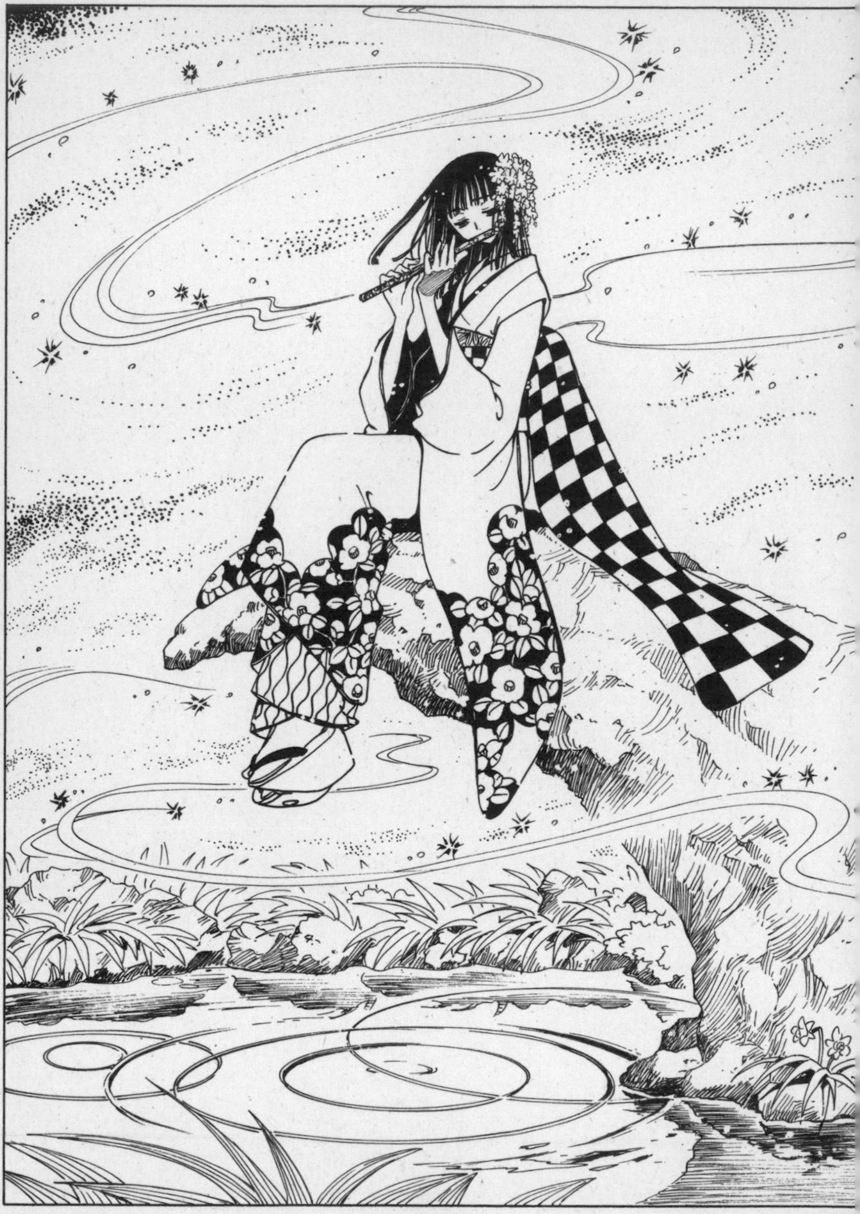

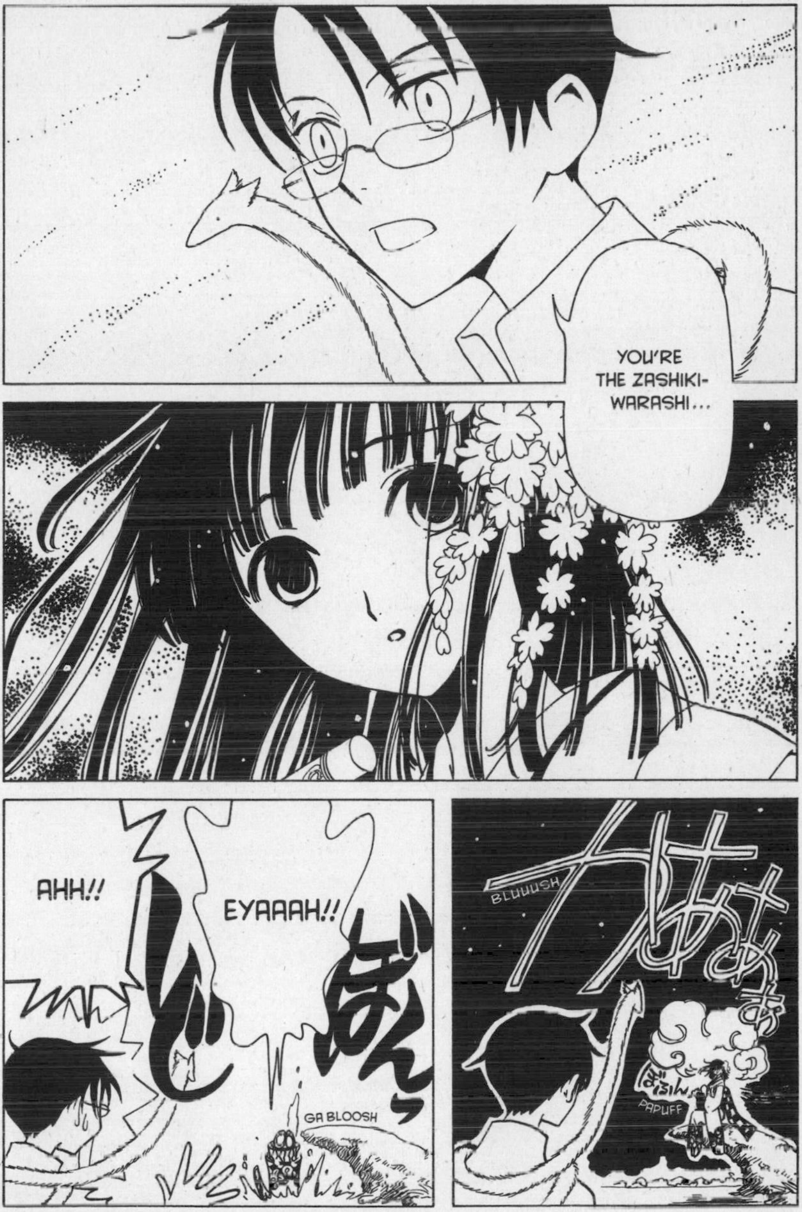
YOU'RE THE ZASHIKI-WARASHI...
BLUUUSH
PAPUFF
EYAAAH!!
AHH!!
GA BLOOSH

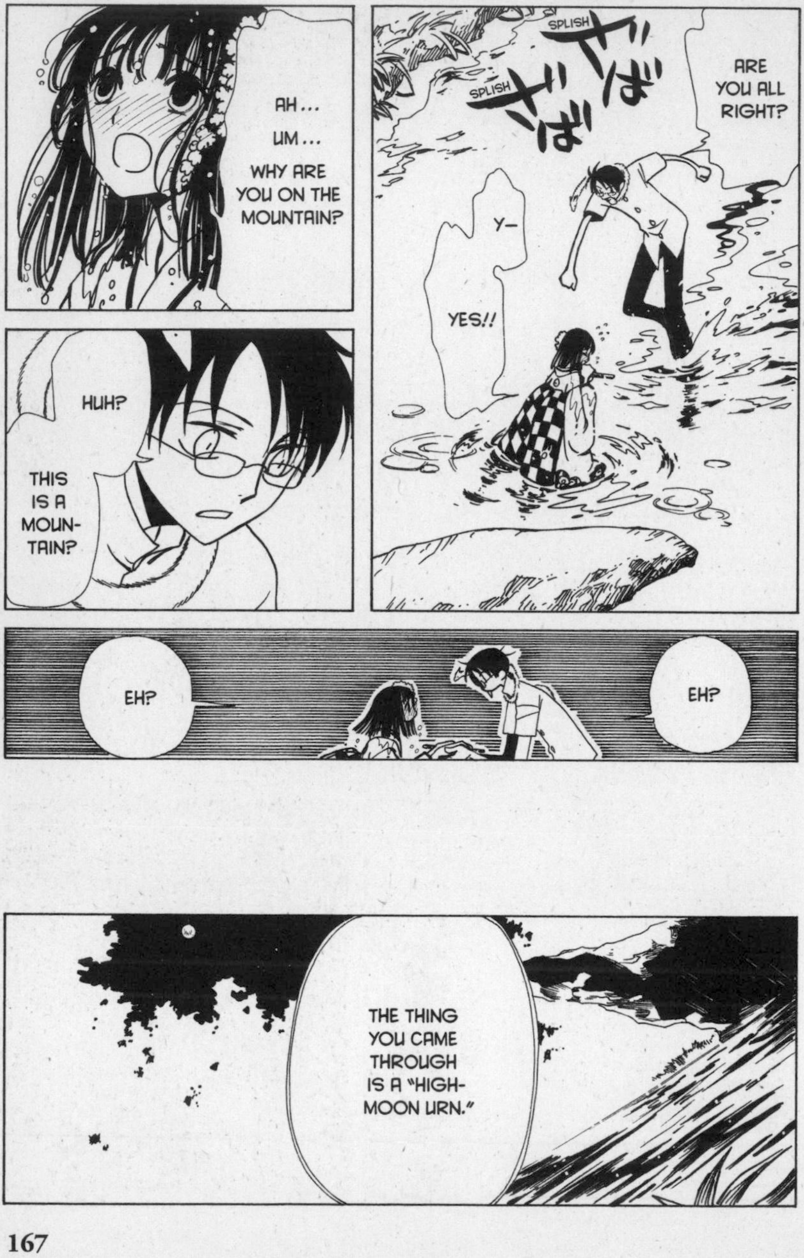
ARE YOU ALL RIGHT?
SPLISH
ざば
SPLISH
ざば
Y—
YES!!
AH...
UM...
WHY ARE YOU ON THE MOUNTAIN?
HUH?
THIS IS A MOUN-TAIN?
EH?
EH?
THE THING YOU CAME THROUGH IS A "HIGH-MOON URN."

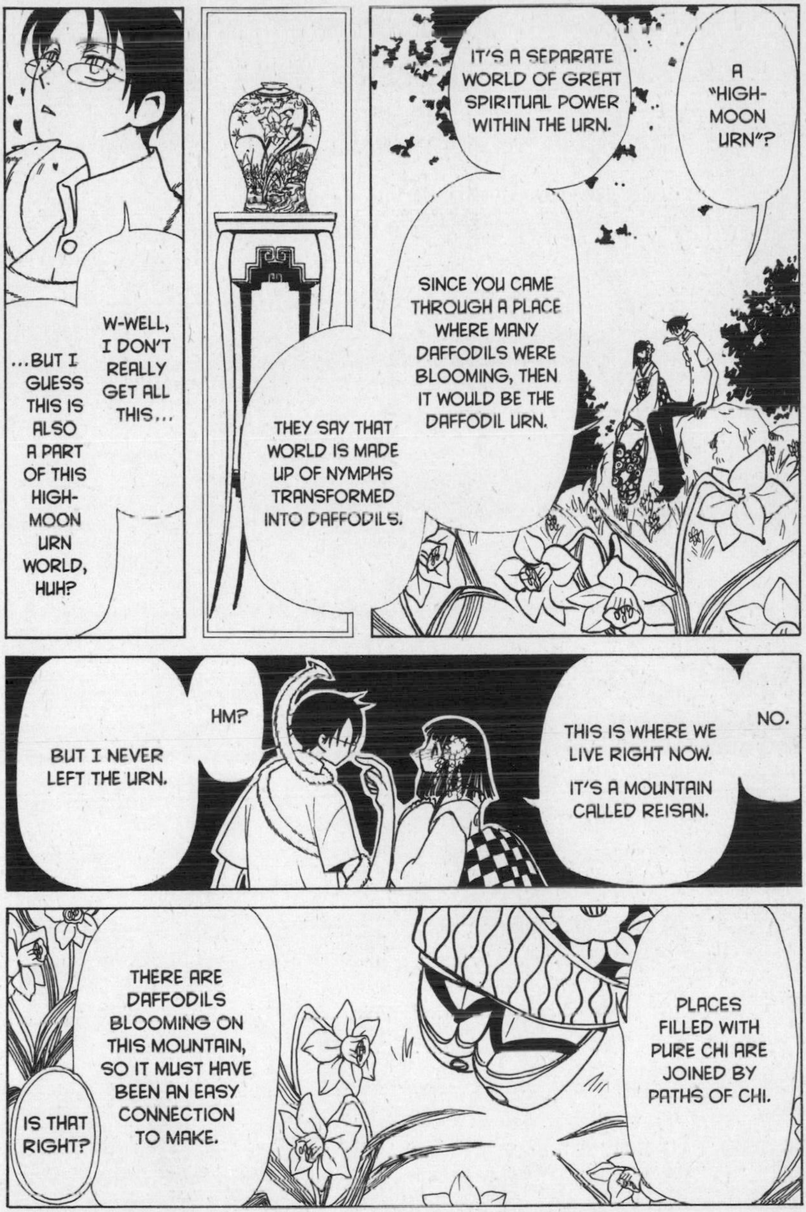
A "HIGH-MOON URN"?
IT'S A SEPARATE WORLD OF GREAT SPIRITUAL POWER WITHIN THE URN.
SINCE YOU CAME THROUGH A PLACE WHERE MANY DAFFODILS WERE BLOOMING, THEN IT WOULD BE THE DAFFODIL URN.
THEY SAY THAT WORLD IS MADE UP OF NYMPHS TRANSFORMED INTO DAFFODILS.
W-WELL, I DON'T REALLY GET ALL THIS...
...BUT I GUESS THIS IS ALSO A PART OF THIS HIGH-MOON URN WORLD, HUH?
NO.
THIS IS WHERE WE LIVE RIGHT NOW.
IT'S A MOUNTAIN CALLED REISAN.
HM?
BUT I NEVER LEFT THE URN.
PLACES FILLED WITH PURE CHI ARE JOINED BY PATHS OF CHI.
THERE ARE DAFFODILS BLOOMING ON THIS MOUNTAIN, SO IT MUST HAVE BEEN AN EASY CONNECTION TO MAKE.
IS THAT RIGHT?

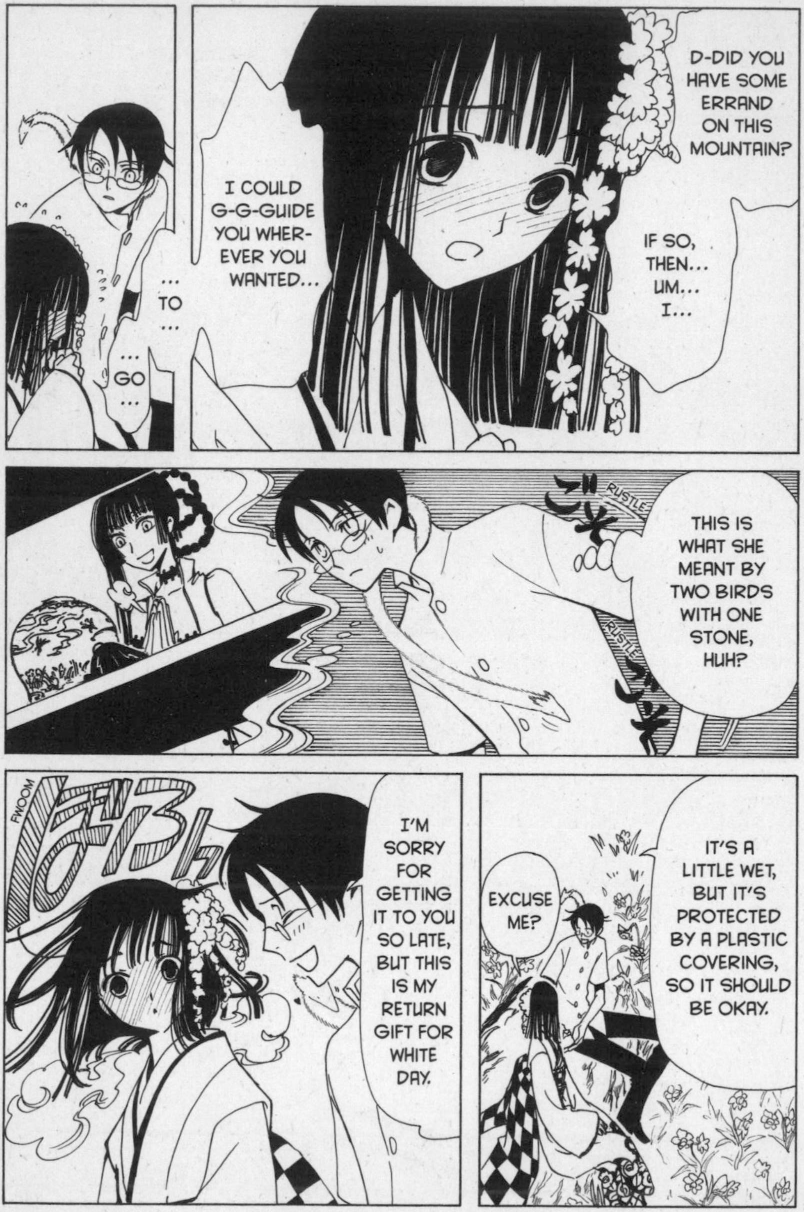
D-DID YOU HAVE SOME ERRAND ON THIS MOUNTAIN?
IF SO, THEN... UM... I...
I COULD G-G-GUIDE YOU WHER-EVER YOU WANTED...
... TO ...
... GO ...
RUSTLE
THIS IS WHAT SHE MEANT BY TWO BIRDS WITH ONE STONE, HUH?
RUSTLE
IT'S A LITTLE WET, BUT IT'S PROTECTED BY A PLASTIC COVERING, SO IT SHOULD BE OKAY.
EXCUSE ME?
I'M SORRY FOR GETTING IT TO YOU SO LATE, BUT THIS IS MY RETURN GIFT FOR WHITE DAY.
FWOOM

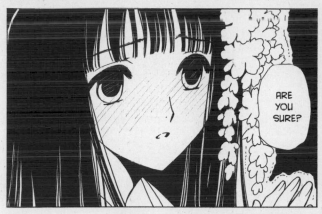

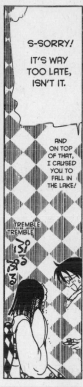

S-SORRY!
IT'S WAY TOO LATE, ISN'T IT.
AND ON TOP OF THAT, I CAUSED YOU TO FALL IN THE LAKE!
TREMBLE TREMBLE
ぷるぷる
ARE YOU SURE?
Y-YEAH.
I COULDN'T FIGURE OUT WHAT'S A GOOD GIFT FOR A GIRL.
FLIP
I WANTED IT TO BE FOOD.
BUT SINCE I DIDN'T KNOW WHEN I'D SEE YOU AGAIN, FOOD WAS NOT AN OPTION.

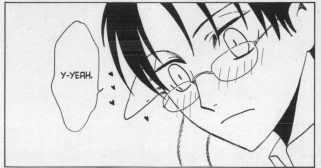

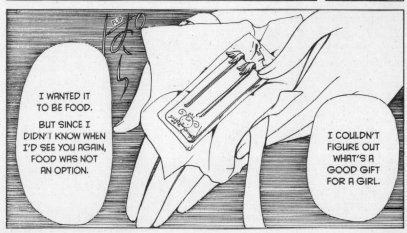

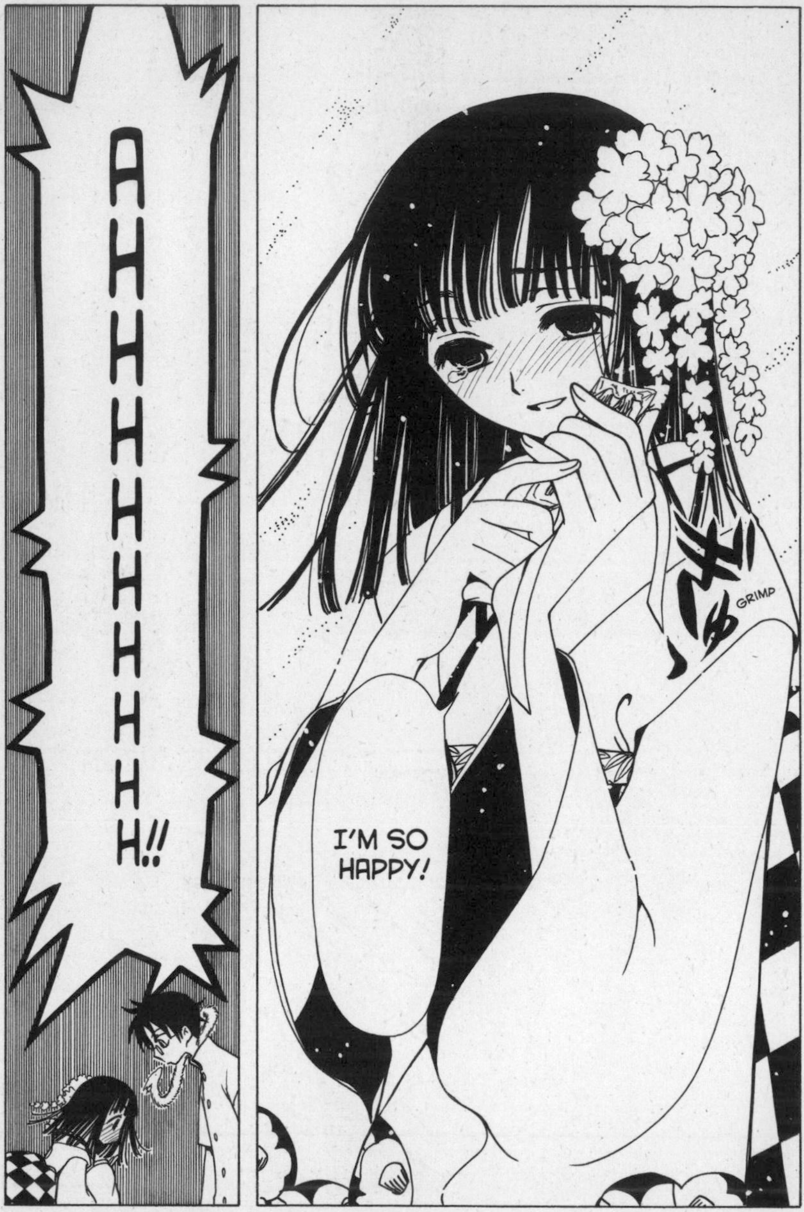
GRIMP
I'M SO HAPPY!
AHHHHHHHHH!!

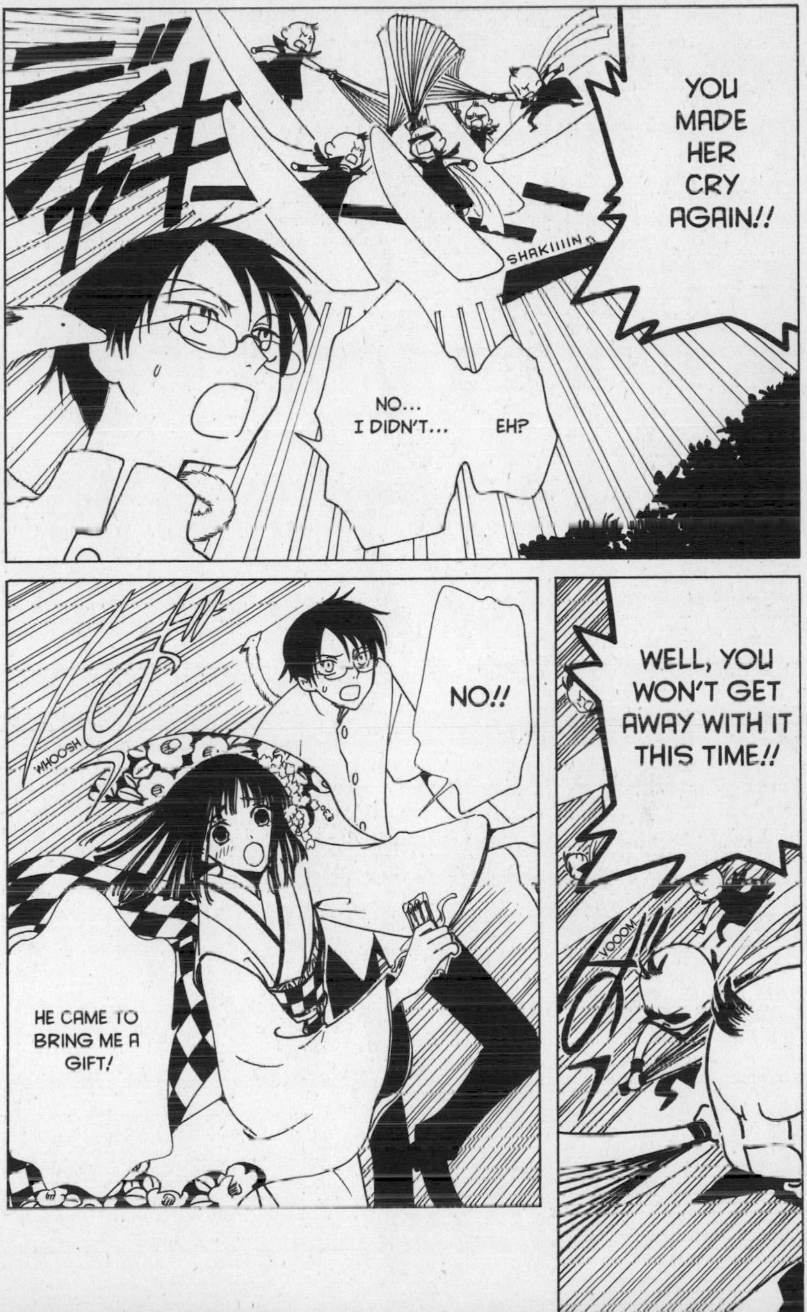
YOU MADE HER CRY AGAIN!!
SHAKIIIIN
NO... I DIDN'T... EH?
WELL, YOU WON'T GET AWAY WITH IT THIS TIME!!
VOOOM
NO!!
WHOOSH
HE CAME TO BRING ME A GIFT!

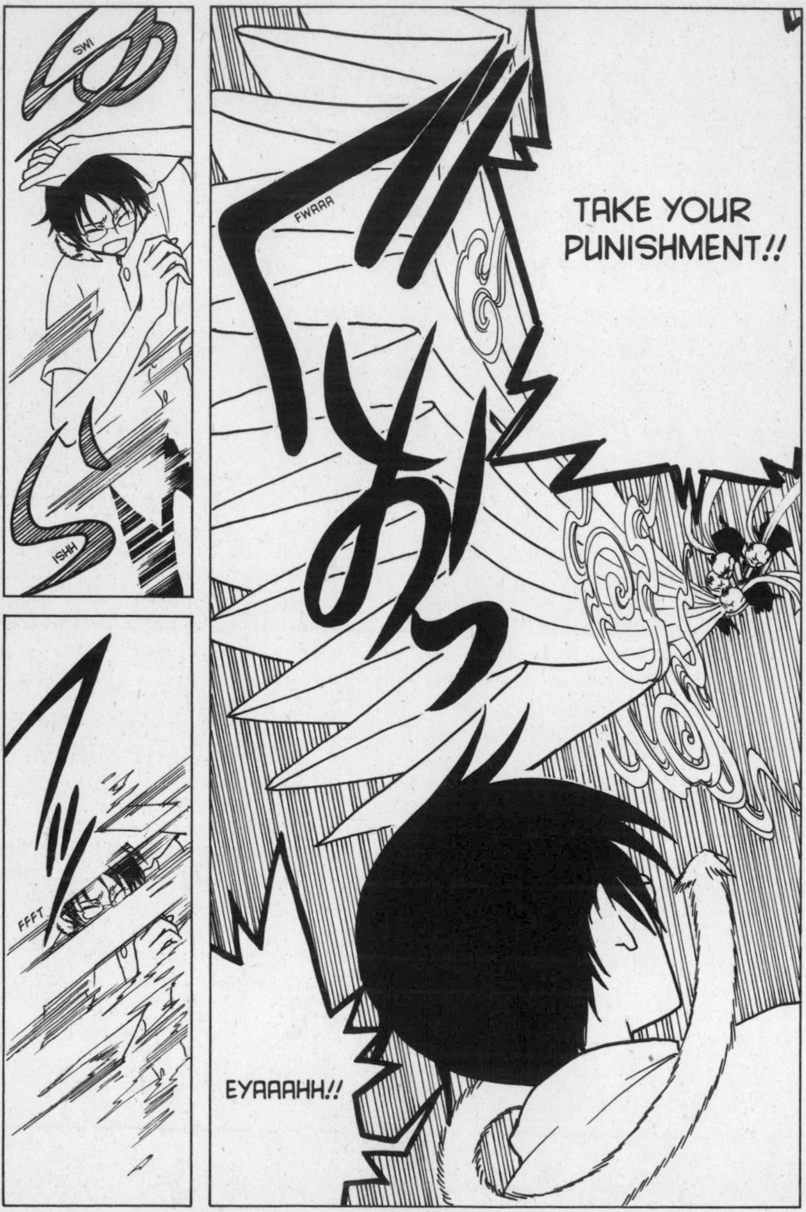
TAKE YOUR PUNISHMENT!!
FWAAA
EYAAAHH!!
SWI
ISHH
FFFT

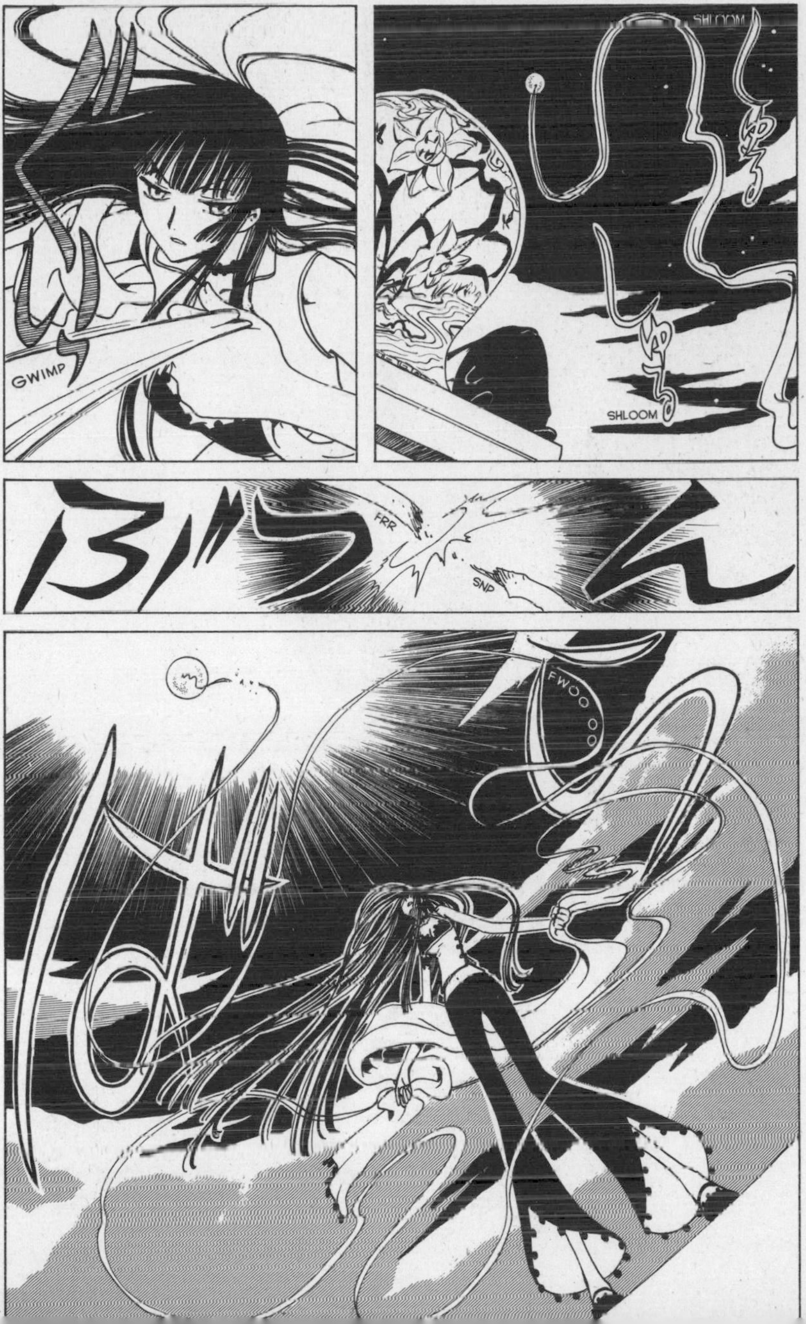
SHLOOM
SHLOOM
GWIMP
FRR
SNP
FWOOOOO

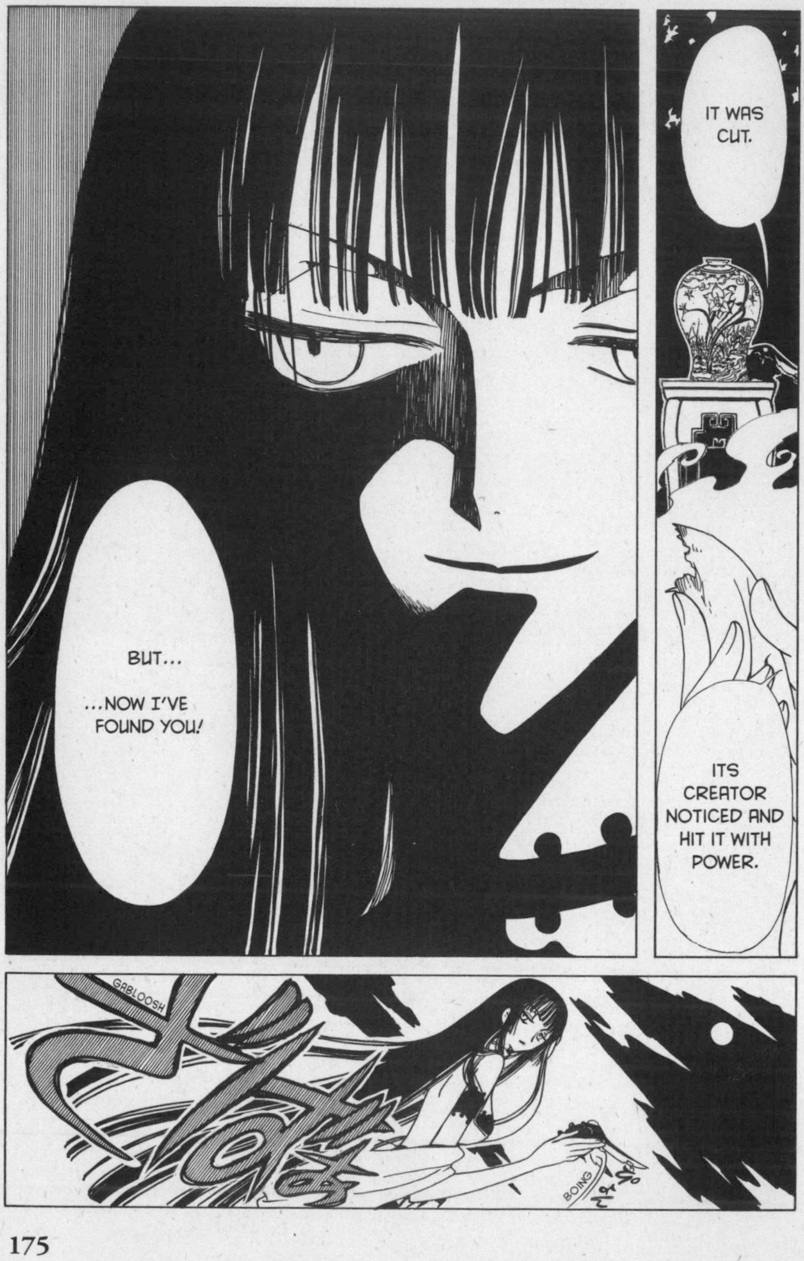
IT WAS CUT.
ITS CREATOR NOTICED AND HIT IT WITH POWER.
BUT...
...NOW I'VE FOUND YOU!
GABLOOSH
BOING

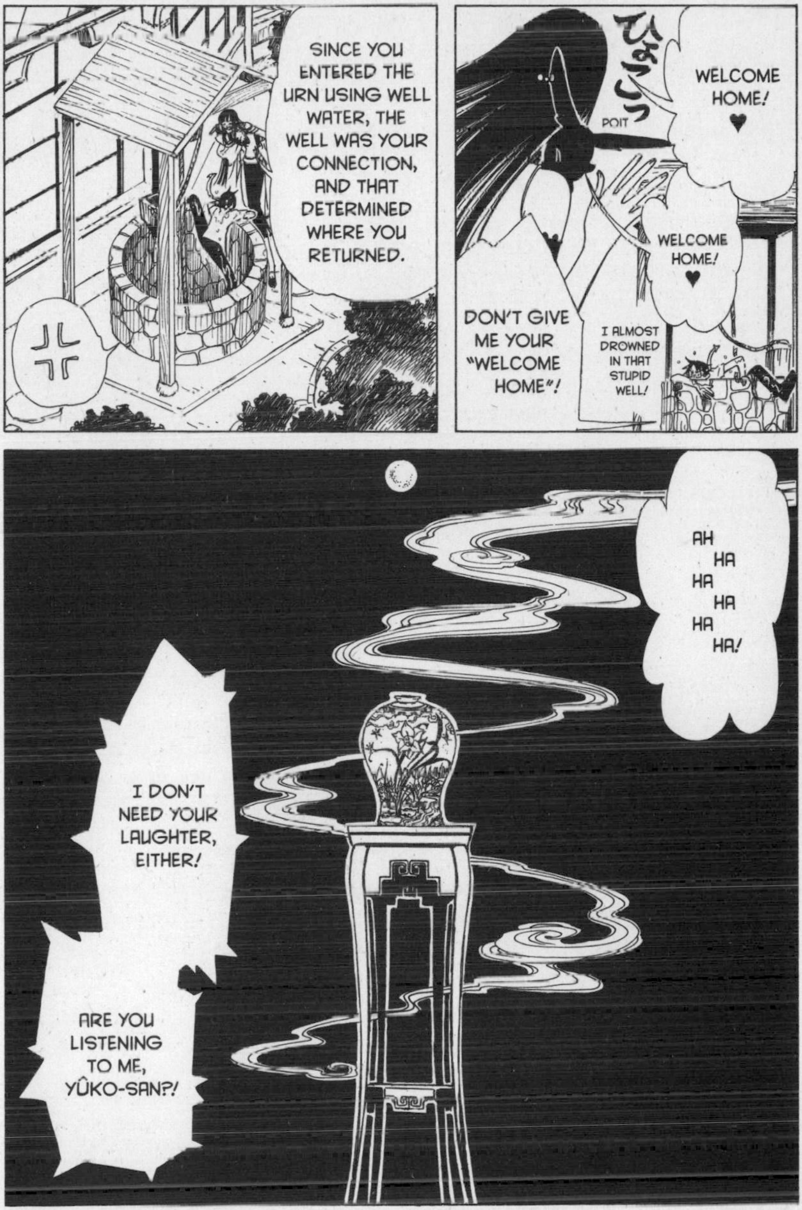
WELCOME HOME! ♥
ひょこっ
POIT
WELCOME HOME! ♥
I ALMOST DROWNED IN THAT STUPID WELL!
DON'T GIVE ME YOUR "WELCOME HOME"!
SINCE YOU ENTERED THE URN USING WELL WATER, THE WELL WAS YOUR CONNECTION, AND THAT DETERMINED WHERE YOU RETURNED.
AH HA HA HA HA HA!
I DON'T NEED YOUR LAUGHTER, EITHER!
ARE YOU LISTENING TO ME, YÛKO-SAN?!

⇥ Continued ⇤

in *xxxHOLiC* Volume 6

About the Creators

CLAMP is a group of four women who have become the most popular manga artists in America—Satsuki Igarashi, Tsubaki Nekoi, Mokona, and Ageha Ohkawa. They started out as doujinshi (fan comics) creators, but their skill and craft brought them to the attention of publishers very quickly. Their first work from a major publisher was *RG Veda*, but their first mass success was with *Magic Knight Rayearth*. From there, they went on to write many series, including *Cardcaptor Sakura* and *Chobits*, two of the most popular manga in the United States. Like many Japanese manga artists, they prefer to avoid the spotlight, and little is known about them personally.

CLAMP is currently publishing three series in Japan: *Tsubasa* and *xxxHOLiC* with Kodansha and *Gohou Drug* with Kadokawa.

Honorifics Explained

Throughout the Del Rey Manga books, you will find Japanese honorifics left intact in the translations. For those not familiar with how the Japanese use honorifics and, more important, how they differ from American honorifics, we present this brief overview.

Politeness has always been a critical facet of Japanese culture. Ever since the feudal era, when Japan was a highly stratified society, use of honorifics — which can be defined as polite speech that indicates relationship or status — has played an essential role in the Japanese language. When addressing someone in Japanese, an honorific usually takes the form of a suffix attached to one's name (example: "Asuna-san"), or as a title at the end of one's name or in place of the name itself (example: "Negi-sensei," or simply "Sensei!").

Honorifics can be expressions of respect or endearment. In the context of manga and anime, honorifics give insight into the nature of the relationship between characters. Many translations into English leave out these important honorifics, and therefore distort the "feel" of the original Japanese. Because Japanese honorifics contain nuances that English honorifics lack, it is our policy at Del Rey not to translate them. Here, instead, is a guide to some of the honorifics you may encounter in Del Rey Manga.

-san: This is the most common honorific, and is equivalent to Mr., Miss, Ms., Mrs., etc. It is the all-purpose honorific and can be used in any situation where politeness is required.

-sama: This is one level higher than "-san." It is used to confer great respect.

-dono: This comes from the word "tono," which means "lord." It is an even higher level than "-sama," and confers utmost respect.

-kun: This suffix is used at the end of boys' names to express familiarity or endearment. It is also sometimes used by men among friends, or when addressing someone younger or of a lower station.

-chan: This is used to express endearment, mostly toward girls. It is also used for little boys, pets, and even among lovers. It gives a sense of childish cuteness.

Bozu: This is an informal way to refer to a boy, similar to the English term "kid" or "squirt."

Sempai: This title suggests that the addressee is one's senior in a group or organization. It is most often used in a school setting, where underclassmen refer to their upperclassmen as "sempai." It can also be used in the workplace, such as when a newer employee addresses an employee who has seniority in the company.

Kohai: This is the opposite of "sempai," and is used toward underclassmen in school or newcomers in the workplace. It connotes that the addressee is of lower station.

Sensei: Literally meaning "one who has come before," this title is used for teachers, doctors, or masters of any profession or art.

-[blank]: Usually forgotten in these lists, but perhaps the most significant difference between Japanese and English. The lack of honorific means that the speaker has permission to address the person in a very intimate way. Usually, only family, spouses, or very close friends have this kind of permission. Known as *yobisute*, it can be gratifying when someone who has earned the intimacy starts to call one by one's name without an honorific. But when that intimacy hasn't been earned, it can also be very insulting.

Translation Notes

For your edification and reading pleasure, here are notes to help you understand some of the cultural and story references from our translation of *xxxHOLiC*.

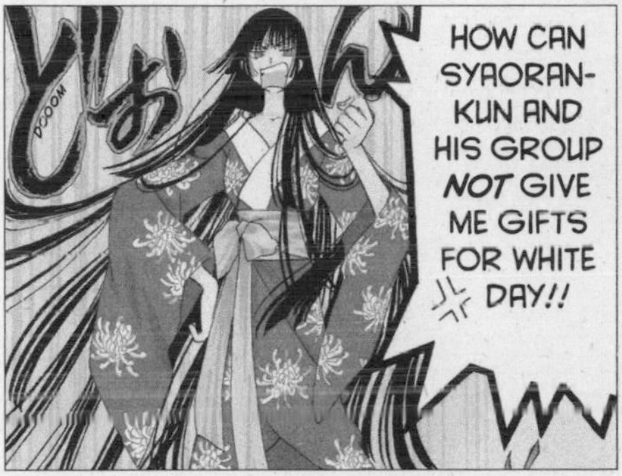

DOOOM
HOW CAN SYAORAN-KUN AND HIS GROUP *NOT* GIVE ME GIFTS FOR WHITE DAY!!

Valentine's Day in Japan, page 4

(For a more detailed explanation, see *xxxHOLiC*, Volume 4.) Unlike Valentine's Day in America, Valentine's Day in Japan is an opportunity for the women to give chocolate to the men. Of course, there are committed couples and obligational business relationships where chocolate is given, but the main objective is a way for a girl to reveal to a guy that she likes him. If her feelings are requited, the guy is then supposed to reciprocate one month later on March 14, which is called White Day. A gift of something white indicates that the guy "accepts" the girl's feelings. (Of course, if a man is given a Valentine's Day gift out of obligation, he is obligated to give a gift in return on White Day.)

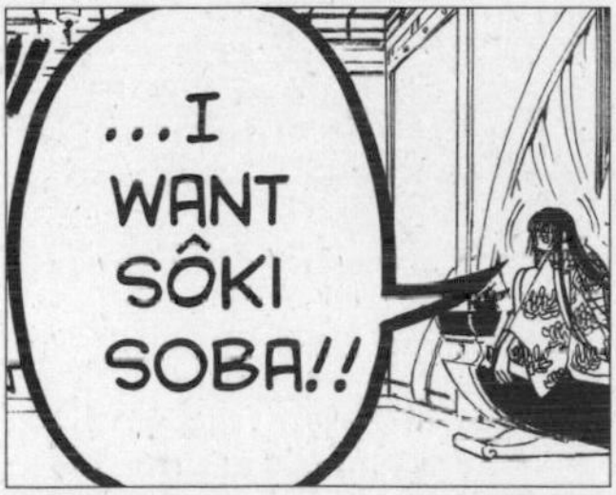

...I WANT SÔKI SOBA!!

Sôki Soba, page 5

Soba ("noodles") are to Okinawa (even more than the rest of Japan) a regional main course much like hot dogs are to America or tortillas to the Mexican diet. Since soba is so inexpensive and readily available, even the presence of the U.S. military bases has not been able to overwhelm soba's importance in Okinawa. Quite the opposite! Soba generally becomes a favorite of foreigners, as well. Okinawan noodles are thicker and firmer than

the noodles popular in the rest of Japan, and *Sôki Soba*—"spare-rib noodles"—are one of the Okinawan favorites.

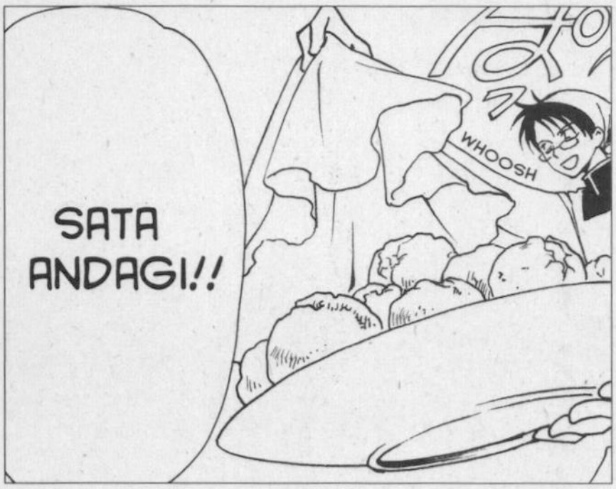
SATA ANDAGI!!
WHOOSH

Sata Andagi, page 6

Since Okinawa's tropical atmosphere is good for sugar, *sata-ya* (sugar factories) are one of the traditional Okinawan industries. And one of the uses of Okinawan black sugar is *Sata Andagi*, also called Okinawan doughnuts. They are made of a simple recipe consisting of sugar, eggs, vanilla, flour, milk, salt and baking powder mixed and deep fried into a crispy confection. *Sata Andagi* is probably the most popular sweet in Okinawa.

The Rainy Season (*Tsuyu*), page 7

June is the rainy season in Japan; it rains nearly every day and is pretty much cloudy all month. It's usually looked on with dread by the denizens of Tokyo, but the rainy season still has its romantic implications in its relationship to the umbrella. Two names inside a

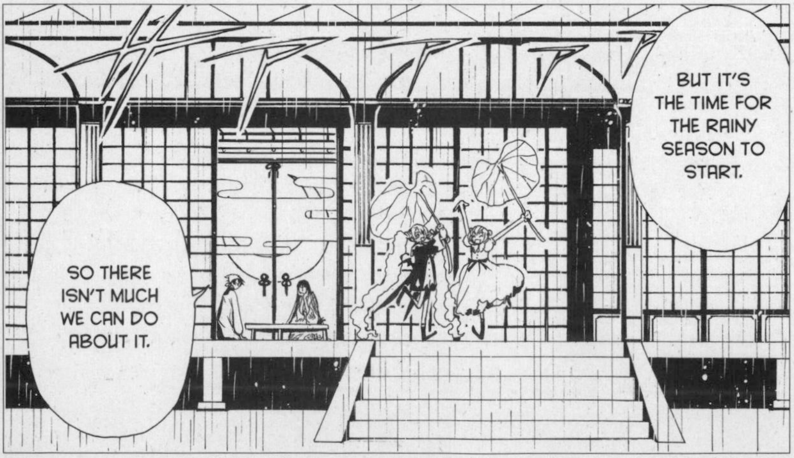
BUT IT'S THE TIME FOR THE RAINY SEASON TO START.
SO THERE ISN'T MUCH WE CAN DO ABOUT IT.

heart is an American children's symbol for love, and the Japanese equivalent symbol is two names under an umbrella. Many Japanese romantics have conveniently "forgotten" their rain gear during the rainy season, hoping that they'd be invited to walk home together under the shelter of a certain someone's umbrella. In prewar Japan, it was one of the few allowable intimacies in public. That isn't so much of a problem in modern Japan, but the umbrella has still retained some of its romantic aura.

Nobita, page 11

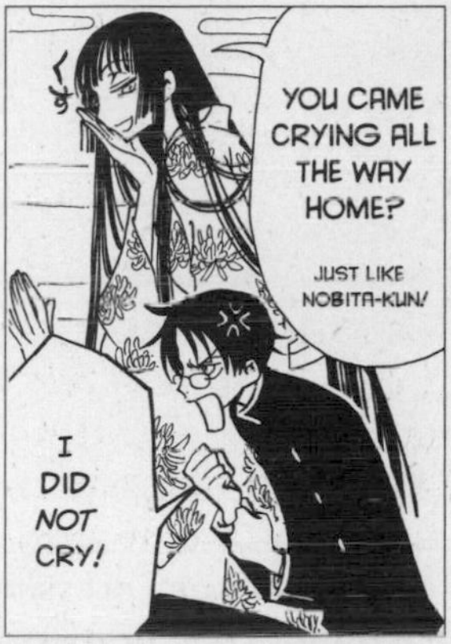
YOU CAME CRYING ALL THE WAY HOME?
JUST LIKE NOBITA-KUN!
I DID NOT CRY!

Americans have been introduced to many iconic characters from Japan—characters such as Tetsuwan Atom (Astroboy), Godzilla, and even Ultraman, but one of the icons that hasn't made it to the Western Hemisphere with any force yet is a blue, snowman-shaped robotic cat from the future named Doraemon. He's the greatest best friend a person could have, offering unflagging loyalty and a gadget for every occasion. The person he's most dedicated to is a grade-school boy, Nobita. Nobita is lousy at sports, unpopular, not too bright, often bullied, and constantly looking for the easy way out, and when anything goes wrong, he always runs crying all the way home. He's become Japan's symbol for the crybaby.

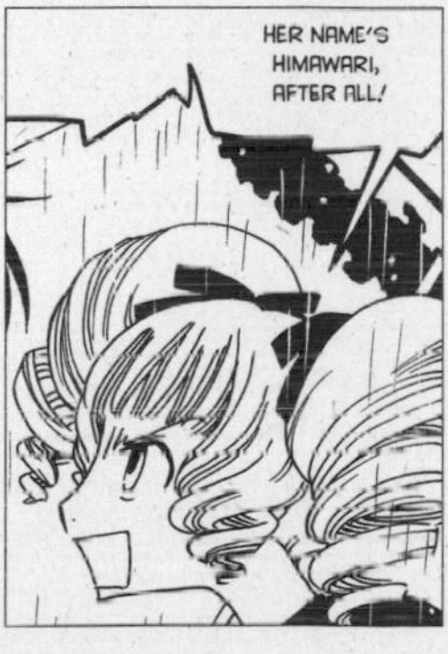
HER NAME'S HIMAWARI, AFTER ALL!

Himawari's Name, page 19

Himawari means "sunflower," so with such a sunny name, it's easy to understand why a rain spirit would be wary of getting close to her.

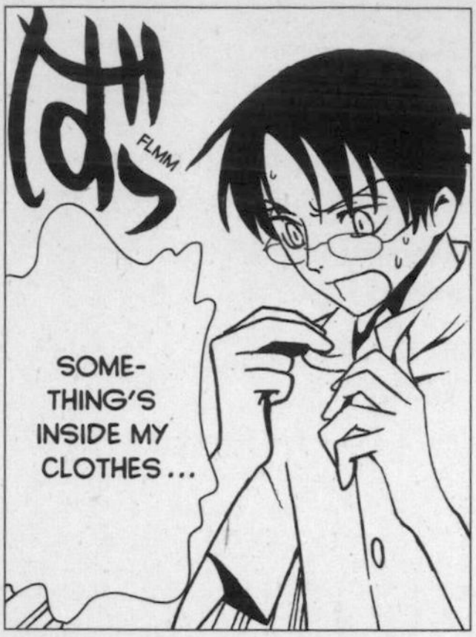
FLMM
SOME-THING'S INSIDE MY CLOTHES...

Pipe Fox Spirit (*Kuda-kitsune*), page 72

A traditional magical creature from Tôhoku region (northern part of the main island of Honshu). Some of the traditions related to Pipe Fox Spirits are: Those who own Pipe Fox Spirits avoid weddings like the plague. When farm items and produce are stolen or if a crop goes badly, it is often blamed on Pipe Fox Spirits. People possessed by Pipe Fox Spirits become rich. And it's said that the only people who can catch a Pipe Fox Spirit are ascetics who live beneath the Mitake Shrine outside of Tokyo.

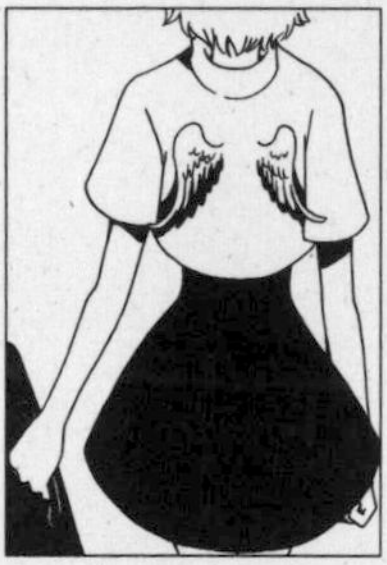

Cosplay, page 77

Short for Costume Play, cosplay has a broader meaning in Japan than the same concept in America. It can mean creating costumes to look like one's favorite movie or anime characters, but it can also mean dressing in the style of one's favorite singer, or making a fashion statement with outrageous clothes and cosmetics.

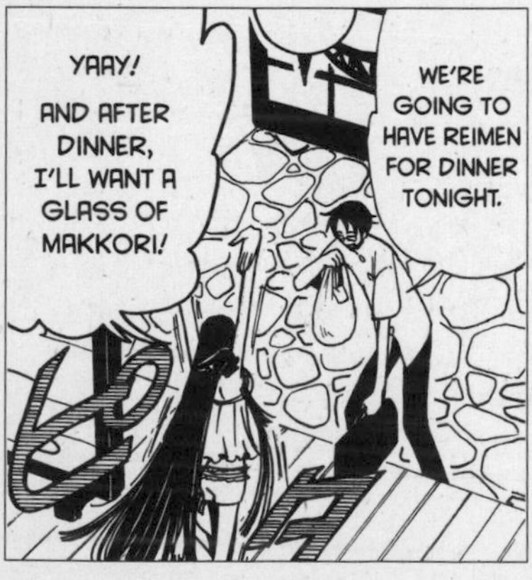
WE'RE GOING TO HAVE REIMEN FOR DINNER TONIGHT.
YAAY! AND AFTER DINNER, I'LL WANT A GLASS OF MAKKORI!

Reimen and Makkori, page 79

Reimen are noodles, usually in soup, served cold. It is especially popular during the hot months of summer. *Reimen* is often flavored with kim-chee or other spicy Korean flavorings . . . which is exactly why Yûko wanted *Makkori*, a Korean rice wine, for afterwards, keeping the Korean theme.

Night Fair, page 94

Usually connected to temples or cultural centers in the summertime, the night fairs feature lanes lined with stalls that sell food or run games like the goldfish catch. Children are allowed to stay out late at these fairs, and the standard dress for visitors is the cool "yukata" cotton kimono.

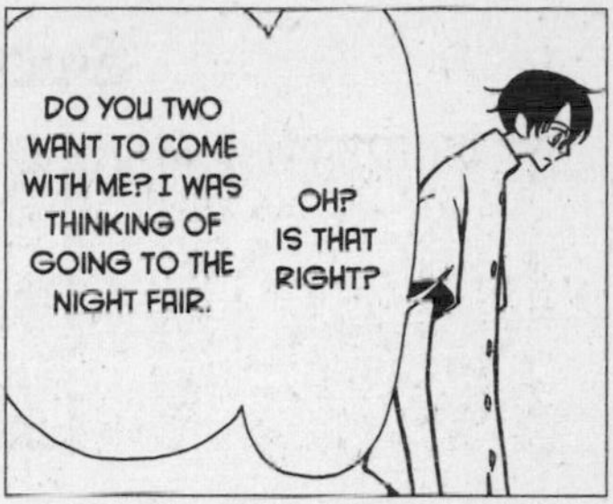
DO YOU TWO WANT TO COME WITH ME? I WAS THINKING OF GOING TO THE NIGHT FAIR.
OH? IS THAT RIGHT?

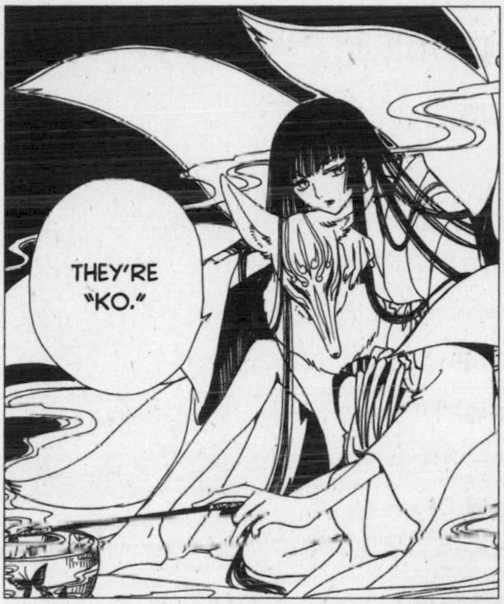
THEY'RE "KO."

Ko, page 130

The kanji for *Ko* is made up of three *mushi* ("insect") kanji, and also means vermin, worm, bug, bad temper, or bad company.

Reisan, page 168

The name of the mountain, *Reisan*, is made up of two kanji, "Spirit" and "Mountain."

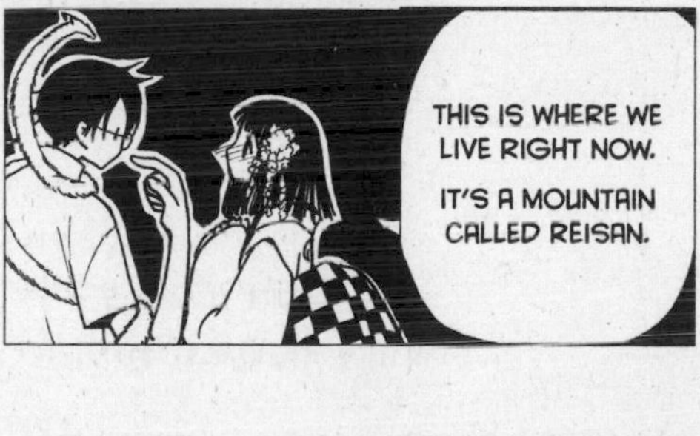
THIS IS WHERE WE LIVE RIGHT NOW.
IT'S A MOUNTAIN CALLED REISAN.

TOMARE!

[STOP!]

You're going the wrong way!

Manga is a completely different type of reading experience.

To start at the *beginning*, go to the *end*!

That's right! Authentic manga is read the traditional Japanese way—from right to left. Exactly the *opposite* of how American books are read. It's easy to follow: Just go to the other end of the book, and read each page—and each panel—from right side to left side, starting at the top right. Now you're experiencing manga as it was meant to be!